HOW TO HAVE
AN OUTSTANDING LIFE

HOW TO HAVE
AN OUTSTANDING LIFE

Paul Smith

NEW
HOLLAND

First published in Australia in 2005 by
New Holland Publishers (Australia) Pty Ltd
Sydney · Auckland · London · Cape Town

14 Aquatic Drive Frenchs Forest NSW 2086 Australia
218 Lake Road Northcote Auckland New Zealand
86 Edgware Road London W2 2EA United Kingdom
80 McKenzie Street Cape Town 8001 South Africa

10 9 8 7 6 5 4 3 2 1

National Library of Australia Cataloguing-in-Publication Data:

Smith, Paul A, 1951–.
How to have an outstanding life.

ISBN 1 74110 229 4.

1. Self-actualization (Psychology). 2. Success. I. Title.

158.1

Publisher: Fiona Schultz
Managing Editor: Angela Handley
Editor: Jenny Hunter
Designer: Karl Roper
Production: Linda Bottari
Printer: McPhersons Printing Group

This book was typeset in Cleargo 10 pt

Cover photo: Getty Images

Warning! Warning!

You've already flicked through this book, haven't you? Confused? Baffled? If you're right-handed, you probably started from near the end of the book. If you're left-handed, you started somewhere else. I don't know where. Left-handers do things differently, and so do I.

This book is not for ordinary people. It's not even for normal people. I say that proudly and with a lot of passion. I've helped a lot of sports champions, both teams and individuals. All champions are champions because they're never ordinary and never normal. They stand out from the crowd. That's why the crowds come to see them. I want you to be a champion at the things that are important to you. I want you to have an outstanding life, by standing out from the crowd.

The look of this book might be puzzling, because it chases success from many different directions. This book is a combination of a jigsaw, a collage and a kaleidoscope. Many sections fit tightly together, but many sections also overlap, so that you should look at it from many different angles, at many different times.

On closer inspection, you'll find two books side by side — a dialogue from me, plus companion exercises to actively stretch your mind.

This book is dedicated to my mother for giving me some wonderful gifts. She showed me that learning can happen anywhere and at any time. She also taught me that we should enjoy sharing what we learn. These strong beliefs led to my love of psychology. Thank you Mum.

Contents

Introduction
Jogging Along the Highway of Life

At the end of many of my seminars I share a handful of very valuable objects with my audience. Here's what they look and feel like:

> They're small solid cores of rock, like little cylinders, stretching one to five centimetres long. When you rub them with your fingers you feel their smooth texture. When you hold them to weigh them, you discover they're surprisingly heavy for their small size.

What are they? Rarely does anyone come close with an answer. I've found and collected more than a hundred of these objects on my many jogs along a busy country highway. Jogging is a wonderful exercise, it's wonderful therapy, it's a wonderful source of creative ideas. These little rocks have made my love of jogging even stronger.

Over 200 million years ago, the region where I live was on the ocean floor, rich with many animals looking like corals. These are my rocks. They're the fossils of ancient sea lilies, a poor name because they're colonies of animals, not plants. This ocean floor was covered with ash and lava from huge volcanoes and the fossils became part of an incredibly hard rock layer, which was eventually mined, crushed, and used in the construction of roads and highways all over New South Wales, my home state.

The sea lilies have left their mark, a mark that has lasted over two hundred million years. Think deeply about a big question: How will you leave your mark on this planet? I'll tell you my own personal answer. I want to leave my mark in the minds of others, not just my family and friends, not just everyone who attends my seminars, and everyone who reads my books, but also millions of people who I'll never meet. I get some strange looks when I share my dream.

I want to leave my mark by sharing, and following, great ideas that will help others have better lives. I'm addicted to sharing these ideas whenever I find them. A friend once told me I was a *share-aholic*, but there's no negative side to this addiction. I love hearing Zig Ziglar, the motivational speaker, say in his unforgettable voice, 'You can get everything you want in life, if you just help enough people get what they want.' He's normally inspiring salespeople, but we all have something to sell, and to give away. This is the philosophy that has built this book.

I'm now going to say something that might amaze you. Every time you do one of my mind stretching exercises, every time you read a page and think about what I've written, you and I will become closer. From your success, my success will grow! Let's spend some time together, and go jogging along the highway to success. Let's leave our mark on this planet in the best possible way.

Chapter 1
Secret Formula
For All Success

Are you ready for a huge mental exercise? It involves only one word. If you had to give a one-word summary, a single word to explain what you want from this book, why you picked it up, what would that word be? My word for you is … success. It's staring at you up in the title. You want even more success in your career and your life, don't you? Heads nod everywhere whenever I ask that question. But, I'm also certain you want to help other people to be more successful in their lives — success for your colleagues, co-workers, team-mates, clients, customers, students, patients, friends, neighbours, even strangers. Most importantly, you want success for your loved ones. If you hear yourself agreeing, you've got the right book in your hands.

I wear many different caps — a psychologist, a corporate trainer, a public speaker, a relationship counsellor, and a therapist helping depressed and suicidal clients. But it's only my work in sports that gets me into newspaper and television articles. I'm very proud of my track record of success as a sports psychologist, and a journalist from *The Australian* newspaper once interviewed me for an article on sports psychology as a career choice. She asked me, 'What's the most important skill you need to become a successful sports psychologist?' When I gave her my answer, she had a laugh. I told her you have to know how to ask strange questions that put people into strange situations. Why? So they think differently, so they look at their lives from different angles, so that they learn more about themselves. You boost their awareness. When this happens we're on the road to success.

Let's kick off with some awesome daydreaming and go to a place built around success — the Olympics. I'm giving you the opportunity to win a gold medal at the next Olympics. What sport and event do you want to enter and win a gold medal? I've thrown this question at more than a hundred groups, business, sport, school teachers, and it's surprising how many synchronised swimmers I discover in my audiences. I'm running in the 10,000 metres.

Now you're at the Olympics, and it's about an hour before you compete for the gold. You're sitting in the dressing room, fully psyched to win, when you feel a tap on your shoulder. You look up and you see your number one opponent, standing there, and before you know it, this person pushes a pill into your hand. What do you do? The most common response is to throw the pill back. One footballer said he'd jam the opponent's head into a toilet bowl.

But, you're far too rational to do that, so you calmly ask, 'Well, what does this pill do?' Your opponent immediately says, 'The pill isn't an illegal drug, you won't fail a drug test. But when you take this pill, and we compete against each other today, I'll guarantee that you'll perform 1 per cent, 2 per cent, 5 per cent, 10 per cent, 20 per cent, maybe even 50 per cent ... below your peak performance.' I'll say that again, *below* your peak performance. What do you do now? Nobody, and I mean nobody out of thousands of people who've heard this story, has ever said, 'Okay, I'll take the pill'. Everyone agrees that would be totally dumb, and that's why I call this pill the dumb pill.

I'm now going to make a huge statement. (I often tell my audiences when I'm going to make a huge statement, so they won't miss it.) You sometimes act as if you've taken a dumb pill. Don't feel insulted, because I do the same thing, and we're not alone, because every person on this planet sometimes acts exactly as if they've swallowed a dumb pill. We all take dumb pills when we stop learning, when we stop looking for, or listening to, new ideas to help us grow and improve.

Even world champions can sometimes take dumb pills. Ian Thorpe held several world swimming records when he went to the 2000 Olympics in Sydney. The media said Thorpe was unbeatable. All he had to do was fall in the water and he was guaranteed another gold medal. But, he lost to the Dutch swimmer Pieter van den Hoogenband, who was the European champion. Why did Thorpe lose? Maybe it was due to the battle between dumb and smart pills.

When Hoogenband and the Dutch team arrived in Australia, they immediately took a couple of smart pills. They trained in Newcastle, away from the distractions of Sydney. Then they took another smart pill. Videos of Thorpe's swims were analysed in great detail. They knew exactly what Thorpe did at every stage of every race, and worked out what Hoogenband could do to counter him at the Olympics.

A few years back I did some sessions with NSW swimming squads and I asked a couple of the coaches what the Australians did to especially prepare for any possible challenge from Hoogenband. You know what I was told? Nothing. If that's true, that would have been like taking a giant dumb pill.

Why do we sometimes find it hard to look for, or look at, new ideas? To get an answer let's do a quick medical test. It's very accurate. Have a good feel around your right ankle, your ankle, not someone else's. Now feel around your left ankle. Feel anything? I hope not! Sometimes we have an invisible chain around one of our ankles and that tells us that we're suffering from the baby elephant syndrome.

What am I talking about? Here's how they used to train baby elephants in circuses. They attached a long chain to one of the ankles and then secured it to a large spike hammered deep into the ground. There was no way the elephant could escape. As the elephant grew much larger, they kept the same chain on, and by the time the elephant was fully grown, all they needed to have was a couple of links of the chain dangling from the ankle, and the elephant would never try to escape. Why? Psychologists call it conditioning, but you get a clearer picture if you see the elephant being held back by past memories, past memories of when it was too small to escape. We're often held back by ideas and experiences from the past. This can happen so easily and that's why phobias are so common.

How often do you suffer from baby elephant syndrome?

Please remember the connection between the dumb pills and the baby elephants. One very confused giant basketballer told me, 'Smithy, I just don't understand your story about those pink elephants!' It's not pink elephants, it's not white elephants, it's baby elephants. Remember, everyone takes dumb pills sometimes. So, be on the look out for any of those times when you've just swallowed one, and you might be held back from going forward, because of ideas from the past.

There is good news because you can easily build up your resistance to dumb pills, by regularly asking yourself questions, questions like, 'What have I learnt this week?' or 'What have I learnt today?' or, and this is one of my all-time favourites, 'What have I learnt from this problem?' When you regularly ask other people what they've learnt, you end up with a huge proactive team, with no sheep. The best sports coaches I've worked with, do this. The number of questions they ask outweighs the number of answers they give. Great coaches, great managers, great parents, ask great questions.

I'll show you what I mean, right now. Hold on to your seat because this question might give you a shake. Why haven't you written a best-selling book on how to have an outstanding life? All right, you might argue you're not a sports psychologist. Throw away the sport part of this book. You might say, 'Well, I'm not an expert on motivation and success'. I'll then ask you, 'Why aren't you an expert?' You might be thinking you haven't done any-thing outstanding in your life. If that's true, why haven't you? In the next 300 pages I want to inspire you to chase outstanding success, and help many others around you, especially those you love, to be outstanding as well. Then, in a few years time I might buy your book.

Now that I've got you fully warmed up, let's move onto my most valuable insight into success — the secret formula for all success. I've read hundreds of books about success. I've spoken to, and worked with, some of the most successful sportspeople and businesspeople in Australia.

Out of all my thinking about success, I've put together my own formula for all success. It works for sport, for business, it works everywhere in life, and it's made of only three parts. The three ingredients are A plus B plus C equals Success.

Have you ever seen the crazy movie *Blazing Saddles*? It was made back in the 1970s and it still lights up my day whenever I watch it. One of the many reasons it's successful is that all the actors look like they're enjoying themselves. That's an extremely important message.

There's another high energy visual package that always gives me a lift. You'll see it when we meet at one of my seminars. Be prepared for a 2-minute glimpse of life at its best. I've shown this mini-video hundreds of times, and it's still possible for me to get a tear in my eye. The video has no title but I introduce it as *Blazing Wheelchairs*. It shows the incredible success that came after what many would only see as a tragedy. It shows the Australian Men's Wheelchair Basketball Team winning their gold medal at the Atlanta Paralympics. These men, plus their British opponents, are champions in the truest meaning of the word.

Characteristics of champions

What mental strengths do you show?

In the diagram above you can see many of the characteristics of champions. The wheelchair basketballers showed all these characteristics, every one of them. But I've left out the most important core. What is necessary before any of these champion qualities can grow? What has to come first? The answer is our first ingredient in the secret formula for success.

Go back to the crazy *Blazing Saddles* movie. You have to have that passion, a love for whatever you're doing, whether it's sport or work. Success comes from enjoying yourself, getting excited, having fun, or just liking what you do.

How passionate are you about your life? There's a very simple way of knowing your answer. Become aware of how often you smile and laugh. It's such a simple test, but it's so accurate. Ask others to find out how they see you. It can be quite an eye-opener. For some of my clients, it has produced a profound awakening. On the other hand, some business executives and sports coaches tell me that you have to be 'deadly serious' to be successful. I disagree, very strongly. Look at those two words together — 'deadly serious'. What a horrible combination! Think about it. Instead of following this bleak advice, go out and join a true winning team. Smile, laugh, be passionate. The energy from your passion can do incredible things. Love your life — it's a gift.

What's the second ingredient for success? You have to be able to see where you're going. When the Australian team went to the Olympics they were given no hope of winning gold. But they thought differently. They shared a vision of proving everyone wrong, and becoming the Olympic champions. When you have your vision of the future you have power in the present. They could see themselves returning to Australia, coming out of airports with their gold medals around their necks, meeting all their cheering supporters.

The last ingredient? The team worked incredibly hard on and off the court. Troy Sachs, regarded as the world's best player, trained up to 13 hours a day, every day, in the six-month period before the Olympics. You need action to be successful.

PASSION + VISION + ACTION = SUCCESS

I'll now explain why each of the three ingredients is so important, why each can't survive without the other two. It's a three-piece jigsaw where each piece is critical. If you have passion and vision without action it's just like sitting around wishing, hoping, praying you'll suddenly become wealthy or happy.

That's why people get addicted to gambling, especially buying lotto and lottery tickets. It's also the reason behind drug addictions. None of these addictions involve taking any real action. Some teenagers I've counselled went to great lengths to get their dope supplies but their efforts simply hid them from reality, and success in life. Before I leave my attack on addictions, I love sharing the next piece of trivia about the connection between lotto and leprosy. You have a better chance of catching leprosy. I don't know why that's left out of lotto advertising. The likelihood of winning a gigantic lotto competition in the United States was given as 135 million to one.

You might also think my next comment is harsh, but it's true. The vast majority of people who gamble, are losers. They never get back what they lose. This is often a sore point when I discuss my attack on lotteries. Often I'm rebutted with the argument, from a dedicated once-a-week dreamer, 'Somebody's got to win.' True, but a hell of a lot of people have to lose at the same time. I rest my case.

Lotteries make lots of losers

Why do we need passion for what we're doing in our lives? Passion makes things happen faster because you enjoy what you doing, so you show more commitment, you work harder.

I'll share with you some images of me with and without passion. As a public speaker, I cannot stand still — I zig and zag in front of, and sometimes through, my audiences, and I'm wired for sound. One lovely lady, somewhere in her eighties, told me after one of my speeches, that I would fly if I waved my arms any more.

I also try to show my passion in my writing. If I'd lived before 1553, I would have been in big trouble. That was the year the exclamation mark first appeared!! I just love using exclamation marks! However, there was a period when I didn't have much passion for my writing. When people asked me how long it took to write this book I used to say four years. The time from when I started to the finish was four years, but for the first 18 months I simply plodded, with no enthusiasm. Then my passion arrived and I put my foot to the floor, or more correctly, I hit a lot of letters on my keyboard a lot more often.

I've seen some job advertisements that are actually seeking people with a lack of passion. Some organisations, especially government, emphasise nine-day fortnights. What's the hidden message there? They seem to be searching for employees who are focused on time-off, instead of time-on. The reward is that you don't have to come to work. No wonder I meet many managers who complain about staff who are simply going through the motions. Isn't that a horrible image?

I saw lack of passion up close when I worked with a high school. A disillusioned deputy principal told me I was wasting my time trying to inspire the teaching staff. He told me to visit the school library and discover what were the most commonly borrowed items by teachers. The head librarian quickly gave me the answer — fishing magazines. Enough said?

At another school I visited, the staff volunteered to have the school crest embroidered on their shirts and blouses. I think they were saying they were proud to teach at their school. I have a huge wardrobe of clothes and caps given to me by sports organisations who were my clients. I proudly wear everything I'm given. Would you wear an item of clothing in public that clearly identifies where you work?

Do you proudly tell people where you work?

There's a silly demonstration I like doing in front of my seminar audiences. It shows what passion and action looks like without any vision. I slowly spin around with my arms stretched out, build up speed so that I bump into and bounce off a wall. It's a lot of activity without any achievement.

I did some consulting for a company where one of their managers was an expert at looking busy when he was doing very little. He looked very active but had very few runs on the board. This was one of his tricks or habits. He often walked around carrying a piece of paper. It fooled a lot of people. Maybe it even fooled the manager himself. Activity without a vision is more than a waste of time, it's super dumb!

Imagine rushing up to the check-in counter at an airport, yelling that you don't have time to say where you're going, 'Just give me a ticket to anywhere'. No-one would do that, absolutely no-one, but many people give little thought to their many destinations in life. Success will not come without a vision. However, be prepared to change your vision or, sometimes, throw it away, without fearing you've failed. Few visions have the power to last a lifetime. Head in the direction of your vision, but life contains many detours that still lead to success.

Something happened in one of my seminars to senior high school students, that shook me and forced me to change all my future talks about vision. A young woman started crying after I said how dumb it was to not have a vision of where you're going in life. Her tears grew, and eventually she had to be comforted by a teacher. She eventually said, still sobbing, 'I have no idea what I want to do'. I asked her, was she looking? She was. I told her, and her school friends, that you're only dumb if you don't care about not having a vision. Great uncertainty was a natural part of being a teenager.

What happens now that you know this secret formula? It gives you three clear guidelines to lift your success, and the success of others. It then gets back to the power of questions. Ask yourself questions about your passion, your vision and the action you're taking. Then ask others about their passion, vision and action. Good questions, big questions, lift awareness and lead to success. I'll never apologise for saying that over and over again.

I once asked a single question that revitalised a sporting career, and a lot more. I received a phone call from a young professional footballer who had just been told he had 48 hours to make a huge decision about his future. It was half way through the season, and his coach was very disappointed with the young man's commitment and performance, both playing and training. Was he going to be serious about playing football? If his answer was no, the coach was going to rip up the player's contract. Back to the phone call. The young man desperately wanted some guidance, and I'd helped him a few years back. I left him with a mental exercise based on this question, 'Why do I love football?' I told him to list 10 answers. If he couldn't do that, he knew he wasn't serious about his sport. What happened? He identified 10 clear answers, and finished the season playing top-class football.

What question leads to depression?

I've preached to you about the power of questions, but I want to make something absolutely clear. There can be a dark side to questions, when they're the wrong ones. Often when I'm counselling a depressed client, I'll show the wheelchair basketball video after I hear the wrong question. It's one of the worst. The question is 'Why me?'

People who ask this question usually have low passion, poor vision, and rarely get active. I like to tell them about the backgrounds of two of the players in the wheelchairs. The co-captain of the team was Sandy Blythe. Imagine you're 19 years old, driving home at the end of the university year, and you're looking forward to spending the summer holidays with your parents. You go to overtake a slow car, it suddenly pulls out in front of you, and you crash into a dry creek bed … and realise you're going to be a paraplegic for the rest of your life. Sandy had to change his vision of his life, but he stayed passionate about playing sport. He now has an Olympic gold medal, has written a best-selling book and runs a successful business.

The other player I talk about is Troy Sachs. Imagine you're born with one bone in your lower leg, instead of two. The leg is fairly useless, so when you're about three years old, your parents tell you it should be amputated. You get an artificial leg, but after you discover the wheelchair, you soon represent Australia at the Barcelona Olympics, when you're only 16. At 20, you're voted one of the best players in all US college sports teams. When you win your gold medal, you set a world record scoring 42 points, and you play the Olympic final with a broken elbow. Sometimes life forces us to change our visions. That's okay, if you still chase your new vision with passion and action.

If a man is called a street sweeper, he should sweep streets even as Michelangelo painted, or Beethoven composed music, or Shakespeare wrote poetry.

Martin Luther King

Let's have a closer look at the role of passion in our careers. I've been challenged by some people who argue you can't possibly be excited by most jobs. In one audience a plumber told me, 'Mate, you're talking crap. I spend most of the day looking down drains and my job sucks. I only do it for the money.' If that's true for you, you're taking years off your life.

I strongly believe if you have the right person in the right job, you can be excited about your work. Others might see mundane, boring, repetitive, dead-end, low wages, trivial, and unappreciated, as well as stressful and even terrifying, jobs. I do something at least once a week that most people are terrified to do. It's at the top of many lists of fears. I speak in public! Am I an idiot because I do something that the majority of the population would run away from? No! I love it because it's right for me. When you're excited about what you're doing in life, you can very quickly give a snapshot of your life. I call these excitement snapshots. Study the exercise 'What are they talking about?' See if you can guess what these 10 people are talking about.

What are they talking about?

Listen to the following people talk about their careers and then name their sources of excitement.

'I've done something with my life. I've made kids happy around the world.'
Mystery career 1:..
'I help build cathedrals.'
Mystery career 2:..
'We are the Michelangelos of the hospitality world.'
Mystery career 3:..
'Ours is the most incredible industry. We touch people — physically and emotionally — and change their lives by helping them to improve their image. We give them a whole new lease of life.'
Mystery career 4:..
'We're still in the entertainment industry — at 25,000 feet.'
Mystery career 5:..
'Everyday I'm surrounded by 100 per cent curiosity and the love of life.'

Mystery career 6:...

'I have no pride. I'll do anything that's necessary to get people involved. I am a dispenser of enthusiasm.'

Mystery career 7:...

'I'm like a fireman — when I go out I want to put out a big fire. I don't want to put out a fire in a dumpster.'

Mystery career 8:...

'I do massive face-lifts. At the same time I give out anti-depressants.'

Mystery career 9:...

'It's just this great big outflow pipe that keeps the pressure nice and even. It just pours all this stuff out. All the insecurities come out, all the fears — and also, it's a great way to pass the time.'

Mystery career 10:...

Here are the surprising answers to the 10 careers.

Mystery career 1: These words came from a very rich man just before he died a few years ago. He made his fortune from one chemical discovery. His name? Walter Diemer. His name means nothing to you, but there are cleaners everywhere who hate what he invented — bubble gum!

Mystery career 2: Three stonecutters in a quarry were asked to describe their jobs. The first said the work was back breaking but he gave 100 per cent commitment. The next worker said he produced perfect blocks of rock. The last worker said, 'I help build cathedrals'. All three did the same job, but each showed different levels of passion, and different visions.

Mystery career 3: Whenever I think of Michelangelo, I have to look up at the ceiling, and think of the finishing touches he put on the Sistine Chapel in Rome. Did you know he had 13 other painters who helped him? These modern day Michelangelos are the room-cleaning staff of the Ritz hotels. Instead of dragging themselves to work every day to clean another 20 rooms all over again, they see themselves putting on the finishing touches that make the Ritz hotels possibly the best in the world.

Mystery career 4: The man who won the North American Hairstylist of the year award.

Mystery career 5: He's probably one of the world's greatest eccentrics — Sir Richard Branson. When he decided to start his first airline, he was told he knew nothing about airlines. This was his response. Success easily transfers from one area to another, when you've got plenty of passion.

Mystery career 6: This was how a kindergarten teacher saw her job.

Mystery career 7: Dispenser of enthusiasm. Isn't that a brilliant description. Are you a dispenser of enthusiasm? The man who said this was the conductor of a symphony orchestra.

Mystery career 8: When a journalist asked Harrison Ford why he keeps making movies, he gave this reply. His career isn't driven by money, it's passion, excitement.

Mystery career 9: We're not listening to a plastic surgeon, this man is a house painter.

Last of all, career 10: Who's the world's most successful living author? He's written more than 50 best-selling novels, many of them have been turned into movies. Stephen King described his career this way.

How would you describe your career in an excitement snapshot? My snapshot is, 'I stretch minds to lift lives'. Do you have one already?

Australian businessmen on the run

Why are these five Australians wanted all over the world?

WANTED

Deadly DOUGIE DAFT

for ....

Gorgeous GEOFF BIBLE

for ....

Jumping JAC NASSER

for ....

Rugged ROD EDDINGTON

for ....

Dirty DAVID MACKAY

for ....

$$ BIG REWARDS $$

What does this tell you?

Who the hell is Herb Klodell?

There's one name you should remember when you think about happy passionate employees. He's the world's best and friendliest employee. He has to be. The world's largest company said he was. Who? It's the retailer Wal-Mart Stores. They held a competition amongst their 1.3 million employees to find the friendliest employee. They selected Herb Klodell, a 66-year-old ex-marine, ex-high school maths teacher, ex-salesman. He retired and then began as the doorman at a Wal-Mart store in Austin, Texas. Apparently, he is a genius when it comes to greeting customers and other employees. He's sensational at his job. Are you? Would you be voted the happiest employee where you work?

'Australian businessmen on the run' is an exercise about vision, big vision. What's the answer? Why are they all wanted men? We're not talking about Christopher Skase and the gang of other Australian businessmen who've fallen foul of the law over the last few decades. All of the businessmen on my poster are, or were, CEOs of gigantic multinationals.

Forty years ago, Doug Daft was a teacher at a high school in Sydney. Now he sits behind his desk in Atlanta, Georgia, and runs the worldwide operations of Coca Cola. I saw a report that listed his yearly salary package as $160 million!

Jac Nasser resigned a few years ago as CEO of the Ford Motor Company. He grew up in a poor part of Melbourne, his Lebanese parents couldn't speak English, and he left school at 14.

Geoff Bible is the boss of a gigantic conglomerate made of Kraft, Nabisco and Philip Morris. Then there's Rugged Rod who used to be a pilot with Ansett Airlines but he's gone on to be the CEO of British Airways. Last is Dirty Dave. He's just become the CEO of Kellogg's.

Australians are aware of our incredible achievements in sport and entertainment, but we've also reached the same high levels of success in the business world, as well as in science and medicine.

What does this tell you? (That's a beautiful question, isn't it? 'What does this tell you?' I use this question a lot, especially when I'm talking to myself.) It tells me Australians can be world champions in anything. How? These five businessmen all had high ambitions. Having an ambition is when you have a clear picture, a big clear vision, of what you want in life and you're excited about it. It's like saying, 'I want to do this and I know I can do it!'

This message is not restricted to Australians. Any person, from any nation, can be successful when they mix passion and ambition. Like ego, ambition is sometimes seen as a dirty word. Maybe it is, when it comes out of a hard, cold, uncaring mould. But this will rarely happen when it's blended with your principles. Later in the book we're going to talk a lot about, and look closely at, your principles.

Where are the successful ambitious women?

You've just read a question that I've seen in the eyes of hundreds of young women, especially high school students. I've given examples of incredibly successful men, Australian businessmen, but I've left out what they so desperately want to hear. There are plenty of glass ceilings in the business world, but I hope I've helped inspire plenty of women to go out and ignore those invisible barriers.

However, there is one world where women are now free to excel and even dominate — literature. Three authors, JK Rowling, Jean Auel and Millie Benson, have helped to shatter some of those barriers placed in front of, or above women. You're probably well aware of the first two authors. Both have had phenomenal success. But who is Millie Benson? She wrote 23 of the 'Nancy Drew' novels published between 1930 and 1953, and also wrote more than 100 other books, many while she held down a full-time job. She was a real trail blazer for women. Her books introduced a resourceful, intelligent young heroine who was courageous, and hated housework. Millie's books were translated into 17 languages and sold 30 million copies. She was still writing for a newspaper just months before she died in 2002, aged 96. There are some literature snobs who might look down on extraordinary commercial success of these three women. Bah, humbug. All three share the same humanitarian spirit that made Charles Dickens' works so popular with all levels of readers.

How can you become a champion in your career? I know one small council in local government that received five major awards, some of them national, in just three years. That's awesome! That's a champion council. Take a bow Tumut Council. It is a council hidden in the Snowy Mountains of NSW. I've been sharing this story with businesses outside of local government. Why? To show you can be a champion anywhere.

There are thousands of reasons why people don't become champions. Many are hooked to one word — 'realistic'. Those who warn others to 'just be realistic', rarely think like winners. It goes along with 'if only' thinking. In some businesses I've heard, 'That might work, if only … we were a bigger company'. But, I've also heard, 'That would work, if only we were a smaller company'.

Once you start asking yourself and others, 'What if … ' it's only a small step up to a favourite question used by champions, 'Why not?' This question breaks down another barrier to being a champion — being frightened to take risks. Later on we're going to look closely at you and your thoughts about taking risks. Look forward to that.

Future champions are hiding everywhere

Two of Australia's sports stars became world champions in 2003 — Matthew Hayden and Lauren Jackson. Both of them must have constantly asked, 'Why not?'

Anyone who follows cricket, anywhere in the world, knows that Matthew Hayden broke the record for scoring the most runs in a single innings. When he was a teenager he was told he would never play for his state, Queensland. He proved them wrong. He then broke into the Australian team, several times, and was dropped after the experts said his technique was not good enough. He proved them wrong. How? At the press conference after he set the world record he said, 'You don't know how many hundreds of hours I spent on the beach thinking how to get back into the Australian team.' That's passion and vision. By the way, he was on the beach because he lives on Stradbroke Island. His wife gave an extra insight when she told of all the sand dunes 'we ran up'. That was just some of the action that lead to his success.

Lauren Jackson achieved so much in 2003, she was undeniably the best female basketballer in the world. She was voted this season's Most Valuable Player in the American Women's NBA. Listen to how great an achievement this is. No other foreigner has ever won this title, nobody as young as the 22-year-old has, and no player ever has whose team missed the finals. To follow this up, she was then voted the best player at the World Club Championships in Russia. When she came back to Australia to recover from an injury, she revealed her next big dream — to win gold at the next Olympics for Australia. In 2004, Lauren's brilliance helped her team, the Seattle Storm, win their first WNBA Championship. Champions keep looking for new ways to be successful. Are you?

Why not be a champion for the rest of your life?

When people hear the word 'champion' most automatically think of sport. Why not music? Who is, or who was, the world's greatest rock and roll band? My vote would be for The Beatles if we looked at their output and impact on the world, in music, fashion and even philosophy.

The group that kept breathing down the Beatles' necks in the 1960s was The Rolling Stones. Still introduced at their concerts as the world's greatest, they've definitely won the longevity crown. This has surprised many, including me, amazed that the ravages of long-term drug use has not shortened their careers or their lives. Maybe the intense creativity of Sir Mick Jagger and Keith Richards has protected them. Sir Mick summed up his refusal to retire gracefully when he said, 'Either we stay at home and become pillars of the community or we go out and tour. And we couldn't find any communities that still needed pillars.' I like that.

Your age is nine-tenths what you think it is, and humour helps you stay young. I'm with Sir Mick. I've already decided I'm not going to retire. At the other end of the champion-seeking spectrum are those who seem satisfied with fleeting success. Like those one-hit wonders, who rely on a single successful song to attract audiences. You can now add those normally anonymous people who become micro-celebrities in reality television programs. Here today, forgotten next week.

Champions have spectacular visions of their future successes. Their ambitions astound others. What stops so many people from being ambitious? What stops so many young people shooting for the stars? For a start, some people connect saying 'I'm ambitious' with arrogance. As I said before, that's only true if you've lost your principles.

I often hear another answer, whether I'm counselling distressed clients or listening to managers who are rarely leaders. It's a phrase that kills ambitions. It exterminates risk-taking and stifles progress, especially when building relationships. In therapy, I often hear 'I can't'. Short and sharp but an extremely powerful way to stop you in your tracks.

One of my clients was once on an 'I can't' overload. He was spraying statements like 'I can't understand my daughter' and 'I can't talk to her'. I asked him what his response would be if someone aggressively told him that he couldn't do something. My client's reply was, 'Who says I can't?' He stuck a large copy of this statement in his bathroom so it would remind him every morning of something very important. He quickly realised the only person stopping him from enriching his relationship with his daughter was himself. How much do you hear yourself saying 'I can't'? Listen closely to those who you want to help — your family, friends, co-workers. Quickly ask them, 'Who says you can't?' Relight that ambition flame straight away.

Here's a question about your career vision. Can you see your business, your company, your school, your hospital, or whatever organisation you're connected to, being the best in your state? What about the best in Australia? Why not? What would you have to do to make it the best?

There are institutes or think tanks popping up all over the country. How could your organisation become a respected Think Tank for Outstanding Success? You have to start by mixing some passion with a vision. Here's another strange situation to get you thinking. You've just been randomly selected to show international visitors some highlights of your organisation, highlights to impress your visitors. What would you do? What would you show them? I proposed a similar scenario to the general manager of a basketball team in Australia's NBL. I asked him what could he show to visitors from the San Antonio Spurs, the NBA champions in the US. You know what his response was? He shrugged his shoulders. I saw why his club has only ever won one Australian championship in over 20 years.

How do you look at success?

There's a very quick way of learning so much about the way you personally look at success. I've given you a strange diagram — I call it 'The success wheel'. In each rectangle, write the name of a successful person you admire. (I encountered a manager at a large corporation who left the page blank. He told the group he didn't admire anyone. I was flabbergasted.) After you've chosen your heroes, look for the connections between them. What do they have in common? This will point you in the direction toward your own achievement of success.

I learnt something bizarre about myself when I first did this exercise 10 years ago. I wrote in Mandela, Gandhi, Viktor Frankl, a brilliant and caring Austrian psychiatrist who spent four years in German concentration camps, and Weary Dunlop, the Australian doctor who is regarded as a saint by the Australian soldiers who had to build the Burma railway for the Japanese in World War II. I realised four of the men I admire the most had all been in some sort of prison! I shared this insight in a seminar with prison guards and one of them told me, 'You're never going to find a Mandela or a Gandhi in our prisons'. My reply was, you might.

The success wheel

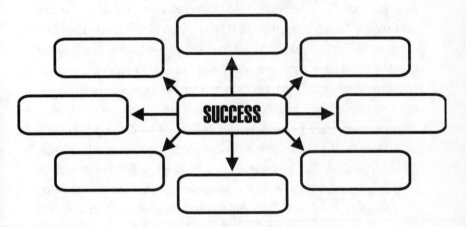

Be careful when you look at someone because success, even greatness, might be in disguise, waiting to explode sometime in the future. Imagine you're looking at a young black man sweeping floors in a factory, it's his first job. In 50 years he becomes one of the most powerful men in the world — he's Colin Powell. Then there's the milkman who became a legend in movies — Sean Connery. How about the general manager of a local government council who began his career on a garbage truck? A future great success might be right in front of you, anywhere.

It's hard to separate success from happiness, and both of them depend on your perspective, how you look at your life. Tiger Woods gave an answer worthy of a Zen master after he was asked what was the happiest time of his life. His reply, 'When I was 11. I got straight As, had two recesses a day, had the cutest girlfriend and won 32 tournaments. Everything's been down hill since.'

Before we move on, I want to tell you how this exercise showed I had a bit of racism in me. I became aware of this when I was in the middle of giving a talk at an Aboriginal college in the inner suburbs of Sydney. Some negativity crept into my mind before I gave my talk. Would the students see me as a white person intruding, would I be ignored, rejected or even verbally abused? I could not have been more wrong. After my talk, one student called out as I left the school grounds, 'See you brother'. During my talk, I asked the students to share their heroes. The first young girl who answered said Dr Victor Chang, a heart transplant specialist who was murdered in a Sydney street. Her second choice was the author of the book, *The Power of One*. (She didn't know his name was Bryce Courtney.) I didn't expect such impressive answers. Another girl then told us her heroes were Dr Martin Luther King, and God. I had a good look at myself after that session.

If you've been really paying attention, you might be thinking I've hardly talked about the third ingredient of our formula for success — action. You're right, so let's rectify that. Action leads us to the most popular word used by sports coaches, after the F-word; it's commitment. In the exercise 'Showing extra commitment' below, I've put together some guidelines so that you will be more aware of your commitment. When you want to boost your commitment, look backwards before you go forward.

Showing extra commitment

Over the last 12 months, I showed a **commitment** to the important things in my life by:

....

....

....

....

....

Over the next 12 months, I will show **extra commitment** to the important things in my life by:

....

....

....

....

....

Over the last 12 months, I **helped others** in my life by:

....

....

....

....

....

Over the next 12 months, I **will help others** in my life by:

....

....

....

....

....

Here's how and why I first put the exercise 'Showing extra commitment' together. About three months before the Atlanta Olympics, one of my clients was an 18-year-old swimmer who had been chosen to go to Atlanta. You'd think she would be happy and excited, wouldn't you? The exact opposite was the case — she had started having panic attacks because she was worried she couldn't keep up her commitment for the last few months. I cured her panic in one session. She gave me the clues. She said she was frightened she would choke and embarrass herself in front of hundreds of millions of people watching on TV. She said, 'I'm frightened all my years of commitment will be a waste of time'. Really? I asked how many years she had been committed to her swimming. She began at six years old. I got some blank paper and told her to describe the effort she had put in over the last 12 years of her life. We filled up two pages. I asked, 'What does this tell you?' I just love that question. She said it was awesome and I agreed. I then asked her, what else did it tell her? She smiled at me, such a beautiful smile, and said, 'It'll be easy to stay committed for just another three months'. Once she clearly became aware of her past commitment, she used this as a springboard to increase her workload, and show even more commitment. I can't give you a fairy-tale ending and say she won a gold or even a bronze medal, but she did swim a PB — a personal best.

The success of this exercise is based on a big principle. The heart of commitment is about finishing, rather than starting. Anyone can start. Many big finishers were slow starters, late bloomers. I'm one of them. I didn't discover my passion and vision for a rewarding career until I was 39. And, watch your last three steps. What? At football training, during sprint sessions, one great coach always watches for those who ease up three steps short of the finish. They're telling everyone what they're also likely to do in a game.

You might be asking why the last two questions are part of the last exercise. How is helping others connected to commitment? I'll explain.

One of the best parts of being a sports psychologist is meeting great coaches. I've learnt so much about success in life by listening to what great coaches say, and watching what they do. Great coaches have a philosophy based around caring for others, giving more than they receive. For me, this caring for others is a real sign of strength, great strength. If you've seen the TV program on Wayne Bennett's life story, you'll know exactly where I'm coming from. He's the one who watches the last three steps.

Let me share with you a brief story about giving and receiving. This story means a great deal to me. It's about a friend of mine, a different Wayne, Wayne Pearce. He had a great career as a rugby league player for Australia and he often captained NSW in their yearly battles with Queensland. He holds the record for being the only person to captain NSW to a 3–0 whitewash of Queensland and then do the same thing as a coach.

Back in 1997, I was the psychologist with the Balmain Tigers, the club Wayne was coaching. It was the second last game of the year, and if we lost, that was the end of the season. Balmain had to play a red-hot Parramatta team and the Tigers' form had been wobbly. It was a Friday night game, and

I did my bit with a pre-game team hypnosis session, but there was something far more powerful going on that I was totally unaware of. The last 30 minutes before a game are precious to coaches and Wayne was just leaving his seat in the grandstand to go down and talk to his players, when someone asked if he could speak to a girl, a girl who had cancer. I know plenty of coaches who would have put it off until after the game. Wayne spent the next 15 minutes talking to the girl. That night the Tigers thrashed Parramatta, and early the next morning, the girl died. Her mother said that night was the happiest she had seen her daughter in years. Wayne told no-one about it. That's even more class. I only found out after a friend of his told a reporter.

Are you strong enough to give more than you receive?

I'm certain whenever you help anyone to be more successful, some of that success comes back to help you, even if you're completely unaware of the connection. What's really special is that you're often rewarded with things that money just can't buy. I was once attacked by a cynic for believing this. I was told later that he was very self-centred — that's a nice way of saying he was selfish. I'll give you a quick insight into your personality. Because you're reading this book, I am very, very confident you're not selfish. Success is superficial when it's built around selfishness.

Chapter 2
Life's a Lot Like Sport

My most cherished sports book has a title that always tantalises me. Its full title is *Beyond Winning: The Timeless Wisdom of Great Philosopher Coaches*. I'd owned this wonderful book for several years before I saw its essential message. Unfortunately for me, I only skimmed over the introduction before jumping into the heart of the book. Something drew me back one day to read the book again, more thoroughly this time. Hidden in the introduction was this sentence, '*To coach is to believe in something*'. I immediately asked myself, what do I believe in? Since then, I regularly ask coaches, and lots of other people, this question. I get a lot of stunned reactions.

Many of my psychologist colleagues avoid going into this area with their clients. They don't want to enter a 'no-go zone'. Maybe they might feel its an area that's too personal, like a zone of mental intimacy. However, I've found the exact opposite. People enjoy the mental shake-up when they are asked to think about their principles. That's an important statement, and it's taken me many years to realise how important it is. Wars, crises, tragedies, all make us stop and look at our principles. But so do the best forms of humour.

Like millions of other Australians I became addicted to a television series called *SeaChange*. Stretching over three successful years, it was one of the most popular Australian television series of all time. One critic claimed Shakespeare would've been proud to have been its author. I agree. The series was so thoughtful, one episode was discussed at a conference on the role of fathers in modern society.

Amongst the quirky humour and the twists and turns in the storyline, there was an ongoing and magnificent study in human principles and values. One episode stands out for me. The central character in this series was a disillusioned lawyer and mother, who leaves her hectic life in

Melbourne to become a magistrate in a quiet seaside town. She picked up the flame I want to pass on to you. She asked all those around her, 'What do you believe in?' The answers from these fictional characters were a good sample of the rich variety in the real world. The reply from a disillusioned and bitter reporter was 'Swimming'. Every morning he isolated himself from the rest of the world by swimming far off the beach. The young policewoman quickly said, 'I believe in everything that Catholics believe'. This answer touched on my triple view of religions — they can be vibrant sources of life, long-term anaesthetics, or simply insurance policies. The Buddhist monk visiting the town stated simply, 'Love and forgiveness'.

Closing the episode was the wisdom from the caravan park manager. He told his son, 'Life would be boring if we knew everything'. Yes, yes, yes! That tells us so much. Principles — what we believe, what we stand for — are timeless, but that doesn't mean there is only one way to look at them, only one way to describe them. Our lives are a constant search to learn about our own principles. The clearer we see them, the easier they are to follow.

Here is a simple exercise to show you where we're heading. Copy the following words onto separate small pieces of paper.

ACHIEVEMENTS, CHANGES, GOALS, DREAMS, ETHICS, PLANS, PRINCIPLES, RESULTS, STRATEGIES, SUCCESS, TACTICS, VALUES, VISION

Rearrange the words so that you form four separate groups. Now arrange the groups in a stepwise sequence. You can build your own 'Ladder of Success'. That is, decide what group comes first, then second, then third, and then last. Which group formed your first step, the base, the foundation of everything else? Have a look ahead (see 'My ladder of success' on p. 39), and see if we've constructed the same ladder. Now focus on the image of a giant ladder. How smart is it when you try and jump onto the ladder and miss the first step? There's a good chance the ladder will become unstable and fall with you on it. That's the same with your life. With a stable strong base you can go as high as you want.

Let me share with you some of the pathways I've taken to find my life principles, my beliefs. I have come to the very strong conclusion that sometimes you're meant to receive wonderful insights into life. Keep your eyes open and your hearing switched on because I don't think these messages arrive regularly. Because they are random, you can miss them. One day, a few years ago, I was bombarded from three different directions. Early in the day a friend mentioned that he thought life revolved around two things, pleasure and pain. This was not earth shattering as the father of psychiatry, Sigmund Freud, preached the same view. And more recently, Anthony Robbins, the gigantic speaker and author, expounded the same view.

On with my story. Later the same day someone commented to me that the only two things certain in life were death and taxes. Benjamin Franklin originally proposed this humorous assessment over two hundred years ago. Pleasure and pain followed by death and taxes. My mind was now prepared for something big. That evening I was watching an episode of the television series, *Chicago Hope*. The head of the hospital had entered a coma. Another doctor, who had previously died, came to visit him. In this dream sequence, the dead doctor hands across a piece of folded paper. On it was written 'Meaning of Life'. I was hooked and had to watch the rest of the show to find what was inside the note. At the very end, the note was opened to reveal, 'Giving and receiving'. That's what I believe!

A few days later, I was listening to an audiotape series called *The Psychology of Achievement*. The speaker and author was Brian Tracy, a highly successful consultant to many blue-chip corporations in the United States. After listening to several hours of psychological techniques and anecdotes on business success, I was truly not prepared for, or expecting, what I heard next, 'The purpose of life is to form loving relationships'. This ended a powerful group of messages that were thrown at me in a three-day period. I'm so glad I was aware enough to catch these messages. How aware are you?

There was one night when I learnt a lot about life. I was called in to do emergency grief counselling with two teams of young rugby league footballers. They were 15 years old. During their last game, one player collapsed and then died in hospital. I saw in front of me 30 faces that showed pain, disbelief and even anger. I knew I had to choose every word carefully if I was going to help these young men.

I borrowed an idea from Wayne Bennett, the rugby league coach who I've already mentioned. Wayne has coached the mega-successful Brisbane Broncos for nearly two decades, as well as coaching Queensland and Australia. He has written a book called *League's A Lot Like Life*. I told the young players that I thought this message was true, but the reverse was much more important, 'Life's a lot like League'. Life and football, or any other sport, are full of unexpected problems, small and large, and the champions cope better than others. They get stronger by dealing with problems. This, in a nutshell, is my view about sports psychology.

Anything I teach as a sports psychologist has to apply to life as well as sports. I greatly admire all coaches, whatever their sport, who share this philosophy. Near the top of my list is Phil Jackson, one of the most successful basketball coaches of all time. In his book *Sacred Hoops*, Jackson wrote, 'When I was named head coach of the Chicago Bulls in 1989, my dream was not just to win championships but to do it in a way that wove together my two greatest passions: basketball and spiritual exploration'. His core philosophy for his team was, 'Not only is there more to life than basketball, there's a lot more to basketball than basketball'. Jackson mixed ideas from Zen Buddhism, Native American customs and Christianity. He encouraged his players to practise visualisation and meditation. Jackson taught his team to win by the principles of awareness, compassion, and most of all, selfless team play. During the finals, the most important part of any basketball season, he often read a passage from Rudyard Kipling's *Second Jungle Book* to his players. After reading this poem to my seminar audiences, I always ask: Why would the world's best basketball coach make the world's best basketball team listen to a poem from a children's book? What is its incredible message?

Now this is the Law of the Jungle
as old and as true as the sky;
And the Wolf that shall keep it may prosper,

but the Wolf that shall break it must die.
As the creeper that girdles the tree trunk
the Law runneth forward and back
For the strength of the Pack is the Wolf,
and the strength of the Wolf is the Pack.

There's another inspiring Australian coach who has achieved so much on and off the football field. Rod Macqueen, possibly the most successful rugby union coach of all time, also tapped onto the power of this poem when he wanted to define the philosophy of his coaching. It's hard to keep a great message hidden. Different coaches have taught me a lot about life. One of my favourite learning positions is leaning against a wall in a dressing room listening to a wise coach. More often, coaches have inspired me through their books.

My book shelves contain four books written by one coach. No other coach makes more than two contributions to my personal library. The word legend is frequently thrown around loosely, but it's totally appropriate when used to describe rugby league coach Jack Gibson. This man revolutionised rugby league and his strong influence over other coaches in Australia has stretched more than three decades. His four books are rich in wisdom and they're essential reading for any sports coach, in any sport, and more than that, they're valuable even if you have no interest in any sport at all. That's why I sat up and absorbed a powerful message he gave to an inexperienced coach. Jack was asked what was the most important attribute of a coach. That's a huge question. His answer was huge as well. It was 'trust'. I think trust comes from honesty, and it's impossible to separate the two. I can't, can you? I've never found I could trust a dishonest person. There's a fascinating book called *The Millionaire Mind* that reveals the thinking of 733 self-made millionaires. The author of the book, Thomas Stanley, asked this huge range of millionaires to rate the factors that lead to their success. Way out in front, was honesty!

My ladder of success

RESULTS, CHANGES, ACHIEVEMENTS, SUCCESS

↑

STRATEGIES, PLANS, TACTICS

↑

VISION, DREAMS, GOALS

↑

VALUES, PRINCIPLES, ETHICS

How trustworthy and honest are you?

A popular exercise, guaranteed to be a discussion starter, and sometimes an argument provoker, is to rate professions according to honesty. This exercise is actually part of a regular scientific study carried out in Australia by the CSIRO. Some variation exists between the ongoing studies, but a general pattern shows that Australians usually regard the top three most honest occupations, in descending order, as doctors, dentists and school teachers. I get lots of applause when I share that with teachers. At the bottom are newspaper journalists, advertising people and car salespeople. One teacher told me this end represents the top of the most despised list. Hold on if you're in this group and you feel like throwing my book across the room. These analyses are based on perceptions, not facts, and they only represent superficial generalisations. Billy Connolly, one of my favourite comedians and philosophers, attacked the mantra of some men-hating feminists who claim, 'All men are the same'. Billy suggested if you compare Adolf Hitler and Jesus, you'll soon see the variety that's possible in men. That also goes for all professions. You'll find good and bad in all of them.

Many of the successful sports teams I've worked with share a simple technique to promote even more success. Their coaches design game plans and strategies that are condensed into clear concise printed summaries. Sometimes called 'tip sheets', these summaries are only one or two pages long, and are devoured by the players. A tip sheet is the bible for the upcoming game. These tips are a mixture of insights, suggestions and instructions. So brief and simple, but so incredibly helpful.

A few years ago, I saw how you could gain much bigger benefits if you expanded this technique to look at life. I was given this message during a session I had with a young footballer who was playing poorly and in a long slump. As his father was no longer alive, he had grown very close to one of his many uncles. Like a loving parent, this uncle had just given the player some sincere advice. The young man found the handful of ideas very moving. I told him that I felt the same way. When a message is based on love, the idea contained in the message is timeless. For the rest of the session, I encouraged him to take over the role of his uncle and produce his own list of powerful advice, 10 best tips for life, that he could share with the rest of his large family. It was an emotionally uplifting session for both of us, and the player soon achieved spectacular results on the football field.

Since then, I've repeated this exercise over and over again, with individuals and groups, small and large. It's been wonderful. I deliberately say wonderful, because I've seen the sense of wonder grow in people's faces as they start to see their lives more clearly. I want you to now experience your own wonderful lift. This exercise will help you to learn a lot about your future pathway through life. It will be so easy if you start by recalling some advice you were given that helped you a lot. This advice probably strengthened the bond between you and the other person. Right? Turn the situation around and think of someone you care strongly about and imagine that person is now in front of you asking for your best advice.

Why not share your best thoughts with yourself?

Take your time. Go back and reconsider the importance of the many themes we've already talked about. Then fully digest the Hockeyroos Mission

Statement. This 10-point statement was put together by one of Australia's most successful teams. The Hockeyroos dominated women's hockey, winning world championships plus gold medals at the Atlanta and Sydney Olympic Games. Championship thinking produced championship results for this magnificent team. Borrow great ideas, the Hockeyroos did. Does their bottom line sound familiar? That was originally said by President Kennedy when he challenged his fellow Americans to put a man on the Moon. The Hockeyroos did more than borrow Kennedy's advice, they followed it to the very last word.

Hockeyroos Mission Statement

We will win in Atlanta by being the best we can be because Olympic gold is the ultimate challenge in our sport. We will achieve this by playing beyond our previous performances and by never, never giving up. I will be the best I can be by:

1. Continually challenging myself to go beyond my comfort zone.
2. Making the necessary sacrifices.
3. Believing in my ability and the strength of my purpose.
4. Valuing excellence, determination and dedication in both training and match play.
5. Having faith and confidence in, and being supportive of, my team-mates.
6. Not making excuses but taking responsibility for my development, performance and for my lifestyle.
7. Seeking feedback and making contributions to the program.
8. Being tolerant of differences in others and respecting them for who they are and what they have to offer.
9. Accepting disappointments and frustrations and overcoming them by working together.
10. Having faith in the course of action chosen for the team and being committed to it knowing that it may not always be my preference.

We choose to do this thing **not** because it is easy but because it is hard.

While you're reading and thinking, building your own personal philosophy of success in life, expect a sense of wonder. It's there for us all to enjoy. When you feel it, you'll know you're on the right track. Maybe you're thinking I've promised too much. Have you ever watched children look at something new? That's the sense of wonder for life that was once strong within all of us. I loved the long-running television series *The Wonder Years* about a boy entering and leaving adolescence. Becoming more mature often dulls the awareness that every day in our lives can hold something wonderful.

10 best tips to be a winner

1. ....
2. ....
3. ....
4. ....
5. ....
6. ....
7. ....
8. ....
9. ....
10. ....

How important is this exercise? Here's an image I like using. If I had to tear out the two most valuable pages from this book, and throw away the rest of the book, then the last page would still be in my hands. It's one of two pages that regularly achieve magical changes. The other page? Well, you'll find it later on when I introduce you to the power of self-hypnosis.

Your '10 best tips' are important because your list can quickly expand into many more valuable insights and pathways to success. This will especially happen if you follow the footsteps of the legendary basketball coach, John Wooden. In the United States, he was frequently selected as Coach of the Year, and in 1971, he even received the accolade of *Coach of the Century*. Wooden's clear philosophy of life led to incredible achievements. He clearly described his philosophy of success in a unique way, a way so memorable that his former players often remembered it for the rest of their lives.

Back in the 1930s, John Wooden built a five layer pyramid, consisting of 15 blocks. He labelled each block with a key to success, a broad concept that he briefly described. You studied the messages in the pyramid from the base upwards. For nearly 40 years, Wooden began every basketball season with a discussion of his unchanging 'Pyramid of Success' (see page 44).

You can build your own impressive pyramid. You can also benefit from the insights from others if you construct a pyramid from the 'Best Tips' of all members of a large group. This is a rewarding and eye-opening exercise. It leads to true team bonding. I've led many sporting teams through this activity, especially at pre-season camps, and then seen players consulting their team pyramid throughout the competition season. Where? Often players stuck copies in their lockers and some told me they placed their pyramid on a shower wall at home. To show you the great results you can expect, look at the pyramid put together by one of my favourite sporting teams — the Balmain Tigers Rugby League Club.

Here are the steps I like to follow. Collect and compare the different 'Best tips' from everyone around you. You will quickly see that some advice is very popular. Many group members will offer the same important messages. Identify the five most important common messages from your group and place each message on a different basement block. Continue this process for the second layer, third layer, fourth layer and the crowning message.

Sometimes some advice, especially when it's in the form of a short quote, has a very attractive sound to it. However, when you look more closely, some appealing advice is really shallow, hollow and empty, like a sea shell mimicking the sound of the sea. I've come across advice that I reject, but others strongly believe. A long-time chairman of Coca-Cola liked to say, 'The world belongs to the *discontented*'. This message was also on the walls in many offices at Coke's headquarters. It's not for me. Australian cricket captain Stephen Waugh has written many best selling books, and one of them has the title *Never Satisfied*. This philosophy is also preached by Deepak Chopra and a former high flying, but now disgraced Australian business entrepreneur. One member of a family of multimillionaires told me their success was driven by their unwritten motto, 'Stay Insecure'. George Bernard Shaw proposed that 'all progress depends on *unreasonable men*'. I've counselled many depressed clients who followed these four philosophies.

Pyramid of Success

Leadership
Actions speak louder than words. Be a great role model.

Dignity
Be more concerned about your character than your reputation.

Respect
For yourself, for your supporters and your opponents.

Initiative
Take that extra step to attack new challenges.

Concentrate
Stay focused. Know exactly what you are doing.

Persistence
Be positive and overcome any setback.

Encourage
Strengthen yourself by helping others.

Preparation
Cover every detail with careful planning.

Honesty
Act so others can depend on you.

Courage
Endure and expect hardships.

Enthusiasm
Enjoy what you do. Life is a search for happiness.

Learning
Absorb good ideas from everyone. Seek help to constantly improve.

Desire
See yourself achieving the best! Have a clear vision of success.

Confidence
Believe in yourself at all times, without being arrogant.

Commitment
Give 100% —work harder and smarter.

What causes the dark side of sport?

I admire so many champions in sport, possibly the great coaches more than the great athletes. However, I should make something absolutely, 100 per cent, clear. There are many things in the make-up of professional sport, all over the world, that stink! To show you where I'm heading, slowly digest some hard hitting thoughts. Michael Parkinson, the highly respected TV interviewer and lover of sport, gave British soccer this blistering review in 2003. Take a deep breath, because this is powerful stuff. In the London *Daily Telegraph*, he wrote

> … it needs fumigating, sterilising and purifying, not to mention deodorising, disinfecting and decontaminating. Taken in isolation, the drinking, the whoring, the racism, the violence, the cheating, the lying, the false pride, the arrogant self-interest masquerading as team spirit, the conniving, the failure to admit blame and to accept responsibility, the fatuous excuses, and the utter dumb, gormless stupidity of the players would be enough for grave concern. Put it all together, join the dots and what you have is Dodge City without the sheriff. It is what happens when men and money come together in an unregulated and unprincipled mayhem and all the normal rules governing human behaviour are treated with contempt.

Again, I emphasise I love so much about professional sport, but I'm still going to stand in Parkinson's corner. Some coaches, sports managers, commentators, and many sports fans condone contemptible actions, carried out by some sports stars. Parkinson hit it on the head when he diagnosed these problems on the lack of principles. His diagnosis applies to many areas of life, away from sport. Do you remember the title of this chapter? Say it out loud. Life's a lot like sport. The beauty and fascination of sport is that it encapsulates what is best about life. Unfortunately, sport sometimes contains the worst aspects of life as well. Plenty of sports fans overlook that fact.

Possibly this is a reverse of the tall poppy syndrome. AFL footballer Wayne Carey was regarded as one of the greatest players, and happily married, but this did not stop him throwing away his reputation. When he was caught having an affair with the wife of a close team-mate, he was forced to leave his club but, wait for it, several other clubs then chased him with open arms. When cricketer Shane Warne completed his 12-month suspension for taking an illegal drug, many fans and fellow players called for Warne to be forgiven, and be immediately selected to play in the Australian team. After all, he's one of the greatest bowlers of all time. We've now discovered a host of US track stars who failed drug tests but were permitted to compete in the Sydney Olympics. The basketball star, Kobe Bryant, was still under the cloud of a rape accusation when he was wildly cheered by the crowd as he ran onto the court.

I'm a big believer in forgiveness, and I'm certain many of the world's problems would disappear if the surplus of forgiveness in sport spread into the rest of the world. A lack of principles produces shallow sports stars, conniving corporate leaders and superficial politicians. Some sportspeople, businesspeople and politicians feel that ethics is the English county next to Sussex.

Before we leave this chapter, slow down and stop for a moment. I want to share some sobering thoughts about borrowing wisdom from others, even from me. Some people often grab for a quote or a saying when they want to support their own view. Using the wise thoughts of others is healthy as long as it does not lead to tunnel vision. No person owns the truth. Opinions that totally clash are sometimes given as examples of truth. The next exercise will help you remember this for a very long time.

Conflicting advice

In this exercise, form 14 pairs by matching the statements that **contradict** each other.

1. Ignorance is bliss.
2. Absence makes the heart grow fonder.
3. If it ain't broke, don't fix it.
4. Imagination is more important than knowledge. (Albert Einstein)
5. Don't put all your eggs in one basket.
6. Too many cooks spoil the broth.
7. Out of sight out of mind.
8. There's a sucker born every minute. (PT Barnum)
9. Pride goes before a fall. (Proverbs, The Bible)

10. There's always room for improvement.

11. Fools rush in where wise men fear to tread.

12. The devil you know is better than the one you don't.

13. A silent fool can still appear to be smart. (Abraham Lincoln)

14. You can't teach an old dog new tricks.

15. It's never too late to learn.

16. Slow and steady wins the race. (Aesop)

17. All men are created equal.

18. Ego is not a dirty word. (Skyhooks)

19. A brave man speaks his mind.

20. Variety is the spice of life.

21. Two heads are better than one.

22. Wonders will never cease.

23. It is a capital mistake to theorise before one has data.
    (Sherlock Holmes)

24. He who hesitates is lost.

25. There's nothing new under the sun.

26. Time is money. (Benjamin Franklin)

27. Greater the risk, greater the profit.

28. Knowledge is power.

Chapter 3
Last Questions You'll Ever Hear?

It's a great pity most of us avoid thinking about dying. Why? Because, if we visualise the end of our lives, it opens our eyes to many things. It can teach us a lot about true success. Spend some time visualising this and you'll get more accurate and valuable insights than any horoscope. If you're taking your last few breaths on this planet, it's likely plenty of questions will flash through your mind. If you ask two questions — *Is that it?* and *What's next?* — I think you've got problems. There are two other questions, you won't ask yourself, but you still might hear them.

Elisabeth Kübler-Ross was a remarkable woman who lead the way in changing many of our attitudes toward death and dying. Her works were landmarks that lead to greater scientific study of these critical areas of the human life cycle. One fascinating study looked at people who had 'crossed over', those who had died and returned to life. After interviewing a large number of these people, Kübler-Ross found a common thread. Many recalled that they were asked two questions during this life-death transition period. When I first heard about this discovery I was on the edge of my seat. The first question was, *Have you learned enough?* The second question was, *Have you loved enough?* Wow! What beautiful questions. Knowing these questions can be wonderful news. Why wait to be asked these questions?

I love learning. Do you? We can use a lot of metaphors for life and one that stands out for me is that life is a banquet. There's so much before us, spread out, for us to taste with our bodies, and our minds. I regularly drive past a Greek restaurant with a banner stating, 'All you can eat for $30'. I always mentally rearrange the message to, *All you can learn and love for life.*

I do a lot of strange things to give my audiences lasting impressions. One of my favourite stunts involves a Superman top, you know, one of those with a giant red 'S' on the chest. After I unbutton my shirt to reveal my secret identity, I ask if anyone has seen a far stronger super hero who wears a giant 'L' up front. Up in the sky, it's … Learning Man, or Learning Woman.

If only we would accept that learning gives us incredible strength, like steroids for the brain. Call anyone a 'know-it-all' and you know the reaction you can expect. However, I've heard many people in sport who proudly describe themselves this way. Oh yes, they don't say 'know-it-all' but they use descriptions that end up with the same label. They've been swallowing those dumb pills that numb their desire for learning. It's amazing so many young athletes, in so many different sports, still keep ignoring great advice like this. A coach suggested to a young cricket star that he do some mental skills training with me. His knee jerk response was, 'I did all that at the Cricket Academy'. He did all that! Then there was a struggling football coach who told me he could teach a course on mental preparation. I've got no doubt he could have. Unfortunately some courses are taught very poorly.

Quite often the more experience you gain, the more you realise how much you didn't know in the past. A friend of mine, Paul Sironen, a rugby league footballer who played many times for Australia, was kind enough to write in his biography that I made him aware of the importance of sports psychology. He wished he'd been taught more mental skills at the start of his career, instead of near the end. Stephen Waugh, captain of the Australian cricket team and one of the greatest batsmen in cricket, echoed Paul's thoughts. After a lecture from a sports psychologist to the Australian cricket team, Stephen said everything made good sense. In fact, it was all common sense, but it had taken him 10 years to learn what he had heard in just an hour.

Let's go back to my dumb pills. I want the image of taking dumb pills to stay with you. It's a silly image, even an outrageous one, because it's something you would never consciously do. So make sure you don't do it subconsiously. Set out every day to learn, to improve, to grow. Do some mind stretching every day. It's a great exercise when you stretch your mind, it never returns to its former shape. Muscles can shrink, healthy minds don't! You've got a great head start because humans were designed to learn. We can all be excellent learners, intelligence has got nothing to do with it. Want some powerful evidence that humans are tremendously effective learners? Do you know anyone who has had a phobia? They're common, believe me. Over the years my clients have described a plethora of phobias. How are they linked to learning? Phobias grow from learning too much, usually from a single incident. Mark Twain painted a memorable image of this form of overgeneralising. He said once a cat has stepped on a hot stove it will not only keep away from a hot stove, it will never step on a cold stove. Phobias are learnt, and that's why psychologists have tremendous successes helping people to unlearn them.

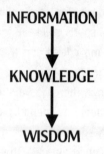

INFORMATION

KNOWLEDGE

WISDOM

It's what you learn after you know it all that counts
John Wooden (Extraordinary basketball coach)

There are countless opportunities for us to learn much more helpful behaviour than phobias. Look around you. We live in a world saturated in information. Every time you pick up a large newspaper, like the *Sydney Morning Herald* or *The New York Times* you're holding more information than you would have encountered in a whole lifetime 100 years ago. Then there's the Internet. However, if you only consume information, your learning will be malnourished. My view is that we are drowning in information but starving for knowledge. Knowledge exists at that level above information. When you are very, very lucky, sometimes you will find amongst all that information around you, wisdom. It's the knowledge that never has a use-by-date.

Was your education like having a lobotomy?

I'm often asked to recommend books. Would you believe that the list of authors I put together for the next exercise has offended some people? Some have felt insulted, as if I've criticised them, calling them ignorant for answering 'No' to the question. They missed the point I was trying to make. These authors can help you in your search for wisdom, so can thousands of others, many you've already read, many I've never seen. My list of authors contains some of my favourites, plus a couple whose ideas I reject. That's a huge part of learning. You have to search to find out what you believe, and what you don't. It can be annoying reading ideas that get up your nose. However, this is still a part of true education. One Australian author said good education is upsetting. It upsets, because it disturbs complacency, intellectual laziness and mindlessness. She compared relaxed, comfortable, sedating education to having a lobotomy. You don't have to be brain dead to be ignorant. I know I'm always missing out on valuable skills and ideas, and so are you. I think that makes life even more interesting and stimulating, doesn't it?

What do you know?

Have you read any books written by any of the following prolific authors?

· Deepak Chopra, e.g. *Ageless Body, Timeless Mind*
· Stephen Covey, e.g. *The 7 Habits of Highly Effective People*
· Dalai Lama, e.g. *The Art of Happiness*
· Edward de Bono, e.g. *Six Thinking Hats*
· Wayne Dyer, e.g. *Wisdom of the Ages*
· Daniel Goleman, e.g. *Emotional Intelligence*
· John Gray, e.g. *Men are from Mars, Women are from Venus*
· Robert Kiyosaki, e.g. *Rich Dad, Poor Dad*
· Tom Peters, e.g. *The Circle of Innovation*
· Anthony Robbins, e.g. *Awaken the Giant Within*
· Martin Seligman, e.g. *Learned Optimism*
· Dennis Waitley, e.g. *The Psychology of Winning*

If your answer is 'No', you are not fully using your personal resources. You are missing out on valuable ideas and skills.

Research is a great way to locate valuable parcels of wisdom. Like other words that attract me, research is a word that can be looked at in different ways, and I love things that are different. There are two excellent ways to research. First, first and still first, is read, read and read!! Ignore the chant, 'I don't have enough time'.

The second way to research stares right at you and tells you what you have to do. Search backwards and rummage through the pile where you tossed all those insignificant observations. I've found a lot of treasure in my insignificant pile. I think learning in life is like the fossil-hunting I do while I'm jogging. To collect many of the fossils I find I have to stop and go back one or two steps to look more closely. I also use the same techniques with reading. I've discovered many valuable things by rereading books, sometimes books I haven't touched for years, as well as returning to books I've previously dismissed as not containing anything valuable.

Many of the recent movie blockbusters have been built around science fiction or fantasy themes, enabling the viewer to travel in space and time. Long before computer technology allowed these epics to come alive, what was there? There were books!

This was made so clear to me in a deep discussion I had with a friend who lived in the 18th century. No, don't start worrying that I've lost the plot. My friend was, or is, Dr Isaac Watts, who shared his thoughts with me through a book he wrote around 1750. His book, *The Improvement of the Mind*, was loaned to me by the football legend Jack Gibson. The book was precious as it had belonged to Jack's father, and his copy was over 150 years old. As I've said earlier, it's amazing how important ideas will fall into your lap. Watts shared many great insights, including a timeless assessment of the benefits of reading. He said, '*By reading we acquaint ourselves, in a very extensive manner, with the affairs, actions, and thoughts of the living and the dead, in the most remote nations, and most distant ages*'. Great stuff, Dr Watts. Our minds, our brains can produce more spectacular special effects than anything generated by a computer.

Expect more moments of great learning!

There can be many turning points, breakthroughs, special moments in our lives. The best of these times happen when you gain deep insights into life. I've already talked about some of those that have helped me to see the world differently. I now believe a large amount of the great learning we experience is completely unintentional and completely unexpected. I vividly remember another one of these times, so clearly that my thoughts now give me a bit of a tingle.

I arrived, fairly late, at a conference for sports coaches, expecting to relax and learn by just being part of the audience. Instead I was suddenly asked to replace a speaker who had met with an accident. I found it impossible to say no to someone who was desperately pleading. The organiser told me I had a tiny 30-minute time slot. That's tiny for me because I can talk for hours, even underwater. Then things started to sink in. The topic was enormous, 'How To Build A Winning Team'. This was definitely a predicament as I pride myself on the quality of my speeches, and I had less than 30 minutes to prepare. How could I do justice to this incredibly important topic? I take at least a few days to prepare every talk I give. How could I condense so many ideas? Nearly everything I taught in all my seminars would be relevant.

I left the auditorium, went outside to have a quiet stroll, to be alone with my thoughts. It didn't take long before I received a huge, but painless, injection of self-awareness. I thought of many winning teams I've worked with, and I put my own input under the microscope. How had I helped? I got a beautifully simple answer. The answer was right in front of me because I was following the basic steps there and then. First, become aware of the new challenge. Second, analyse the situation. Third, take action. What you see below are the first notes I wrote on the conference overhead screen. I told the audience that we all have to keep on our toes and have our eyes open to know where we stand, and where we're heading. That got a few laughs. After I finished speaking I met a basketball coach who regularly drilled his players with his sequence for success — *Look, Think, Move*. We were definitely on the same wavelength.

AWARENESS

↓

ANALYSIS

↓

ACTION

↓

SUCCESS

The first step for me, or any coach, leader, manager, or anyone who wants to be part of a winning team, is to be aware of what's happening in and around the team. Be alert, attentive, awake. Be alive! Zig Ziglar, the American motivational speaker, shares the same philosophy. He describes himself as a travelling optometrist. He goes around the world giving people new glasses so they see the world differently and more clearly. That's a very smart image that we should all use. We should all be regularly having awareness check-ups to see if we need new prescriptions, prescriptions to look at our lives differently.

This part of my 30-minute talk was well received. There were even nodding heads. That's a great sign for me. Then I changed tack. At the time, I wasn't sure why I was doing it, but I'm so glad I did, because I confronted myself and the audience with a far more deeper issue. Here I was with a hundred pairs of eyes staring at me, and I was about to inspire them with words like team spirit and synergy, and instead, out comes the word selfishness. I was as surprised as everyone else. I said, above all, I thought *selfishness* was the prize example of the benefits of awareness. I hope I just got you like I got the raised attention of my audience. Were you thinking, like they were, that sounds stupid? I'll expand on it.

Low levels of awareness, not being aware of others, leads to high levels of selfishness. I told my audience how I've seen selfishness rear its ugly head in teams and even seen team-mates come to blows. I've also seen selfish coaches in sport and selfish managers in business. When I got to this point at the conference, I made sure I said it very slowly and deliberately. I finished my talk by saying some very successful people often act selfishly, but I don't want to be part of their type of success. I had never previously spoken to sports groups, players or coaches, about being selfish. Why? Maybe I didn't want to offend. It's a touchy subject. However, it's a subject I now realise can't be ignored. Since that speech, I regularly challenge my audiences and individual clients to assess the levels of selfishness in their lives. You have to be aware of it before you can eliminate it.

It was not until after the conference when I did more self-analysis, that I discovered the likely inspiration for my detour into a discussion of selfish-ness. I had probably been prompted by some acts of ecological vandalism I'd seen a few days before. Around beautiful Jervis Bay, near where I live, trees had been attacked, chopped down with axes, all in the name of real estate. The trees blocked views of the bay, so they were illegally removed. The same selfishness occurred in streets around Sydney Harbour when huge healthy trees were found to be dying from poison. The values of many properties would soar when the trees no longer blocked magnificent views. Not everyone thought these were outrageous examples of selfishness. A journalist said it was highly understandable, and she blamed irresponsible councils for planting the trees in the first place, 50 to 100 years ago.

Selfishness is predictable. It happens when personal goals outweigh or even blot out team goals. In sport, I remember a great English cricketer who was dropped from the national team because he often batted to improve his aver-ages, his statistics, instead of batting to help his team win. In other team sports, there were players who thought they owned the ball. Once they got possession of it, they were unlikely to pass it on to someone in a better position. When I've spoken to some of these players, they appeared to be genuinely surprised at the ill feelings others had toward them. They weren't aware!

Language can give the most accurate forewarnings of selfishness. Selfish statements often send seismic waves before selfish acts shake the scenery. I enjoyed writing that! As part of one of my business consultations I interviewed a manager who had a fairly good track record. However, the problem was he never reached impressive heights. I quickly solved the mystery when I heard three of his statements, 'I hate going to meetings', 'I've got a million things to do' and 'I don't want to know about their personal problems'.

First, there was a paradox about him and meetings. There was an office joke that he was very religious when he was informed about another meeting. Frequently he would complain, 'Jesus, not another meeting'. I discovered his only problem with meetings occurred when he was not in charge. He was very fond of calling meetings for his team members, but there was a backflip when he had go to a meeting with higher level managers. He liked being the big fish in a small pond. That's selfish symptom number one.

Second, his busy workload seemed to become much busier when he was asked to be more hands-on, to get in and share the workload with his team. He was a good finger-pointer, but poor at shaking hands.

Third, like many managers and sport coaches, he believed in magic. This is their fantasy. Something magical happens whenever any employee arrives at work. Personal problems magically disappear. Personal problems can't touch you once you are at work. If you believe this, you never need to listen closely to your team-mates or co-workers. You just have to rely on the invisible power of magic.

This short case study of one manager has many variations as there are countless symptoms of selfishness. What's your self-diagnosis? Has anyone ever said you were selfish? Common reactions are either guilt, if you agree, or anger, if you think it's an unfair accusation. This leads you to two possible paths. One, you can reconsider your behaviour and then act by altering it in the future. Two, you can simply ignore what you've been told. Plenty of people walk along this second path.

Who's bigger than Batman and Robin?

My dual nomination for membership of the Super Hero Club is the Dalai Lama and Stephen Covey. What a dynamic duo! So intensely different in so many ways, but so alike in one essential way. They both preach the same message with different labels. From all over the world, students travel to be with the Dalai Lama in northern India and thousands hear him on his world speaking tours. Over 750,000 people around the world attend seminars with Stephen Covey or take part in training courses run by his organisation. Both Covey and the Dalai Lama have spread their thoughts even further with many best-selling books. Their link? One talks about intimacy, the other talks about interdependence. The message is the same! They are both trying to help people learn more about the role of love in our relationships, and at the same time, diminish selfishness.

When the Dalai Lama links the art of happiness with the finding of intimacy, he's talking about much more than sexual intimacy. He has broadened the definition of intimacy to include not only the romantic or sexual connection with that special somebody. Sexual intimacy is a truly wonderful sharing process, but the pursuit of sexual pleasure is far more common, and for some people it's not too distant from simply scratching an itch. True intimacy is much more. It's about caring, sharing and bonding with many people.

Much of Covey's teachings are based on his identification of the seven habits of highly effective people. He acknowledges that the driving force behind these habits is the belief that, 'Interdependence is of a higher value than independence'. Throughout his best-selling manifesto he reminds us of the maturity continuum. Dependence begets independence. Both then combine to give birth to interdependence. We're back to sharing, caring and bonding. How can two opposites, dependence and independence combine? Listen closely to the Lebanese poet Kahlil Gibran in his masterpiece, *The Prophet*:

> *… let there be spaces in your togetherness …*
> *And stand together yet not too near together:*
> *For the pillars of the temple stand apart,*
> *And the oak tree and the cypress grow*
> *not in each other's shadow.*

A business leader proudly told me he was 'fiercely independent'. My reply was, 'That's a shame'. Not surprisingly his jaw dropped. Once you're fully aware of the maturity continuum, how maturity grows, you see that independence is really a sign of not being fully developed. Rogue nations, like South Africa under apartheid and Afghanistan under religious zealots, view themselves as being bravely independent, but they end up being isolated from the world community. Full maturity is only reached with interdependence. To update an old poem, 'No person is an island'. Interdependence is not only a tongue twister for some, it's something many don't grab because they're totally ignorant of its existence. It's not as if interdependence is a characteristic only found among humans. It's been around for hundreds of millions of years. Just take a look at a group of lions.

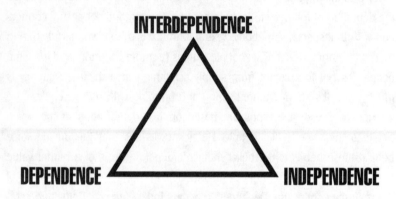

Interdependence is of a higher value than independence

Behind the facade of masculine dominance there's constant cooperation. That's more interdependence in action.

Why is independence regarded as such a prize and interdependence rarely gets a look in? Maybe we can blame politics. Throughout the 20th century a succession of countries broke away from colonial rule and the map of the world has certainly changed since the breakdown of national conglomerates such as the Soviet Union and Yugoslavia. Ethnic groups all over the world, in places as diverse as the Balkans, Indonesia, Iraq and Canada, still crave independence. East Timor became independent after a bloodbath and quickly realised it could not exist without military protection and food aid from the United Nations.

Independence is a form of leaving, rejecting restrictions, finding freedom. It's full of excitement. Eyes are hypnotically focused on the rewards of independence. Interdependence comes from discovering the wisdom of caring, sharing and bonding. This pattern of how maturity grows is repeated over and over. Successful nations grow this way, successful families grow this way. This sequence is not only natural, it's the most logical path. Caring can only grow stronger by sharing. Caring means nothing if it simply remains as thoughts. It must be followed by the actions of sharing. And bonding? When the sharing exists in both directions, each partner giving and receiving, you have reached that level of bonding that the Dalai Lama calls intimacy.

Maybe you're thinking you don't have enough time and energy to pursue such lofty goals. You sure do! Strong bonds can grow from so many small things. A powerful catalyst is to remember that every best friend was once a perfect stranger. Compliments help to give birth to these vital relationships. Do you get many compliments? Do you give many compliments? Some are obvious like, 'You look sensational' and 'You sure did a great job'. But there are many more ways to compliment like smiles, nods and laughter, hugs and pats on the back and saying the magical phrase, 'Thank you'. I'm still waiting for someone to say I look sensational. That would be flattery, and flattery sometimes contains insincerity. Stay sincere.

Do you ever ignore, reject or hurt those you love?

Even more basic, and more important, than giving a compliment, is acknowledging someone. One high-powered CEO shared his secret of success. He proposed that his team of managers and employees only respected what he inspected. I disagree. Instead of inspecting, looking over the shoulder to check on someone, you can gain respect, and show it at the same time, by acknowledging people, and what they have done. It's so simple. I saw one manager who rushed through a large factory, cheerfully asking, 'How's it going?' and 'How are you?' but he didn't once wait to hear any answers. This was superficial acknowledgement. The workers were totally aware of it, and the manager was totally ignorant of it. I know, I asked him. Such tiny incidents are often remembered for a long time.

Monty Roberts, the legendary horse whisperer tells of a painful incident that ate away at him for a long time. In his book, *Horse Sense For People,* he recalls his father ignoring him when was 10 years old. He saw his father walking down the main street in their small town and he called out, 'Hi Dad! Dad, hello! Dad, hey!' His father's response? Nothing! Years later, when confronted about this, his father simply argued he had nothing to say to his son. Monty Roberts went on to be the opposite of his father, and became a great humanitarian, a superb trainer of horses, and an expert at connecting with other people, especially with his dozens of foster children. Whether Roberts is bonding with humans or horses, he taps into the power of love, and I don't mean the song.

We can all connect with others with an everyday action that we normally overlook — shaking hands. I was hit with the great value of this action when I was working with the NSW Cricket Team. The players were doing a joint training session with a football team and I sat on the ground, like a buddha, some distance away. I finally noticed something special was going on. One after another, the footballers were slowly finding their way to one of the cricketers, Michael Slater, who had just been selected to return to the Australian team, after an absence of 16 months. He had fought his way back, against the odds, and every footballer was saying, with a handshake, 'Well done!' They were also saying they cared about him, and with each handshake, they bonded. I later asked Michael how many people had shaken his hand that day. He said, hundreds. I told him to enjoy every handshake, especially in the rest of his career.

Someone else took a long time to recognise the importance of holding a hand. As George Harrison was dying from cancer, his friend and honorary big brother, Sir Paul McCartney, sat beside him holding and stroking his hand. Here were two men who had sung 'I Wanna Hold Your Hand' thousands of times, but it was only at this time that McCartney realised he had never held his friend's hand. An emotional moment, and a moment of great learning.

Be a bleeding-heart do-gooder

Some people don't realise their words and actions place obstacles and barriers in front of their growth process toward interdependence. Caring can be quickly denigrated with terms such as 'bleeding heart' and 'do-gooder'.

Those who freely help the misfortunate have to duck economic rationalisms such as, 'There's no such thing as a free lunch'. This old saying, popularised by the economist Milton Friedman, is only a short step away from the belief that the poor deserve to be poor. You must be lazy if you're poor or unsuccessful. Beliefs like these can be used to justify indifference, coldness, meanness and even cruelty. Several governments around the world now chant the mantra of zero tolerance for crime. I think it can also be used as a cover for zero caring. When confronted with such unbending negativity, I like to return fire with the awesome piece of wisdom from one of my heroes.

Service to others is the rent you pay for your room here on earth.
Muhammad Ali (Boxer, poet and philosopher)

I was given extra resolve when I read an observation made by Rich de Vos, co-founder of Amway. He had discovered that the statement, 'God helps those who help themselves', does not come from the Bible. It's definitely not a Jewish or Christian principle as it comes from the ancient Greek storyteller, Aesop, and originally was 'The gods help those who help themselves'. The more caring view was beautifully shown on a sign I saw outside a church in Sydney. It proclaimed 'God helps those who help others'. The word 'themselves' had been deliberately crossed out. Brilliant advertising and a brilliant message! It caught my attention even though I was driving along a busy road.

Bonding is also surrounded by conflicting views — positive and negative ones. At historical celebrations, politicians will wax lyrical about the importance of maintaining bonds and links to the past. In sports, team-bonding is usually thought to play a big role in the team's success. On the other hand, bonding in personal relationships can be seen in a very negative light. Unfortunately, I frequently hear many negative descriptions when I do marriage counselling. You might hear a partner being described as the ball-and-chain or the warden. This bonding is akin to being stifled, you're being held back from doing what you want to do. Bonding people, developing true intimacy, is like a special kind of alchemy. It's like the difference between a five-watt light bulb and a laser. They both have the same amount of energy but the laser can reach the moon and bounce back to earth. The laser has all its waves going in the same direction. Together, people can do amazing things!

Forgiveness is a sensational way to show your love for others, and your great strength. Who was the last person you forgave? This power of forgiveness was certainly used by two of the greatest leaders of all time. I've got one great quote, with two authors.

> *The weak can never forgive. Forgiveness is the attitude of the strong.*
> Mahatma Gandhi and Nelson Mandela

It's a lot easier to search for wisdom and love at the same time, than you might think. Possibly this was the motive behind the cross-country trip carried out by those three wise astronomers in 4 BC. (If you're confused, 4 BC is the accepted date for the birth of Jesus.) Maybe they wanted to learn more. If they were wise, they wanted more wisdom. Back to the present, the spirit of these ancient scholars could be reincarnated in three young men who are inspiring school children to change the world. How? By tapping into the power of kindness to combat religious prejudice. We cringe when we hear jokes starting with the words: a Catholic, a Jew, and a Muslim. However, this is not a joke. Three young men, a Catholic, a Rabbi and a Muslim, are touring schools throughout NSW to encourage students to *find 1000 acts of kindness at each school*. They have started something big. Look out! How many acts of kindness have you done recently?

Another trio of awesome women

In my first chapter, I talked about three women who have achieved so much as authors. I want to introduce another great trio, and you've probably never heard of these three wonderful compassionate women. Their lives, full of caring for others, show the intimacy that the Dalai Lama wants us to find, and the interdependence that Stephen Covey wants us to reach.

First in my magnificent trio is Australian welfare worker Geraldine Cox. She set up and manages an orphanage in Cambodia. For over 10 years, she has protected and saved countless children from the vile pedophiles who flock to this impoverished country.

Second is Pamela Baker, the lawyer and angel who defended thousands of asylum seekers in Hong Kong. In her life, which ended in 2002, she constantly stood up to what she saw as the cruelty and injustice.

The third is across the Pacific in Tijuana. Sister Antonia, another angel, works and lives in one of Mexico's worst prisons. Once a divorced mother with seven children, she is now in her late seventies, and for nearly 30 years has comforted and helped thousands of murderers, drug dealers and thieves. No prisoner will hurt her. A warden says she always spreads the message of peace and love.

Whenever I read stories of such magnificent achievements, I tend to get a bit emotional, and then I get inspired to go out and make a difference.

Chapter 4
That Disgusting S-word

I have to start by giving you a *huge apology.* You're just about to see a filthy disgusting word, the S-word. We all know it. We've all said it. I've heard lots of colourful language, swearing, especially in sports dressing rooms, but this word is at the top of my list of offensive words. It causes so many problems, even death. The word is … *stress.* One of my most popular seminars is called *Turn Stress Into Success* and I emphasise the importance of this title, because I see success at the opposite end to stress. Stress is a form of failure! And it's not an unavoidable necessary part of modern life. If you disagree, then you're just letting failure become more dominant in your life. I always ask my audience to put up their hands if they have any stress in their lives. Guess what? All you see is a sea of hands.

If stress is everywhere, who should we blame? We should point the finger at a Canadian scientist named Hans Selye. It's all his fault! He started stress back in 1956 when he wrote a book with the title, *The Stress of Life.* Selye single-handedly changed a rarely used word into a word that's regularly on the tips of our tongues. Up till 1956 people said things like, 'I've had so much work to do this week'. But, they never said, 'This week has been so stressful' or 'I've been stressed out all week'. Once we started using the word stress to describe our problems and hassles, the image of stress grew into worse and worse descriptions. Have another look at the images on page 65. When we use any of the words, out loud or silently, we actually h-u-r-t ourselves. It's even worse because when we hurt ourselves, we usually h-u-r-t others around us, especially those who care about us. Sorry about the spelling lesson, but I want to tattoo this link onto your subconscious. Words create images, pictures, that control our thoughts. Using colourful negative images of our problems just helps to make the pain of the problems grow. The first rule for having less stress in your life — stop saying and thinking the word stress and all of its connected images.

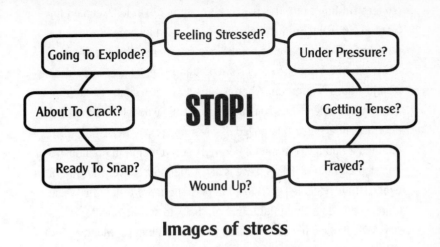

Images of stress

Look at the special collection called 'Stress-building talk' and 'Stress-busting talk'. You can see how lopsided the lists are. This is because of a preponderance of negativity out there. I've found it's very common for people to hook together a couple of negative images, one after another. You use one, then there's a flow-on effect, especially if the other person you're talking to, also says something negative.

Here's a dialogue I heard between two young businessmen in a lift. The first statement was, 'I've been run off my feet today'. The immediate response was, 'Yeah, I'm swamped with work. I'm absolutely flat out'. (Incidentally, I'm not in the habit of eavesdropping — it was a very small lift. I had followed them into the building after they had both just thrown away cigarette butts onto the pavement. That's a quick way to preview how many stressed workers there are in a building — look for the cigarette butts.) Can you imagine how energetic these two men were when they reached their desks to restart their work? They had very effectively de-motivated themselves. I felt like telling them that you have to run a marathon before you're really run off your feet.

Stress-building talk

Today was a disaster, a catastrophe. I'm shattered, devastated. I feel smashed. I'm swamped with work. I'm absolutely flat out. I'm run off my feet. I'm burnt out. This place is a nightmare. I'm just keeping my head above water. I'm just hanging in there. I'm in free fall without a parachute. This is make or break time. There are not enough hours in the day. If it's not one thing it's something else. It never ends, does it? It just goes on and on. When it rains it pours. It's either a feast or a famine. Trouble always comes in threes. I'm always closing the barn door after the horse has bolted. It's like flogging a dead horse. I'm damned if I do and damned if I don't. I'm on a hiding to nothing. It's one step up from hell. This place is like a madhouse. Everything went wrong. The wheels fell off. I lost the plot. The more I tried the worse it got. I can't do a thing right. I'm right back to square one. No job is safe. Why bother? It's useless. Back to the salt mines on Monday. The weather is too good for a Monday. Thank God it's Friday.

Stress-busting talk

There's never a dull moment. Being busy is better than being bored. I'm always in the thick of the action around here. It only appears chaotic from the outside. This place keeps you on your toes. I love the challenges I have every day. I'm sailing better than the Titanic. Feeling good, looking better. The only thing that worries me is kryptonite. Thank God it's today.

I've also heard strong stress talk that was separated by 12 months. I spoke to a manager on the phone and she told me her company would not be doing any training because, 'We're snowed under. We're in the middle of restructuring.' A year later, I gave her another call and this time she said, 'We're just keeping our heads above water. We're in the middle of enterprise bargaining.' Maybe the water came from the snow melting?

Sometimes we can completely, totally, absolutely, miss the importance of what we've said, even when we say it over and over. I'll give you a quick example. I'm going to ask you a question that I think I've asked a few thousand times, 'How are you?' One of the most common responses I hear from my clients is, 'Not too bad'. Did you say that to yourself? Think about that short answer. Ten years ago I heard lots of people saying, 'Not bad'. Do you feel the drop in energy when you say or hear 'Not too bad'? You can quickly reverse this energy drop with a five-part chant that I use with all sorts of groups. Things usually start slowly, but after a few repetitions, there are smiles everywhere as everyone gets louder and louder. I ask our little question, and everyone calls out:

I'm good, I'm really good, I'm great, I'm excellent, I'm sensational!

Try it now, say all five parts out loud … if you're not on a plane or a train. How did it feel? A young critic at one high school sat in the front row with his arms and legs crossed, refusing to join in with his friends. He argued that I was trying to brainwash him. When I returned to his school a week later for another seminar, the principal rushed up to me and hit me with, 'Do you know what you did to this school?' Then with a grin, he told me about the spread of the word *sensational* throughout the school. I wasn't surprised because I get similar feedback from lots of schools and businesses. There's one place where I get lots of opportunities to tell people that 'I'm sensational'. It's at supermarket checkouts. Blank faces usually light up.

Sometimes we use stress-building words when we're trying to help someone. Every year the *Sydney Morning Herald* publishes study notes for students sitting for their final high school exams. They call it the *Survival Guide*. What do you associate survival with? I get pictures of someone hanging onto the side of a cliff, danger, life and death situations. But … saying and thinking the right words can do incredibly positive things.

What words will add years onto your life?

Words can bruise and batter us, but they can also help us live longer! Would you like to know how to add eight healthy active years to your lifespan? You can, if you listen to the results from the *Nun Study*. It all started in 1930, when hundreds of young nuns in the United States were asked by their Mother Superior to write a one-page summary of their lives. Each autobiography had to be less than 300 words and include place of birth, parentage, interesting events of childhood, education, and the influences that led to the choice of their career. Have you got at least 15 minutes to learn a lot about yourself? Why not close this book, sit somewhere quiet, and write your own 300-word autobiography? See you after you're finished.

The life summaries written by the nuns in the 1930s were only rediscovered recently. The nuns used lots of words like *happiness, love, hope, gratitude and contentment,* and lived to an average age of 94 years. Nuns who didn't use many emotion-rich words lived an average of 86 years. That's a big difference for women who all lived very similar lives. One of the happy nuns is 106 and still rides her stationary bike every day.

What does your life summary sound like? Did you include many of those positive emotional words that show you also have a love of life, a love that quickly extinguishes stress? I recommend you write a one-page autobiography once a year to make sure your picture of your life is positive and healthy.

There's more powerful evidence that positive talk plays a big role in your health, and it's from a study done in Sydney. One thousand men and women over 60 years old were asked the same question I've already thrown at you, 'How are you?'

Here's a profile of their health seven years later:

· 22 per cent of the total group died
· 90 per cent of the women who replied 'Excellent' survived
· 70 per cent of the men who replied 'Excellent' survived
· 60 per cent of the women who replied 'Poor' survived
· 50 per cent of the men who replied 'Poor' survived.

The answer to the question was far more accurate at predicting health than any of the medical tests carried out. So, listen carefully to what you say every time you answer this common little question.

Keep breathing and you'll stay alive!

It's that simple, isn't it? This gem came from a man who'd lived to well over 100, was still alert, and enjoying his life. How you breathe, will help you learn more about you and stress. Count the number of breaths you take in a minute, when you're relaxed and not after exerting yourself. A single breath is one inhalation and one exhalation. How many breaths did you take? The average person needs to take 10 to 12 breaths per minute. Some people often breathe at around 20 to 30 breaths a minute. That's stress territory. Use this little test to keep a regular check on yourself, to get a quick rating of how relaxed you are. You can quickly slow down by practising a six-second cycle: breathe in for three seconds and breathe out for three seconds. Try it now. Breathe in 1, 2, 3, breathe out, 1, 2, 3. Do it again. How did that feel?

Have you ever got a speeding ticket? How about exceeding the speed limit by 10 or 20 kilometres an hour? Ever asked yourself why you speed? Your answer might be linked to a much bigger question. Are you speeding through your life? I was given some great advice from a wise man. He was not only wise, he was wealthy, healthy and happy. That's a tremendous trifecta. He told me, 'Paul, you'll get far more done in your life and you'll enjoy yourself much more when you slow down to the speed of life'. Did you hear that? Not the speed of light, the speed of life. Sound travels at 300 metres a second. Light travels at 300,000 kilometres a second. How fast are you travelling?

On page 70 is another self-assessment, a mini-questionnaire which I designed because nearly everyone drives a car, and cars have a strong link to stress. Cars don't produce stress, they just let you show how stressed you are. Your behaviour in your car will tell you a lot about how you're looking at your life. I do a huge amount of driving around my state and on every trip I see the signs of stress. It's not all at high speeds because I study plenty of grim faces in peak hour traffic jams. When I ask high school students to share their scores from the questionnaire, I'm always disappointed, and it's happened at every single school where I've given out this questionnaire. Overwhelmingly, the vast majority of students score 20 or more points — to put them in the highest stress category. It's also disappointing that I have to agree with a study done with roadside repair crews of a motoring association. They were asked to identify the group they most frequently saw speeding on highways. Their answer? It's young women driving hatchbacks. This fits in with bigger and more dangerous trends that are growing in women.

What does your driving say about you?

1. Do you frequently change radio stations while you're driving? YES/NO
2. Do you regularly overtake other cars, or change lanes? YES/NO
3. Do you smoke while driving? YES/NO
4. Do you verbally abuse other drivers when they annoy you? YES/NO
5. Do you usually accelerate rapidly after stopping in traffic? YES/NO
6. Do you eat or drink while you're driving? YES/NO
7. Do you accelerate whenever you see an amber traffic light? YES/NO
8. Do you make rude gestures to other drivers who annoy you? YES/NO
9. Do you chase another car to abuse the driver? YES/NO
10. Do you usually exceed the speed limit by 10 per cent or more? YES/NO
11. Do you normally drive through a traffic light that just turns red? YES/NO
12. Do you often beep your car horn when you're frustrated? YES/NO
13. Do you throw litter out of the car window? YES/NO
14. Do you frequently talk on your mobile phone while driving? YES/NO
15. Do you refuse to let any car move in front of you where traffic has to merge? YES/NO
16. Do you drive very closely to the car in front of you, even when you're at high speeds? YES/NO

Scoring instructions

For questions 1, 6, 13, 14, give yourself 1 point for every YES answer.
For questions 2, 3, 5, 7, 15, 16, give yourself 2 points for every YES answer.
For questions 4, 8, 10, 11, 12, give yourself 3 points for every YES answer.
For question 9 give yourself 4 points for a YES answer.

Analysis

0 points: You appear to be very calm and relaxed.

1–10 points: You might need to relax more and slow down.

11–19 points: Do you feel like you're living in a stressful world?

20–35 points: Step back and take another look at your life.

Are you driving yourself to an early grave?

Have a close listen to some worrying numbers. They give powerful insights into the ways women are reacting to many aspects of modern life. Australian road fatalities have steadily dropped since 1980, but the number of women killed while driving is up more than 40 per cent. When we look at lung cancer in Australia, which is really a measure of smoking, since 1987 the rate in men has fallen 17 per cent, but has risen 24 per cent in women. Surveys across Australia have found only 10 per cent of senior high school girls are happy with their body shape, versus 61 per cent of boys. With binge drinking, it's up in females, steady in males. Women are much more likely, probably three times more likely, to suffer from depression than men. When I give that statistic to women they often say it's because men make them depressed. Please note that depression is the first cousin of stress. In the US, a large study found nearly 18 per cent of women suffer from severe migraines, compared to about 6 per cent of men.

What's going on? I challenge women with my assessment. Some women are flexing their freedom and independence, by trying to be as stupid as stupid men. Men have had a lot more time to practise, but women are catching up fast. Now, if you're a woman and you think I'm painting a grim sexist picture, stay calm. There's one big statistic that says women are stronger than men. About 2,500 Australians kill themselves every year, and 80 per cent are men. Men are far more likely to give up all hope than women are. Why? My own theory is that menstruation has given women plenty of practice dealing with problems.

One last question about driving. Which group of drivers do you think is most likely to show road rage? Most people immediately think of male teenagers. They're wrong! It's my group, not psychologists, it's middle-aged men, and doctors suspect it's because their testosterone levels are changing.

I've heard professional critics, social commentators and even some doctors claim that stress is a myth. I certainly agree that it's not a defined medical or legal condition, but no matter how vague and varied the descriptions of stress are, there's solid concrete evidence of the way we're reacting to stress, whether it's real or imaginary. The evidence is in dollars. How dumb would it be if businesses, schools, governments, all organisations just threw away 10 per cent of their budgets? That's what could be happening. It's been calculated that stress-related illnesses and absenteeism costs Britain 10 per cent of its GDP every year. This figure can probably be applied to the Australian economy as well. Then there's the cost and number of scripts for antidepressants. In Australia, in a single year, we spend about $250 million. That pays for nearly eight million scripts! The figure for the United States must be astronomical.

There can be a much brighter picture than all of these bleak statistics, because there are hundreds of simple, easy ways, techniques and skills to beat stress and have healthier, happier lives. They can help at two different levels — at the surface to gain quick relief, and at a deeper level to put out any sparks before they grow and spread.

How do sports champions beat stress?

I'm certain we can learn a lot from sport to help us with everyday stress. It took me a long while to realise the word stress is hardly ever used by sports-people when they're talking about their sport. When they start talking about their private lives, well, that's a different matter. However, if you want to see an environment with highly charged stress, it's a sports dressing room. The word stress disappears, but you'll still hear lots of negative language, and stress raises its head in the many forms of nervousness. I describe nerves as the temporary face of stress. It can be present for minutes, hours, or even days, but rarely as long as stress exists at work or in the home. But, there's a huge downside of nerves in sport. The consequences can be remembered for years, or a lifetime. Ask any athlete who trained for years and then performed poorly, because of nerves.

It gets worse, because some coaches encourage signs of nervousness. I do my best to do the opposite, and I'm proud to say I've been successful doing that. The good news for you is that the same techniques that I've used to beat nerves and increase success in sport, can also obliterate stress and nerves for you, wherever you experience them — preparing and sitting for exams, giving business presentations, visiting a dentist, even asking someone out for a date. Nervous energy normally reduces your chances of success. If you disagree, I've got a short sermon for you.

A few years ago I was indulging in one of my favourite past-times. I was sitting in front of the television watching the Australian cricket team playing a test. (For those not initiated to cricket, it seems hard to believe that a test is a single game lasting 30 hours over five days. Robin Williams, the zany comedian, described cricket as baseball on Prozac. Cricket might appear slow, but it always gives me an extraordinary opportunity to watch people perform under stress, especially batsmen.) The game had just started and one of the batsmen was playing his first test for Australia. The television commentator, a former captain of Australia, remarked that it was perfectly normal to suffer from nerves in your first international game. The batsman had been selected for this game because he was in superb form with his state team. But he didn't look superb in this game. He looked clumsy. Nerves had caused a dramatic change. Nerves had changed a powerful, elegant batsman into a batsman who looked like he had lead in his feet. Within seconds he was out, having failed to score a single run.

I remind nervous athletes they participate in their sport because they enjoy it. Many acknowledge they love their sport. Why suffer when you're about to do something you enjoy or even love? No-one is meant to suffer. Athletes are frequently given advice, 'Nerves are good for you. They help you to get switched on.' I argue, very strongly, that any statements like these are the great myths of sport, and indeed, of everyday life! It's as if there were an eleventh commandment — 'Thou shalt be nervous before you compete or perform'. Believing this myth can have terrible consequences. Did you know Barbra Streisand and her sensational voice went missing for 27 years? From 1966 to 1993 she did not perform a single paying performance, due to what she called, 'the fear that paralyses'. Nerves help you to feel uncomfortable, and what usually follows is that you make more mistakes or become indecisive. I often hear athletes saying that once their sporting event begins, and they are involved, they settle down and the nerves disappear. Why not settle down in the dressing room? They could then follow the example of a champion of champions:

*I couldn't wait to bat. I never suffered from stage fright. The bigger
the occasion, the tenser the atmosphere, the more I liked the game.*
Sir Donald Bradman (Greatest cricketer of all time)

Instead of helping you to be more focussed, nerves help you to waste
some of your mental energy. Before events, some sportspeople sleep poorly,
they're restless, they can't settle because they're constantly thinking about
the next day's competition. This is like revving up your car for hours before
you start driving. Some athletes like to burn up a lot of petrol.

Here's another way of looking at the negative effects of nerves. Over
millions of years of evolution has helped us to survive in many hazardous
environments. At the top of our personal defence network is our fight or
flight responses. In a truly threatening situation, your brain asks, 'What's the
better way to survive — run like blazes and escape, or stand, plant your feet
and fight?' For either of these choices, the brain decides it would help to
divert a lot of the oxygen supplying the brain and send it to the large
muscles that would be active in either a fight or a flight. Take oxygen away
from the brain and what happens? Oxygen is your fuel for thinking, for concentrating. Less oxygen means your ability to concentrate is likely to drop.
I've seen this happen time and time again in sport.

How have the myths about the benefits of nerves grown? I think they come
from a multitude of definitions of nerves. Being nervous can range from mild
stomach butterflies to stronger symptoms such as frequent running to the
toilet, or even vomiting. I've interviewed many champion sportspeople and
have found that when some athletes reveal they're always nervous before
competing, they're actually referring to a feeling of mild excitement. I don't
think this excitement should be called nerves. Excitement is something I
encourage. Excitement is a healthy positive state. Being truly nervous, being
so jittery you can't sit still for even a moment, being snappy or short tempered, having a painful look on your face, having an upset stomach or
diarrhoea, vomiting, these are not signs of being in a healthy, positive state.

I use one question to discover whether an athlete truly suffers from nerves.
I ask, 'Do you enjoy how you feel before you compete?' If the answer is yes,

I don't believe the athlete actually feels nervous. Let's replace nervous with excited or focussed. It's a giant step toward enjoying your sport more, and being more successful.

If you want to get the most out of nerves, use them to give you a pleasant shiver or a tingle. Imagine that feeling in the few seconds when you dive into chilly water. This leads me to another example of the role of nerves in sport. Back in 1997, Australian swimmer Michael Klim set a world record. On the surface this is not remarkable as Australians have a rich history of world swimming records. This 20-year-old broke the record after swimming an extra 65 metres due to a false start. His event was the butterfly, a swimming stroke considered to be the most physically gruelling. No-one expected a world record after such a disruption. Klim later said the false start helped to wash away his nerves. This is an image to remember. Without his nerves he became stronger.

Here's your treasure chest of stress busters!

This collection of techniques is very special to me because all of them have been successful with many of my clients, producing lots of smiling faces. These techniques can be like an emergency rescue kit, but I prefer to think of them helping you to have more gold in your life. There's even more, because they often give immediate results. Remember the story of 'Ali Baba and the Forty Thieves'? To enter the gigantic cave full of treasure, Ali had to call out a magical password. That's what cue words can do for you. Cue words are part of a package that includes affirmations, body anchors, blot-outs and self-hypnosis. It's a very powerful package!

Every year in Australia, there's an interstate war. New South Wales and Queensland do battle in three games of rugby league. The New South Wales side normally enters the series as favourite, but over the last two decades, Queensland has won the majority of games. Why? The Queenslanders are fiercely determined to gain revenge for the constant thrashings they received back in the 1960s and 70s. Their secret weapon is emotion, emotion that builds an immense pride to be a Queenslander. When the New South Wales team attacks and looks like scoring, someone in the Queensland team might scream out the inspirational call 'Queenslander'. This is a brilliant example of a cue word. It's brilliant because it works time and time again.

Any word or phrase that immediately produces a powerful image in your mind can be a cue word. The more personal the cue word is, the more likely it will be effective. A cue word can be whispered or simply thought of, or even yelled. It can be used sparingly, in crucial situations, or frequently, until it regularly produces the preferred response. Here are some of my favourite examples of cue words in action.

'Mandela' was a cue word that helped a member of a tough Los Angeles gang escape his drug problem and life of crime. When he felt weak or threatened by his former gang members, he silently said the name of the person who symbolised pure courage. Then there was a general manager who had problems controlling his anger, both at work and home, who used his brother's first name. He calmed himself by focusing on the deep love he had for his brother who had been killed in a car accident. One woman on a diet used the cue word 'beach'. She told me that previously she had spent thousands of dollars on various dieting schemes. Her success came after she attached her cue word to the door of her fridge. Obviously, she backed up her sensible eating with moderate exercise, but her word gave her constant inspiration whenever she saw it. Any ideas why it helped her?

Another success I had came after I persuaded a young cricketer to throw away his favourite cue word. His batting deteriorated after he played a poor stroke. He tried to stay focussed by saying 'survive'. Not surprisingly, this cue word was not helping him. I suggested he use a far more positive outlook. He then used the phrase 'baggy green' with immediate success. In cricket, when you're given a green cap, you've been selected to play for Australia.

A swimmer I worked with dreamed up a special way of using her cue word. She embroidered her word onto her pillow case. Every time she put her head down to go to sleep, she focussed on her powerful word. Often her dreams were rich with images produced from the word. She went on to be a national champion!

Sometimes a cue word can be stretched into a sentence. However, this needs to be combined with a powerful dose of emotion. This happened at the Sydney Olympics. The British rowing eight led throughout the final, winning the first British gold medal in this event since 1912. Just before the race started, one of the crew called out, 'Remember, we're doing this for Harry!' Harry Mahon was their coach who died from cancer soon after the Olympics.

Long before I became a psychologist, I greatly benefited from a cue word, even though it took another 20 years before I knew what a cue word was. I worked in a chocolate factory which was nothing like the wonderful Willy Wonka factory. My factory stank, and it was very dangerous. On my first day, I nearly fell into molten toffee. I only stayed for a month, and every morning I woke stressed and dreading what was before me. However, each day at the factory a senior worker cheered me up with a cue word embedded in his friendly greeting, 'G'day champ!'

I've left my greatest success with a cue word till last. One of my clients had been raped, and for more than a year she hadn't left her home at night. She broke her invisible chains, boosting her courage and confidence, using the word 'braveheart'. You won't be surprised to hear that her ancestry was Scottish. Initially, she frequently said her word, before and during her nighttime excursions. Eventually, you only heard a single whisper just before she left her home. When transformations like this happen, I know why I love being a psychologist.

How can you send yourself signals for success?

When you use a body anchor, you're reversing the normal direction of the body language. Instead of sending a subconscious message outwards, you send a conscious message inwards. You build a body anchor anytime you link an inspiring thought with an action in your body language. Usually this is a deliberate action, but not always. It's quick and simple, but watch the incredible results you get.

A client of mine, who played basketball, usually dropped her head and stopped talking after she made a mistake on the court. I later discovered she did much the same thing when she had a problem with her partner. Consequently, her game often fell apart, and her relationship was on the edge. We stopped both these problems with the same body anchor. After any basketball mistake, or a relationship disagreement, she would immediately look upwards and quickly nod. She believed this made her closer to her father who had died, but was always looking down on her. Now she felt free to communicate. In basketball, she encouraged her teammates. At home, she talked about their problems.

An American footballer was having problems catching long passes. His confidence was shot. Using a body anchor, his catching became exceptional. Before he would begin his run, he made a circle with his thumb and forefinger. This symbolised perfection. I shared this story with a sprinter who had been having problems with his starts. He'd been slow to start, and when he tried to rectify this, he suffered two disqualifications for breaking early. He eliminated both these faults by forming his circle of perfection just before he settled into his starting position. He liked his body anchor because no-one would ever notice it, even when he was under the gaze of television cameras.

Desmond Haynes was a sensational batsman with the West Indian cricket team. During a tour of Australia he fell into a major batting slump. Before a game against Australia, he did something strange. He had practised in the nets, and while he was walking back to the dressing room, he lifted his bat high above his head. Normally this is only seen when a batsman has just achieved a milestone, such a scoring a century. That day Haynes broke out of his slump by blasting a century. He used his body anchor before he competed, but they are far more commonly used during competition, right in the middle of the action. I frequently rev up clients with an altered version of Haynes' action. I recommend you copy the famous scene in the *Rocky* movie, punch one fist above your head. It works all the time and has even helped suicidal kids.

Use all your imagination when you're searching for body anchors. Putting your hand on your heart, pulling an earlobe, blowing a kiss, these have all worked. One of my favourites came from a nervous client. He had to give a business presentation, and even when practising, he choked. Somehow we started talking about Superman and the rest fell into place. He told me his goal was to make an impression on his small but important audience. That's what Superman does when he takes off. After only a couple more practise sessions, he spoke confidently. As he rose to speak, he pressed his feet onto the floor, to bounce up with the energy of Superman. No-one noticed anything. He spoke, full of confidence, and left his mark like you-know-who.

Many of my clients are smokers. I love telling them no-one should ever give up smoking. You should see the looks on their faces. If smoking is a problem for you, instead of thinking about giving up, think about having healthier lungs, being more active and living longer. We only give up things we like. That's an example of a negative cue word. It reinforces the nicotine addiction. A chain smoker told himself 'pink lungs' and then slowly spread out five fingers of one hand, every time he thought of lighting up. He'd read that each cigarette shortens your life by five minutes. His body anchor reinforced that his lifespan had just increased. He doesn't smoke anymore.

Before we leave body anchors, here's a warning. Body anchors are in a completely separate category to superstitions. Mix them together, and you might suffer the consequences. A body anchor is like receiving an invisible pat on the back, by a process that you control. You give away that control when you rely on superstition. Baseball and cricket are similar in many ways including the widespread use of superstitions. I know international cricket players who follow exactly the same routine when they get dressed. Left sock, followed by left boot, followed by left pad and so on. Some always make sure they walk onto the field with same foot. Stephen Waugh, the Australian cricket captain, was famous for his mental toughness and his red handkerchief. Sometimes when he was batting he'd take out the handkerchief and slowly wipe his face. This wasn't his lucky charm. The handkerchief was his clear reminder that he'd been successful so many times in tight situations. A politician renown for her determination used a similar technique. When Maggie Thatcher made an important speech, she often wore her favourite dress.

Affirmations: say it, see it, do it!

Most of my clients have goals, but few have affirmations. That's strange because goals and affirmations go hand in hand. Goals are statements about the future. These are things you want to do, or what you're going to do. It's like looking towards the horizon. You have to know the direction you're heading. On the other hand, affirmations are about the here and now. Affirmations spark vivid and exciting pictures in your right brain. No, I don't mean the opposite to your wrong brain. You've got a left and right brain, just like you have two lungs and two kidneys. I'll give you a full update on your right brain in a later chapter.

Goals are easily changed into affirmations by writing them in the present tense. Muhammad Ali used the most famous affirmation of all time, 'I am the greatest!' Ali didn't say 'I want to be the greatest' or 'I will be the greatest'. Few people know that Ali started to use his catch cry because he and his trainer believed he would struggle in his first attempt to win the world championship. Later in his career he revealed, 'I said I was the greatest even before I knew I was'.

In 1985, Ivan Lendl was rated the number one tennis player in the world, but he often performed poorly against John McEnroe. Lendl turned this completely around by writing a short affirmation whenever McEnroe was his next opponent. He wrote, 'I look forward to playing John McEnroe'. By 1991, Lendl's win/loss record of 9/12 against McEnroe had somersaulted to 19/15.

Some successful examples used from my clients, in the one family, include, 'My life is so rich and clear without pot' and 'I love my son, I talk to my son, I listen to my son'.

However, a few words of caution. Be careful when you're designing your affirmation as some early attempts are not only clumsy, they're counterproductive. An overweight businessman reported he became more frustrated after he used his favourite affirmation. He was saying, 'I'm always trying to lose 10 kilograms'. Like me, he was a fan of crazy movies, so we did a dramatic revision of his affirmation. He then used 'I look groovy, baby', stolen from the Austin Powers film. Oh yes, he lost his 10 kilos.

I've helped others to upsize their affirmations with more power. Instead of saying and thinking 'I'm giving up smoking', what would be better? How about 'My body says thanks every day'? Even with major problems such as abuse, affirmations have helped. A wife in an abusive marriage, turned her life around after changing 'I'm not going to take any more abuse' to 'I'm strong. He's weak'. I've learnt over and over again, when you put the right combination of words together, the results are sensational. Did I tell how much I love that word?

Humour plus affirmation is a winning combination. My personal all-time favourite comes from a cricketer who was normally a star batsman. When I met him, he'd had a long string of failures. He was getting out largely because he wasn't moving his feet enough. His coach, a big user of negative imagery, was continuously telling him that he had to get the lead out of his feet. Every time he heard this, the player thought of his ankles being wrapped in chains. It was then a case of humour to the rescue. At that time Michael Flattley was touring Australia with *Riverdance,* the Irish dancers. Flattley was such a superb dancer, he held a world record for foot tapping. My cricket friend thought about Flattley, combined it with his cricket problem, and out came, 'My footwork is better than Michael Flattley's'. He soon had success as his chains disappeared.

So, what's the best way to use your affirmations? Start by converting five goals into affirmations, but make sure you pump each of them up with emotional words to stimulate the right side of your brain. You might only need one affirmation for success, but you've got plenty of extra space on that hard disk inside your head. Our brains can easily absorb five big ideas at a time. Advertisers know all about this rule of learning. They also know that when we try to squeeze in any more than seven ideas, our brains get overloaded.

There are several ways of tapping into the energy of your affirmations. Write them on a small card and take it everywhere. Read your affirmations frequently, silently or aloud. At first, visualise each affirmation with your eyes closed. Later, you can combine them with self-hypnosis sessions. I'll be giving you lots of instructions about self-hypnosis. You can also print a large coloured version to be placed somewhere at home. Laminated versions have turned up everywhere in homes, even inside showers. This is where one nervous student got a lot of confidence and improved her studying. Repetition is important as it makes your messages sink deeply into your subconscious. It's learning the easy way.

Super Seven Sports Affirmations

1. I am in complete control.
2. All my actions are smooth, and so easy.
3. I have so much time to do anything I want to do.
4. I feel relaxed, but I'm fully alert and 100 per cent focussed.
5. My confidence is sky high.
6. Everything I do, turns to gold.
7. I'm enjoying every second.

Blot out the bad with the good

I was first introduced to this technique by a therapist who did volunteer work for a rape crisis centre. The basic principle is so flexible, I've used it in so many ways for sports success and also in clinical counselling. I'll give you a sports example to help you get a feel of its awesome potential.

Imagine you're a young gymnast who performs beautifully at training, but during competition your confidence evaporates, and you literally fall in a heap. Your coach relies on her favourite instruction, 'Just be confident!' This was repeated many times with no success. I enter the scene with two blank sheets of paper. On one sheet, we wrote the word 'practice'. On the other is the word 'competition'. At home, in her living room, the gymnast stood on the first sheet, with her eyes closed. After she felt all the brilliance of a typical training session, she opened her eyes and walked several metres away to stand on the second sheet. Here, she again closed her eyes, but this time she imagined herself in competition. Her pain and self-doubt was so great she could only keep her eyes shut for a few seconds. She felt terrible, and she was in her own home! We went back and repeated the process, always building on the confidence she clearly felt when standing on her practice sheet. After five repetitions, she could stand on the competition sheet and see herself performing with confidence. The next day in a real competition, her performance improved out of sight.

You can follow this technique and substitute words like 'feel good' or 'happy' or the name of an enjoyable place on the first sheet. On the other piece of paper, write one word that describes a problem you're having. You can be extra creative and take your second sheet of paper somewhere outside, stand on it, crumple it up after you're finished and then symbolically throw it away. One gigantic footballer took this to the extreme. He took a lot of things to the extreme. His problem word was nerves, so after he blotted it out with the word confident, he tore up his problem sheet, threw it in the toilet, urinated on it and flushed it. He did this before every game in the dressing rooms. It got lots of smirks, but again, it worked.

The art of doing nothing and achieving a lot

Here's a very brief daydreaming exercise that has a big message in it. Imagine you've just got in bed to sleep, when the phone rings. You might feel annoyed that someone has rung you so late. However, when you hear the person's voice you immediately recognise it's a friend of yours. This is what your friend then says to you, 'Sorry about the late call, but I wanted to tell you a few important things I've never told you'. How do you now feel, worried, curious? Your friend continues, 'I think you're a true friend. Your friendship means a great deal to me, and I know lots of other people feel the same way. Everyone knows you're honest. You're so dependable. You've been someone I can always count on and I trust you completely. You've shown plenty of courage when you've stood up for what's right. I know your family and close friends truly love you. I'm proud to call you a friend. Good night.' Two big questions: Do you now feel worse than you were 30 seconds ago? Do you feel nothing?

I always expect 100 per cent success with this exercise, and I'm very rarely disappointed. At one organisation, two managers who were sitting together, said that they did indeed get nothing from it. They shared the same reason. They felt I had exaggerated, gone over the top with the praise from the imaginary friend. As one put it, 'I'm never going to hear anything like that.' That said a lot. I hope you expect to hear praise like this.

If you enjoyed this brief daydreaming exercise, there are many more pathways for you to try. They go under different names like visualisation, creative imagery, and meditation, but they're all connected to self-hypnosis. As Billy Connolly likes saying, it's brilliant! I teach self-hypnosis to all my sports clients and most of my clients who see me for personal counselling. First up is a sampler that combines many of the things we've talked about. I call it, 'Self-hypnosis for success'. Enjoy 5–10 minutes every day doing a self-hypnosis session.

Self-hypnosis for success

Step 1 — Increase your body awareness

1. You can begin by either sitting in a chair, or lying on the floor.

2. Stare strongly at a point straight ahead of you for 10 seconds and then let your eyelids slowly drop.

3. Contract your stomach muscles and diaphragm so that your lungs are completely cleared and refreshed. Do this several times.

4. Now focus on the sensation of whatever is touching the back of your shoulders. Until you had this thought, you were totally unaware of this feeling. Now it is the only thought you have in your mind. Concentrate for 10 seconds.

5. Move your awareness to the feeling on your lower back — magnify the sensation from the floor or the chair pressing on this part of your body. Concentrate for 10 seconds.

6. Move your awareness to your feet. Feel the pressure on your toes, soles of your feet and heels. Concentrate for 10 seconds.

7. Now move to the most powerful part of your body — your head. Feel the sensations of anything touching your head — the floor, wall, back of a chair, everything.

8. Repeat these different external awareness stages in any sequence you wish to follow.

9. You are ready to lift your internal awareness.

Step 2 — Remember your success

1. Think of a time when you were extremely successful — sometime in your life you are really proud of.

2. Let the sensations of that moment of success fill your head and then spread to the rest of your body — through your shoulders, to your back and down to your feet.

3. You feel excited as you relive this successful moment.

4. Your mind enjoys these powerful thoughts and emotions. Your mind, all of your body, is reliving a wonderful time in your life.

Step 3 — Hold onto your success

1. Capture these thoughts and feelings in a single word. This is your cue word. As soon as you think of your cue word, your mind is filled with success.

2. Clench both fists and let out a long slow breath. Feel the extra power now present in your hands.

3. Unclench your fists slowly.

4. Squeeze your hands again and feel the sensations going up into your forearms.

5. Unclench.

6. Squeeze again so that you feel the power of your success moving deeper into your body.

7. Relax and clench your fists as many times as you want.

8. Silently say your cue word when you want an even greater boost.

Step 4 — Return to the present

1. Let all your fingers slowly spread out.

2. Focus on the sensations from everything touching your fingers. This is your link with the present. You can bring your past success to the present.

3. Lean forward slowly so that your back and shoulders are powerfully straight.

4. Take a deep breath as your slowly lift your head, looking upwards.

5. Open your eyes. Whisper your cue word.

6. Then say it louder, as loud as you want. You are ready for even more success in your life.

Get physical, again, again and again

Stress is a mental problem. You can have a wide range of physical symptoms, but it still all starts in your mind. Ahead of you is a physical training manual of de-stressing exercises and successful strategies. Most of them are supported by scientific studies and surveys. I still recommend the others because they've worked time and time again with a wide range of my clients. This is important when you're faced with many unreliable claims. Some of the solutions I'll soon talk about need plenty of commitment, whilst others can happen as quickly as you can click your fingers.

Move your feet, walk. Stress often gets going because you're not going anywhere, except in a car, bus or train. A figure to keep in mind is 10,000 steps. Professor Adrian Bowman, a specialist in public health at the University of New South Wales, revealed the results of a fascinating study completed in 2004. A small device called a pedometer was worn by 160 volunteers to count the steps taken in a day. They found 'blue collar' workers averaged 8,000 steps and 'white collar' workers ranged between 3,000 to 4,000 steps. The lowest score of 97 came from a truck driver and a street cleaner hit the highest with 33,000. Overall, women did less walking than men. If you drive to work, park away from your workplace so that you have at least 10 minutes to walk each way. Stroll instead of rushing.

Hold on to something because I get worked up whenever I talk about this. Turn off your television. Will that cause a revolution in your home? I'd revolt, but only if it went off permanently. You can tell from how often I refer to movies and TV shows that I like watching television. I sure do! But I avoid tuning into programs that are just like electronic wallpaper — those bland shows that just fill in time. Watching television can be an addiction and I'm not exaggerating. Withdrawal symptoms such as concentration problems, were described in a 2002 issue of the *Scientific American*. The research was carried out by professors Kubey and Csikszentmihaly. These two are so respected in the world of psychology, I even know how to pronounce both their names. You can forget their names but don't forget that watching heaps of television weakens your concentration skills, and weakens your resistance to stress-building incidents.

Before this study turned up, I'd been leading my own crusade against excessive TV watching. When television first entered our homes, for me it was in prehistoric 1960, it was sometimes described as a conversation killer. That's still a fair comment. I also like some other negative descriptions — income inhibitor, family freezer, sedative and even a contraceptive. Television is a big cause of the poverty that breeds stress. It's time poverty. When you hear someone say 'I just don't have enough time to do all the things I want to do', that person is time poor. Watching some TV programs is like throwing away some of your valuable time. The typical Australian teenager spends at least three hours in front of the TV every day of the year. How many hours do you think you watch in a week? Get an accurate count and you might be very surprised.

If you're smart with your TV, you can use it to boost a magical chemical that's in our bloodstream. Do you have your own collection of favourite comedies on video or DVD? I do. There's a medical discovery that now shows why this is a smart practice. The chemical immunoglobulin-A, IgA, is found in our blood and it helps protect us against illness. You pump up its levels with just a single laugh! Researchers at Reading University in England found the level of IgA will more than double and will remain 60 per cent above normal for three hours after you laugh.

Join a gang, a non-violent gang!

Loneliness is a form of blindness. Stressed people can be in a crowded office and still feel alone. Reach out and touch somebody, physically or mentally. Be part of a regular group activity such as attending community meetings or doing volunteer work. Researchers at the University of Texas looked at the church-going patterns of 22,000 people and discovered that non-attenders live an average of 75 years, whilst regular weekly church-goers can expect to live an extra seven years. Finding a close companion, a loving partner or a good friend is a great way to avoid heart problems. The Duke University in the United States studied 1,368 heart patients, and found 50 per cent of those with no close friends died within five years. Only 17 per cent of the patients with a spouse or partner died.

You should also do the opposite, and seek out solitude. Enjoy being by yourself. Even Superman needed quiet time, he flew off to his secret Fortress of Solitude hidden somewhere in the Arctic. Your place of solitude doesn't have to be a place of silence. I often seek out parks and beaches, full of people relaxing, and children playing. When you relax, you should get disconnected. Pagers have virtually disappeared, but mobile phones allow contact 24/7. That's stress shorthand, and I avoid using it and believing in it. Many businesses now expect employees to be available every minute of every hour, of every day, of every week, around the clock, without a break. Convenience is replaced by obligation.

Back in the 17th century, French philosopher and mathematician, René Descartes, proposed a brilliant summary of human life. He said in Latin, *Cogito, ergo sum*. It sounds so elegant, doesn't it? It's even more elegant when you discover it means, 'I think, therefore I am'. We can alter Descartes' wise words to look more deeply at life in the 21st century. Jeremy Rifkin wrote in *The Guardian*, that maybe we should be now saying, 'I am connected, therefore I exist'. Without mobile phones for text, verbal and visual messages, without emails and faxes, you can seem to be an outcast. On the other hand, you won't feel you're electronically tagged like pets with microchips inserted under the skin. I've put together my own alteration of Descartes' words, 'I love, therefore I'm alive'. Another French scientific all-rounder from the 17th century, left us with more great advice:

> *All of our miseries come from not being able to sit quietly in a room alone.*
>
> Blaise Pascal (1623–1662)

I regularly ask groups of young people what is their favourite weekend activity. The most common reply is sleeping. Most of them might be suffering from TATT — Tired All The Time. I don't mean they have the debilitating chronic fatigue syndrome. Thankfully that's fairly rare, whereas TATT is rife. Decades ago, scientists thought sleeping was largely a waste of precious time. Oh, how wrong they were! My Apple computer is programmed to come awake in the middle of the night and tidy up. During sleep our brains do the same thing, a lot of mental tidying up goes on after your head hits the pillow. This job is only completed if you sleep long enough — more than seven hours. Many stressed people, and many who aren't, feel guilty going to bed early during the working part of the week. Winston Churchill only slept a couple of hours a night, and typically joked about his condition saying that when he had his regular catnaps, he was able to sleep very quickly. He used his brief time-out breaks to prevent burnout. That was smart, but you'll be a lot healthier and better looking than Winston if you get an average of eight hours sleep.

There's been a serious decline in sleeping over the last century. In 1910, the average adult slept nine to 10 hours a night. Today in Western countries, it's down to less than seven hours. More progress, less sleep, more stress. Some research has confirmed a common sense hunch about what happens when we disturb our sleep patterns. Investigators from the University of British Columbia found that car crashes increased by 8 per cent on the Monday after daylight saving begins in spring, and this figure backflipped when daylight saving ended, as accidents decreased by 8 per cent. One hour extra sleep meant clearer and better concentration.

Your thoughts in the first hour awake frequently control the rest of your day. You can make your day, by staying happy or at least positive in your first 60 minutes. Sometimes morning television makes that very difficult. At the other end of your day, when you return home after work, spend a few minutes sitting in your car, or standing outside. Prepare yourself to give something extra to those who are waiting for you. Your home should be a place of happiness, where you are with the most important people in your life. Have a special shower when you come home from work. Imagine you're washing away all your problems.

How much do you read for pleasure? According to a survey sponsored by the Australia Council, most Australian adults read an average of eight hours a week. The most popular books are crime and mystery — I wonder whether other types of books might be more relaxing. Maybe you should look more closely at the impact of the sorts of books you read. Unfortunately, 28 per cent of adults don't read any books for pleasure.

What's the most stupid part of your body?

I'd vote for the pancreas. You're often likely to feel stressed when you have low energy. You can boost your energy by eating less food and drinking less. Sound stupid? Blame your pancreas. Let me explain. When you consume high sugar and high fat meals, like pancakes and syrup for breakfast, you flood your bloodstream with sugar. Your pancreas goes crazy and takes too much sugar out of your blood and you're starving again in less than two hours. If you eat more protein-rich foods, you can keep your energy levels up for at least four hours. Concentration up, stress down.

I learnt more about stress by looking inside garbage bins at several universities. I regularly visit different campuses, and at every one I now see garbage bins full of empty cans, cans of high energy drinks containing natural stimulants such as guarana. Guarana is nature's caffeine. I love coffee, but when you have more than four strong cups a day, your brain gets too stimulated. One small can of high energy drink is equal to two very strong cups of coffee. British PM, Tony Blair, was rushed to hospital after drinking lots of strong coffee. He experienced heart problems. You're asking for stress because you're putting your brain and heart on a roller coaster. You go up … and then down … a long way down.

It's a nice feeling to get support from someone you respect. Motor racing legend Peter Brock has become a strong advocate for road safety. Guess what he blames for much of Australia's terrible road tolls over holiday breaks? Sugary drinks, caffeine and lollies. In his words, 'concentration goes up and down like a yo-yo'. Thank you, Peter!

Strap on your seat belt, because I'm going to fire off a lot of de-stressors. None of these are blanks. Ready?

Get your hands dirty — do some gardening. Australian retail billionaire, read that again, billionaire, Gerry Harvey grabs a shovel and does an hour's gardening before he heads off to work. He calls it his yoga session.

Take off your watch for an hour. Many busy people look at their watches more than 200 times a day. Sit up straight, bottom against the back of the chair, not bent over, with uncrossed legs. Get a new hairstyle, a haircut, change your appearance slightly, without surgery. Put on some lipstick.

The giant cosmetics company Estée Lauder reported that their lipstick sales always climb during economic recessions. I guess you don't have to be female to benefit because I've seen lots of sportsmen who will put on dresses at the drop of a hat.

Why wait for special occasions to give a gift to someone you care about? Thoughtfulness has magical de-stressing powers. Visit a pet shop. Hold, pat or watch puppies or kittens. Your heart beat will drop immediately. Do what Tina Turner does. She boasted that her technique saved her from a life of drugs and alcohol. When you feel down, do some shopping therapy.

Be smarter than George Costanza

One of the most stressed people you'll ever see is George Costanza, the whining complainer in the TV series, *Seinfeld*. His father once told him that whenever he was stressed, he should take a deep breath and slowly say, 'Serenity now'. George didn't listen when he was given good advice, but you can. Every technique we've talked about has worked for someone, and helped to wipe out that disgusting S-word.

Chapter 5
Take a Good Look at Yourself

Many decades ago when I was a young schoolboy, I had two obvious characteristics. I was a daydreamer and very talkative. Of course, this regularly resulted in me being the target of disciplinary slings and arrows from my teachers. Here's one vivid image I still clearly see before me. A gigantic teacher looking down at me, glaring eyes, and a voice booming, 'Smith, when are you going to wake up to yourself? Take a good look at yourself.' My silence was broken by class laughter. However, I'm using this warning thrown at me, not as a harsh warning, but as some very helpful advice. You already know I get excited when I discover treasure I call 'insights'. Isn't that a wonderful word? It tells you that you have to turn your sight inwards to learn some of the most important things in life. When we look inside ourselves, we have a much clearer outlook on life. Wasn't that teacher thoughtful to yell that message at me all those years ago?

I love the John Travolta movie, *A Civil Action*, where he plays a lawyer who's fighting for a lot more than a legal victory. In one scene, he strongly weakens his own case when he asks a witness a question, and receives a response that was totally unexpected. Robert Duvall, who plays the opposing lawyer, later gives the advice, 'Never ask a question you don't know what the answer will be'.

Listen to my advice. Do exactly the opposite, especially when it comes to questions about yourself. The more questions you ask about yourself, the more power you'll have. I've had plenty of experience with people who avoid asking questions. For them, asking a question is a sign of weakness, as if they're telling everyone they don't know something. Possibly these thoughts took seed back in school. There are two nasty images connected to asking your teacher a question in a classroom. You're either dumb, or you're a crawler.

Knowledge is power.

> Sir Francis Bacon (Scientist, philosopher, possible author
> of Shakespeare's works, full-time genius.)

Self-knowledge is awesome power.

Paul Smith (Psychologist, philosopher, author and part-time genius.)

Before you go accusing me of plagiarism, I'll admit that my message first appeared thousands of years ago in ancient Greece. The inscription on the Temple of Apollo said, 'Know yourself'. It was tremendous advice then, it still is, and always will be.

Let's give your personal awareness a huge boost with more questions, with more mind-stretching exercises. They've produced some unforgettable comments from my clients. One superbly fit triathlete said she felt like she had put her life in the spotlight. You're going to be the star attraction. A swimmer described his sessions with me as mental massages. That's what I want you to feel like too. I promise you won't have to lay down on a psychiatrist's couch to get a full analysis. (Ever wondered why psychiatrists were famous for their couches? Sigmund Freud, the father of psychiatry, didn't like looking directly into the faces of his clients. Other psychiatrists copied his habit, even though Sigmund probably had some problems like his clients. Just a bit of trivia that says a lot about something.)

Many of my sports clients have superb physical fitness, strength and impressive body shapes. But, beneath the surface, there can be the same problems experienced by any stressed businessperson, or someone who is unemployed. Everyone needs mental massages. Putting your life in the spotlight can also be fun. I often use humour and surprises because they can break down a lot of barriers to greater self-knowledge.

I've lined up four micro-exercises that always produce smiles and laughs when I use them in my seminars. They'll loosen you up for greater insights. They'll quickly prove to you that there are no limits to how far you stretch your self-awareness. I've seen athlete's bodies, arms, legs and backs twisted and stretched by an expert. A friend of mine is one of the world's best osteopaths and she specialises in bending bodies in every possible direction. Many sports stars, including world champions, line up to see her because she achieves incredible results. You can become the expert at stretching yourself — not your body, but your mind — and there'll be absolutely no pain. Trust me. Let's go!

Read through the next passage fairly quickly, and count the number of times you find the letter F. Keep your finger off the page, please.

FINISHED FILES ARE THE
RESULT OF YEARS OF SCIENTIFIC
STUDY COMBINED WITH THE
EXPERIENCE OF MANY YEARS.

You probably counted, recounted, and recounted the number of Fs. The most common answer is three, but you now know there are three extra Fs hidden in there. How's that possible? Slowly say the word of. Did you hear it? Instead of an F sound, your brain heard a V sound. The word of appears three times, and each time the letter F just disappeared off the page. Learn an important rule of life from this simple puzzle — we don't have perfect awareness even with the simplest of observations. When you're digging in your heels during an argument, remember you're probably not getting a perfect picture of the problem.

How good are you at Roman numerals?
The two gigantic letters below form the number
nine. You can add one line to produce a six.
How is it possible?

At least half of my audience members usually give up in frustration on this exercise. However, there are always a few who use lateral thinking and draw a single line, the letter S. So simple! Simple if you're prepared to think out of the square. Why not also think out of the circle, or the triangle? Why not think outside of all your usual thinking habits? Compared to the previous exercise, this answer was hidden a bit more, but it wasn't that far from the surface if you were willing to stretch your awareness boundaries. Many things can have many meanings, some correct, some wrong. That's what makes the study of human behaviour and thinking, especially your own, so fascinating. Keep thinking like a detective or like the new breed of brilliant crime scene investigators in television shows. Look for the clues that others overlook.

Among the jumble of letters ahead of you is a hidden word. Cross off six letters and the word remaining will be the name of a delicious fruit.

sibaxlneattneras

The answer to the previous exercise is often used as a clue to solve this exercise. I use this exercise in seminars where I read out the instructions, to emphasise that listening is more productive than hearing. More effort, but more rewards. Much of my success in counselling comes from listening. After a session I'm usually tired, sometimes exhausted because listening takes a lot of effort, when you give a full commitment. It's also a compliment to the speaker. Have I distracted you so you've forgotten about the mystery fruit? The hidden fruit is a 'banana'. It very quickly appears once you cross out 's-i-x-l-e-t-t-e-r-s'. All you had to do was to remove these two words instead of fruitlessly searching for ways to exterminate six individual letters.

The last of our four micro-exercises involves some simple arithmetic. Mentally add the following numbers.

1000 + 40 + 1000 + 30 + 1000 + 20 + 1000 + 10

You can find the correct answer, and the most common wrong answer, near the end of the book. Nearly every one in every audience, gets it wrong. Ask yourself 'Why?' if you're with the majority. It's because there is not one person, anywhere, who has 100 per cent perfect awareness. That's one of the most helpful things I can tell stressed or depressed clients, because it tells them there are so many untouched areas to look for help. There are many solutions for every problem, and I've filled the rest of this chapter with a smorgasbord of psychological strategies for you to find stress solutions that work for you, and maybe others, who you want to help. There will be some appetisers plus some big meals, that will leave you feeling fulfilled, but not stuffed.

I hope you've loosened those limitations that were around your thinking, and now you're ready and keen to jump into that spotlight. Ready to have a very close look at yourself? The next self-inspection exercise will give you a full workover. It was inspired by a weekly column that appeared in the *Sydney Morning Herald* a few years ago. Every Saturday I would keenly scan the answers provided by some celebrity, or someone who was not yet famous. Some answers were delightful, some enlightened the human condition, at least mine. Whatever your answers are, they'll be valuable to you. They'll grow in value if you repeat the whole exercise six months away. I'm certain you'll give some very different answers. That's a jump in awareness to look for! My list of questions still keeps some of the themes from the newspaper profile, but I've produced new questions for you to consider some novel, even bizarre, situations.

Do you really know yourself?

· Whose face makes you smile?...

....

· How would you spend a perfect Wednesday? ....

....

· What were you thinking about the last time you were showering?

....

· If you had to change your name, what would you choose? ....

....

· What would you never give up? ....

....

· When did you last say 'Sorry'? ....

....

· What do you get angry about? ....

....

· What is the best thing you have ever seen? ....

....

· If you could go anywhere back in time, where would you go? ....

....

· What is the most important word in the English language? ....

....

· Which 'super hero' would you like to be for a day? ....

....

· How often do you say 'actually' or 'absolutely'? ....

....

· What is your greatest extravagance? ....

....

· What would you never do again? ....

....

· What do you want more of? ....

....

· If you had one wish to change the world, what would it be? ....

....

· What is the best thing about being alive? ....

....

Are you flowing or just stuck?

Welcome back. Maybe, you're thinking that some of my questions were so silly they were useless. I disagree, but I'm the first to agree that not all awareness is useful. That's where most trivia belongs, in the non-useful bin. Do you know the time on all the clocks in the movie *Pulp Fiction*? They were all set at 4.20. That's a useless piece of extra awareness, because it's not about you. I've heard some businesspeople rant that it's a dog eat dog world, so you have to look out for number one! They're half right. You have to look inside number one — you! Every question I just threw at you looks inside you. What were two biggest words amongst my self-awareness questions? Not the longest, the most important. I put them in the first and last questions: smile and life. You shouldn't separate them. That disgusting S-word pushes them apart.

Earlier on I promised to introduce you to techniques that attack stress at a deeper level. We've reached that point. I've already taken you to the Olympics and now it's time to rev up your imagination again. Think deeply about a different and challenging way of looking at your life. If you were involved in a horrendous train crash and you survived untouched, and everyone thought you were dead, would you use this as a doorway to another life. Would you disappear and leave your career, family and friends? Sometimes I hear someone grumble, 'What a stupid question?' Then I explain that the situation is not pure fantasy and it really happened in London in 1999. The huge pile up caused by the collision of two crowded commuter trains was a blessing in disguise for some of the passengers. They used it as the opportunity to leave lives of disenchantment, dissatisfaction and despair to start afresh.

Those who took this escape route probably suffered from a deficiency of accomplishments. They might have had busy lives that are overflowing with activities, but few of these are accomplishments. You can't feel dissatisfied with your life when you have an abundance of accomplishments. However … however, (when I slowly repeat myself that's a signal I'm about to say something more important than usual) many people confuse activities with accomplishments. It happens at work and at home, even if that's the same place. I say that because many people who now work from their homes say their stress levels have risen.

I get a lot of ideas looking at nature. Once I was walking back home from a long run and I passed two paddocks. The first had a lot of cows with their calves constantly chomping away at the grass. I startled a lot of the calves but they soon returned to their major activity — eating. The next paddock had a handful of horses. They looked beautiful but all they did was walk, sometimes gallop, and mostly chomp on grass. I saw lots of activity, but no accomplishments, except for the new calves.

How different are you from those cows and horses? Ready for a big challenge? Divide the last week of your life into activities and accomplishments. This might tell you more clearly whether you'll think about disappearing after a train crash. What's your verdict about your life? Are there enough accomplishments?

We have some psychological clues where to look for greater fulfilment. It appears our most valuable accomplishments often occur when we experience *flow*. This sounds like a very unscientific term, but it's now used by psychologists to describe a richly rewarding and enjoyable part of our lives. Add two extra life-circles and you've covered all of your life. They are *order* and *chaos*. You can get another valuable review of your life by carefully considering all the components of each of these three life-circles. How often do you experience flow in your life? Is that enough?

Three life-circles

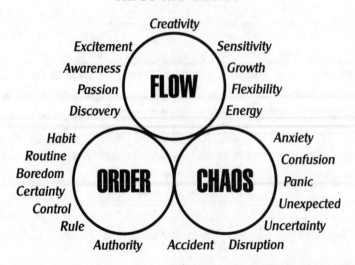

Do you have a big picture?

Life is a game of monopoly. Life is a jigsaw. Life is a cabaret. Life is just a bowl of cherries. Life's a beach. None of these metaphors shine any light for me. In his motivational classic, *Awaken The Giant Within*, Anthony Robbins calls these global metaphors. I strongly agree with him that a global metaphor can be very influential. The right metaphor can put wind under your wings but the wrong metaphor can send you plummeting to the ground.

I'm serious about these crashes. Over 8,000 Australians are reported missing every year. Unfortunately, there are probably many more who are not reported. We have nearly 20 million people in Australia, so that means at least one out of every 2,500 goes missing every year. That's a lot of people to lose, and many of them will never be found. Worse still, 60 per cent of those who vanish are under 16 years old. How many see their lives as misery? How many are on a pathway that can lead to suicide?

After much searching, I believe Mother Teresa's poem on the next page is the very best, the ultimate collection of life metaphors. These are all searchlights! The poem comes from a wall hanging in an AIDS hospice that Mother Teresa supported in New York. Great people practise what they preach.

I'm certain that this poem once changed a young man's life. My client was a classic teenage rebel, proud of his drug problem, and he hardly listened to me until I showed him the poem. He read it and had to admit it contained a few good ideas. But he still shrugged his shoulders, and spat out, 'So what?' I told him who wrote it, and we started talking about Mother Teresa's incredible strength for such a small frail woman. Everyone in the world knew about her. My rebel was so powerfully built, what could he achieve? I knew he was now doing some deep thinking. I could see it through his eyes. What was stopping him from doing great things? He never said it, but he knew what it was. I still clearly remember him calling me a smart arse, with a grin. Years later he had even more tattoos and was now a very caring social worker, helping kids with their problems. We both help adolescents who say, 'My life is a prison,' 'My life is a black hole,' 'My life is hell.'

What is life?

Life is an opportunity, use it.
Life is a beauty, admire it.
Life is bliss, taste it.
Life is a dream, realise it.
Life is a challenge, meet it.
Life is a duty, complete it.
Life is a game, play it.
Life is costly, care for it.
Life is a wealth, keep it.
Life is love, enjoy it.
Life is mystery, know it.
Life is a promise, fulfil it.
Life is sorrow, overcome it.
Life is a song, sing it.
Life is a struggle, accept it.
Life is a tragedy, brace it.
Life is luck, make it.
Life is an adventure, dare it.

Mother Teresa (1910–1997)

What's missing from your life?

Stress often grows into moodiness and much worse. Men prefer to say 'I'm just moody' when they feel down, but I've found it's often a short jump, a very short jump, to depression. One of my greatest rewards as a psychologist is to help a client reverse this jump. As a psychologist, I strongly proclaim that optimistic thinking is the number one way to remove the mental cataract of depression. That's why I've set aside the whole of the next chapter to help you become an expert practitioner, and teacher, of optimistic thinking.

Closely behind optimistic thinking in effectiveness is one of my favourite exercises. I've found stress, as well as depression, can often disappear when we put our lives into perspective.

You can quickly look at your life from all possible angles when you use the exercise 'Four windows of life'. Which windows lead to stressful thoughts? I'm betting you'll agree with me that stress appears when you keep looking at your life through the *Don't Have/Want* and *Have/Don't Want* windows. The first of these two windows is where you can have healthy goals, but it's also where envy exists. This is the if only thinking window. If only I could get a new car, a giant screen television, a bigger house, etc, I'd be happy. Through the other window you'll find illnesses, as well as boring jobs and unhappy relationships. The healthy windows are *Have/Want* and *Don't Have/Don't Want.*

Let's look at your life through each of these windows, one at a time. Here's a challenge for you. Put 24 hours of your life under the microscope by writing down every single thing you have that you want, in one day of your life. And I mean everything! You get out of bed, so you can walk without assistance. If you're like me, you start the day with a magical cup of coffee. Realise you've got clean water and electricity, and plenty of food. The list will be lengthy, if you keep your eyes open. This awareness pushes stress further and further into the background.

Four windows of life

	WANT	**DON'T WANT**
HAVE		
DON'T HAVE		

Here's a simple exercise with a huge message. It's about the fourth and final window. Be very quiet and listen very, very carefully. I stole that line from one of my favourite Bugs Bunny cartoons. Pay special attention to what you don't hear. What didn't you hear? I didn't hear any bombs or missiles exploding. I also don't hear children crying from starvation or AIDS. That's a form of terrorism that happens every day. There are millions of people around the world who would think their prayers have come true if they didn't hear what we don't hear right now. What's the huge message from these missing sounds? When we look at the big picture instead of letting ourselves be carried away with the details, most of our stress simply disappears. Often depression goes too.

I'm prepared to mix many approaches to make clients even more skilful when they look through the *Have/Want* window. You must have gone shopping sometime, for one purpose only, to get your hands on an irresistible special. It's either a bargain because of its price, or it won't be available for long, or ever again. Where and what are the specials in your life, those things so precious, or so rare? Look for them, they're with you now.

A quick quiz about ancient history: What were the Seven Wonders of the Ancient World? Most of my audiences know the pyramids and not much else. You should know a lot more, not ancient history, but what are the wonders in your life? If you don't think you have any, that's stress talking.

In my town, a few hours away from Sydney, garage sales are everywhere on Saturday mornings, and bright-eyed treasure seekers drive from one sale to another. They're extremely keen. I hope you keenly look for the specials, bargains, wonders and treasure in your life. 'Know more about your emotions' will make you more aware of the gifts in your life that we all take for granted — those wonderful emotions. These are your invisible assets. What are the two most important emotions? I don't think you can go past loved and loving. How common are these emotions in your life? Regularly repeat this exercise and share this way of increasing awareness with others who are close to you.

Know more about your emotions

We are capable of a huge variety of feelings. Sometimes we only vividly remember the painful ones. This exercise will help you recall the times when you felt a wide range of healthy positive emotions. Briefly describe situations where you experienced the following emotions.

FEELINGS	SITUATIONS
Relaxed	
Friendly	
Satisfied	
Happy	
Confident	
Excited	
Important	
Strong	
Proud	
Trusted	
Loving	
Loved	
Special	

Great looks plus wealth equals stress?

Helping people to put their problems into perspective doesn't take huge skills, but it requires patience and compassion. These are usually missing when this technique is practised by amateur psychologists.

Recently, a magazine cover blared 'Elle's stress hell'. It referred to Elle Macpherson, former supermodel, who is striving to also be a super businesswoman and a supermum. She's now an ultra-busy, successful businesswoman with two young children. She was savagely criticised for attending an expensive private clinic, at $10,000 a week for therapy, after she broke down complaining about the stress in her life. Possibly she wouldn't have been criticised if she had spent the money on cosmetic surgery. One newspaper critic said how dare Elle think she has a stressful life compared to a mother with an autistic child. Elle should try a reality check and change places with a mother who has real problems. I've heard other high flyers who've also had stress problems, simply dismissed as high maintenance, spoilt and self-centred. They get little sympathy, but they should. Everyone, rich or poor, deserves sympathy when they breakdown, hit the wall, and fall apart. Showing sympathy will help you see your life more clearly.

If Elle attended one of my all-day *Turn Stress Into Success* workshops, I'd welcome her, like I welcome everyone who seeks help. Sometime during the day she would complete 'Rate the pain'. It helps both the rich and poor, and everyone in between, to put negative feelings into a clearer perspective. Expect big things if you share your answers with others. Once, the discussion of this exercise went for nearly an hour. We were all exhausted after it, but we learnt a lot about everyone in the room, including ourselves.

Rate the pain

All of the following emotions are forms of pain, ranging from mild to extremely strong. Give your own ratings by writing each emotion in the appropriate box below.

Abused	Angry	Annoyed	Betrayed
Dejected	Depressed	Despondent	Disappointed
Discouraged	Down	Frightened	Frustrated

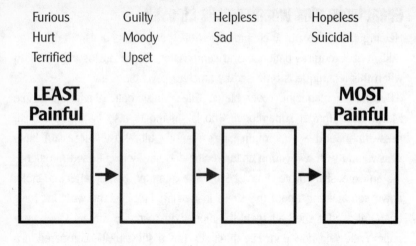

Furious	Guilty	Helpless	Hopeless
Hurt	Moody	Sad	Suicidal
Terrified	Upset		

Now that you've finished, I'll tell you there are no correct answers! There are also no wrong answers. If you repeat the exercises a week later, you'll probably find you don't get the same answers. Confused? Pain and losses can't be accurately measured like the way we dissect time with a stopwatch. It's scientifically impossible. But many people ignore this. They believe the way they see their problems is the only possible viewpoint. Once you believe this, depression can be just around the corner. Stay flexible and alert in your thinking.

Listen to one of the greatest geniuses of all time!

All great relationships are two-way. Both partners have to be prepared to give and take, right? What about money? There's a song that contains the magical insight, 'Money don't care about you!' Why do so many people spend all their lives chasing something that doesn't care about us? I found an answer in Wayne Dyer's powerful book *Wisdom of the Ages*. The chapter titled 'Balance', begins with this beautiful poem:

Every now and then go away,
have a little relaxation,
for when you come back to your work
your judgement will be surer.

since to remain constantly at work
will cause you to lose power of judgement …
Go some distance away
because the work appears smaller
and more of it can be taken in at a glance,
and a lack of harmony or proportion
is more readily seen.

The author? It was Leonardo da Vinci. He left his important message nearly 500 years ago. Money becomes our number one pursuit when our lives lack balance. For me, this lack of balance found in many modern business lives is beautifully summed up by this massive paradox: You can win at work, but lose at life.

Early in our travels together, I gave you some of my thoughts on selfishness. I want to briefly return to this important topic. The head of a large organisation quickly dismissed his regular absence from his children's sporting activities with a sweeping rationalisation, 'It's just one of the many sacrifices you have to do if you want to get ahead in this world.' Whilst he was proud of his badge of dedication, his marriage often appeared colder than permafrost. I wonder what his kids thought of the sacrifices they made for their father's success?

Often kids are more aware than their parents. I love telling this little story. A child asks her mother why her father isn't home for dinner, again. 'Daddy's still at work. He's got so much work to finish.' The young mind suggests, 'Why don't they put daddy in the slow group with the others who can't keep up with their work?'

Another cutting insight comes from Steve Biddulph, author of the bestselling book, *Manhood*. He describes busy working fathers as walking wallets. All overworked parents need to look at the balance in their lives. We all do! You probably know someone who is dreaming of breaking free and getting off the treadmill. An extra bleak image came from a former advertising executive who cashed in and dropped out. He said he used to feel like he was a worker bee feeding a gigantic queen bee. How drained would you be if these were the ways you saw your working career? Unfortunately, many people do.

Being a member of the baby boomer generation, I've lived through a turn-around in our approach to leisure over the last 40 years. The flood of labour-saving devices that started to trickle into our lives in the 1950s was going to give us much more time to enjoy ourselves. We were expecting large amounts of leisure time. What happened? Many of us forgot about the importance of balance. Appliances became more important than accomplishments. Real estate became more important than relationships, and relaxation. Stress became more common than satisfaction.

Money alone sets all the world in motion.

Publius Syrus, 42 BC

Why do so many amongst us lead lives that lack balance? It gets back to your relationship with money. How much does it control you, instead of the other way round? If you're uncertain about your answer, here's a situation that will head you in the right direction. Drum roll … look out. Too late! You've just been attacked from behind and you feel a sharp knife pressed against your throat. The only words you hear are 'Your money or your life'. What do you do? If you even hesitated for a second, you should think more deeply about why do you want money.

Think about why you want money — to give you some food for thought, I've dug up the results of a psychological study about this important question. I found a recent article written by Edwin Locke, an American professor who has been investigating goal setting for more than two decades. His team of researchers identified the 10 core motives for the pursuit of money by entrepreneurs.

Motives for the pursuit of money

Look at the descending rank order found in the Locke study, then build your own 10-point list. After you've built your list, ask yourself this vital question, 'Will my rank order put balance into my life?'

1. Security
2. Personal pride
3. Support family
4. Compensation for effort
5. Freedom
6. Charity
7. Leisure
8. Overcoming self-doubt
9. Impulse activities
10. Social improvement

Why I want money

1. ....
2. ....
3. ....
4. ....
5. ....
6. ....
7. ....
8. ....
9. ....
10. ....

Give me money, it's all I want

These were the lyrics from an early song from The Beatles. Later in their careers, all four of them changed their minds as they learnt you can be rich, but morally bankrupt, you can be rich but emotionally impoverished, and money is not the best motivator. A comedian noted that God mustn't think much of money, just look at the people who have most of it.

I've got nothing against money because it can be a great motivator — when you give some of it away. Compare the attitude to money of some world champions, from sport and business. Formula One driving supremo and respected family man, Michael Schumacher, donated $1 million to

UNESCO. Heavy weight boxer Mike Tyson, jailed for rape, managed to squander nearly $US 300 million. Giorgio Armani, one of the world's premier fashion designers, stoked a controversy by not giving Christmas presents to fashion editors. Instead he gave $550,000 to Down Syndrome charities and pricked a lot of consciences of the me-generation. Sparks flew as many called it a publicity stunt. Then there's one of my favourite eccentrics, Ted Turner. In 1997, he gave $US 1 billion to the United Nations. He explained his decision in one sentence, 'I've learned the more good that I did, the more money comes in'.

South Africa's former cricket captain, Hansie Cronje, is going to be remembered for the wrong reasons. Not for his successful career on the cricket field. Instead, he'll be remembered for fixing matches, taking bribes, and inducing gullible young members of his team to join him. His reputation was destroyed. Worse, his actions pulled down the international standing of cricket, and doubts will linger about the legitimacy of many international games. He admitted that he 'had an unfortunate love of money'. Someone who knows the Bible a lot better than me, said the Bible doesn't attack money. It attacks the love of money. Cronje was a born-again Christian who should have listened more closely. We all should.

When is the best time to have a heart attack?

Sick and morbid question? Think again. The most common time of the week for heart attacks and death from heart disease is on Monday mornings, around 9am. If you want plenty of medical care, then this is the time to avoid. Deepak Chopra, a medical expert on meditation and relaxation, sees this weekly phenomenon as a stunning achievement, because no other species can do this. We can do this because of attitudes to work. Winston Churchill believed the single most important social division was between those who enjoyed their work and those that didn't. I think he was right, do you?

You're going to enjoy the next little exercise. Think happy, think of yourself being happy, think of yourself being happy in as many different places as possible. Clearly identify those places. Did you see yourself being happy at work? Most people don't!

Job dissatisfaction provides cartoonists with lots of inspiration. In one cartoon a frustrated employee is standing outside his office building, and in his mind he connects it to Camp X-Ray at Guantanamo Bay. He also feels gagged, blindfolded and shackled. Stress through job dissatisfaction produces lots of depressing images. One of my clients told me how he reacted to his workplace. Every day when he drove into the car park, he felt his stomach drop as his spirit left his body. He collected it when he returned to the car park at the end of his shift. He looked 10 years older than his real age. David Peake, an Australian organisational psychologist, outlined a common form of evolution that occurs with workers. They begin as keen volunteers, but can quickly become whingers when their ideas and efforts are ignored. Further bitterness turns them into survivors, who are just hanging in there, waiting for their Lotto win or their superannuation payout. When they see no hope of any change, they finally end up angry prisoners. I see lots of clients from these last three stages.

Several Australian surveys show how widespread worker discontent is. Morgan & Banks, the worldwide recruitment specialists, found more than half of the 6,000 Australians they questioned, thought they were in the wrong job. Another 7,000 were asked where they would prefer to be in five years. Forty-five per cent of the sample said they would flee the city and leave the traditional workforce. Running a vineyard was a very popular alternative. Research by Gallup estimated that 20 per cent of the Australian workforce is disengaged from their jobs. Their bodies are present, but their minds are elsewhere. The Canberra-based Australia Institute found 23 per cent of Australians aged 30-59, have in the past 10 years deserted the rat race and found more rewarding lower paying positions. It was once simply called dropping out, then it was seeking a seachange because so many headed for towns and villages near the coastline. Now those searching for the new Holy Grail, a balanced lifestyle, are heading in all directions, so the broader term downshifting was invented. Do you want to run away and run a vineyard, or just change our career? If you do, I'll show you how to do it in later chapters. If you want to stay in your present job, you'll learn how to clearly see why you enjoy your work. I think I've got all the bases covered for you. The game is yet to start.

Why is the number 1,440 so important?

I argue that we're not created equal. Good looks, intelligence, family and financial support, these are just a handful of the characteristics that aren't equally distributed when we enter this life. It would appear the American Declaration of Independence got it wrong.

The only thing equal for every person on this planet is the number 1,440. That's the number of minutes we're given every day of our lives. How you use those 1,440 minutes tells you how committed you are to success in your life. It also tells you how balanced your life is. Wow! Isn't that a lot to get from a single number. Don't ignore this. The rich have 1,440 minutes, the poor have 1,440 minutes. Bigger still, successful people have 1,440 minutes and so do the failures. The failures often complain, 'I don't have time to do that!' Often they're just saying, 'I don't want to do it, because I'm not prepared to work for my success.' However, healthy success doesn't come from being a workaholic. Have you heard someone say something like 'Success comes from hard work. If you work hard enough, you can achieve nearly everything.' Do you agree? I don't! I think it's half right. What do you have to do besides hard work? Think about those smart pills we talked about at the start of the book. You get much more success when you also work smart. Be smart and give yourself time in your 1,440 minutes to relax and enjoy your life. True success comes from having a balanced life.

Einstein can help us with our 1,440 minutes. He proved time can speed up and slow down. It's this last part that fascinates me. Look for the beauty and benefits from doing things slowly. One champion golfer slowed down everything he did in the dressing room before playing. Putting on his shoes and socks took ages. Another champion golfer, Gary Player, taught himself great patience by deliberately driving behind slow cars or trucks.

Has anyone ever tried to insult you by calling you slow? This word has a bad reputation. Why? In a world dominated by rapid changes, you'll hear about the quick and the dead. People who accept this are most likely to be stress sufferers, or stress creators. They're the ones with very little balance in their lives. You'll enrich your life when you identify the benefits of going slow. Go for it, but slowly! Identify 10 slow-down areas in your life where you can gain benefits. Here are the most popular choices: talking, cooking, getting angry, shopping, holidays, walking, driving, studying a problem, making love, aging. What else would you add to your list?

Being short of time, always being in a rush, can do some terrible things. Sometimes it's road rage. I shake people with good stories a well as terrible stories. Here's a terrible story, from Seattle in the United States. A few years ago there was big traffic jam, and many motorists started to get hostile when they realised the problem was being caused by one woman. She was standing on a bridge, about to jump. The crowd started to chant 'Jump, bitch, jump!' She did, and barely survived her massive injuries. Those who chanted, traded compassion for contempt. That happens when your life is unbalanced, and time is more important than people.

Are you an expert mind-reader?

I've probably met a lot more stressed and depressed people than you have. There's one characteristic a lot of them have in common. Many of them think they are experts at mind-reading. That's a big part of their problems. Even on my very best days as a skilful psychologist, it's so difficult to guess what a person is thinking. Once you accept this, you're far less likely to jump to conclusions. Mind-reading and jumping to conclusions, now there's a terrible combination. Unfortunately, they've got many sidekicks that make up the faulty-thinking gang. Psychologists use many different labels to describe faulty thinking. Common ones are catastrophisation and overgeneralising. I like to simplify them all by saying they're just different ways we exaggerate. When you exaggerate a problem or your ability to read minds, you usually jump to the wrong conclusions and say hello to more stress. Jumping to the correct conclusion doesn't happen enough. Can you recall when you were able to do this? I can quickly show you how exaggerating creates big problems, and how you can deal with them.

I'm disturbed. I'm depressed. I'm inadequate. I've got it all!
George Costanza in the *Seinfeld* TV series

What the fool believes, the wise man has the power to reason away.

The Doobie Brothers

Faulty thinking has been around with us since we started to think. On the next page there's a classic example of jumping to conclusions. It's a story from China that's over 2,000 years old.

Here's a real-life example of exaggerating. I'll never ever forget it. I was doing some counselling with a married couple. They were glaring anger at each other, and I quickly discovered it was based on some super-exaggerations. I asked each of them to sum up all their problems in a single sentence. The husband said, 'She always calls me a drunk when she sees me with a beer in my hand'. The wife returned the serve with, 'What do you expect? You never show me any affection.'

I started to smile because I'd just heard the top two danger words that produce exaggerations, two words that build up stress, and breed arguments, and often lead to depression. What are the words? They're never and always. You won't believe what we discovered at the core of most of their problems. The husband revealed that he felt rejected because he and his wife no longer sat on the lounge together, holding each other's hands! I asked him why he hadn't said anything to his wife and I heard a very common answer. 'She should have known.' The wife's frustration also came from a very unexpected source — the garbage bin. She felt she was being ignored because she had to remind her husband to take out their large garbage bin every week. She finally agreed he did it without prompting about once a month. His response was, 'Is that all you want me to do? I didn't think it was important.'

Uncertain or smart?

This story is thought to have taken place in China over 2,000 years ago.

A group of wild horses ran through a village and destroyed many of the crops. The head of the village inspected all of the damage. One villager cried out, 'This is a disaster'. The head man crossed his arms and replied, 'Maybe'.

The next day the horses returned, but this time the son of the head man captured one of the best-looking horses. The villagers cheered the son. One villager told the head man, 'You should be so happy and proud to have such a brave son'. He answered, 'Maybe'.

The son spent all of the next day trying to ride the wild horse. Exhausted, the son lost his grip and fell heavily. He broke his leg. One villager cried, 'This horse will only bring misfortune to all who ride him'. The head of the village simply said, 'Maybe'.

The next day the villagers woke to find they were surrounded by troops. They took all the young men away to join the army. Only the son with the broken leg was left behind. One villager told the head man, 'You are so lucky'. Several villagers whispered, 'Maybe'.

Read the headlines carefully, listen to the news, current affairs programs and political interviews with your faulty-thinking detector on full. You'll discover lots of exaggerating. Is there a day without chaos in the streets, a crisis, a fiasco or a blunder? Professional sport isn't immune from exaggeration. In the National Basketball Association, teams fear the 'doomsday double'. They have to play two games on consecutive days, usually in Adelaide and Perth. It's big news when teams overcome this self-made hoodoo. Then there's the Sydney's annual City-to-Surf mini-marathon. In the run to Bondi, there is one steep section. It's a problem, but when it's called Heartbreak Hill, the problem gets a lot steeper. Exaggerating is a great way to put more steep hills into your life.

How quickly is your world changing?

Changes scare a lot of people. What if there were no changes in our lives? That might give security and stability, but there would also be a lot of stagnation. Think about the following concepts: the GST, night-time cricket and becoming a parent. What do they have in common? They're all examples of paradigm changes. What's a paradigm? It's a word that appeared in science 30 years ago, and has spread into psychology and now into business. A paradigm is a big, new idea that changes the way we look at something.

Sometimes a new paradigm makes you see the whole world differently. New paradigms lead to big changes. I've got three children, my oldest was born over 30 years ago and I can still vividly recall how I became a different person on the day he was born. Many people are afraid of paradigm changes, even if they've never heard of the word paradigm.

Let's put together a collection of paradigm changes that have taken place in the last 20 years. In sport, there was one-day cricket, professionals at the Olympics, professional Rugby Union, steroids and drug testing, just to name a few. In business and modern life, we've had computers, emails, the Internet, ATMs, pay TV, deregulation, enterprise bargaining. In our personal lives, we can become unemployed, get divorced, change jobs, move to a new home, and later on, experience the 'empty nest syndrome'.

What's your conclusion about paradigms? Paradigm changes are all around us, they're happening everywhere. They're a normal part of modern life, and instead of being stressful, you can see them as opportunities for more success in your life. Here's a very quick test about you and paradigms. Do you put salt on your food before you taste it? This silly observation was once part of the selection process that the Ford Motor Company followed when they were interviewing potential new executives. They saw this as a sign of inflexible thinking, and you have to be flexible to be successful. You have to be flexible to enjoy all those paradigm changes that are around the corner for all of us. The only thing that is constant is change.

I truly had a text-book midlife crisis in my late thirties. It was a painful paradigm change. Those who joke about it haven't had one. My growing sense of mortality stirred up dissatisfaction, and I clearly heard a clock ticking. However, I did more than cope, I grew. I got motivated enough to quit my job and begin a whole new career. Now we're finding this unpleasant transition is appearing earlier in life. Do you know anyone who is having a QLC? That's the buzz talk for a 'quarter life crisis'. It's part of the age of discontent. Changes offer opportunities for growth and more success, grab onto these opportunities with both hands. I did, and my life is sensational.

You, me and the frog in the hot water!

Have you heard about the experiment with the frog in hot water? The great thinker Edward de Bono, believes this experiment never happened. A frog was supposedly placed in water that was slowly heated to boiling. Not being aware of the slight changes around him, the frog, fictional or real, suffers a terrible fate.

Lack of awareness can hurt us too, in small and big ways. A couple of weeks ago I went into my garage, hopped into my car, turned the key, and nothing happened. Flat battery. A mechanic later asked me the brutal question, 'Did it go all of a sudden? Didn't you get any warning?' Sure enough, he was on the right track. There had been little signs, but I ignored them, just like the frog. Paying attention to little things can give you big rewards. After this long look at yourself, you're well on the way to inoculate yourself, and others around you, against stress, depression and its dark shadow.

> *The quality of one's life depends on the quality of attention. Whatever you pay attention to will grow more important in your life. There is no limit to the kinds of changes that awareness can produce.*
>
> Deepak Chopra (Doctor and philosopher)

Chapter 6
Optimists Are Winners!

I'm never nervous before I give a speech, but once I got a bit worried just before I was about to speak. I was the next speaker after Tommy Raudonikis at the NSW Rugby League Academy. Tommy was a fierce competitor as a player and a coach, and his face still shows the scars and indents from his lengthy and distinguished career. He's always a passionate communicator, a rough diamond, with a heart of gold. However, I was still concerned because I was going to disagree strongly with something he had just said. Standing in front of a group of young football stars, he dramatically prodded a finger into the region of his heart and loudly told everyone, 'You can't measure what's behind here, you can't measure ticker, you can't measure tenacity'. I gave a sigh of relief when Tommy finished his speech and immediately apologised as he had to leave for another appointment. But, I still waited till I'd heard, 'Tommy has left the building' before I said, 'Tommy was wrong!'

Tenacity or perseverance grows from optimism. High optimism equals high perseverance and, over the last 20 years, psychologists have collected over-whelming evidence to show that optimism can be accurately measured. That's why I was so certain Tommy was wrong. Optimism doesn't guarantee success, but it greatly increases your chances. You can still make mistakes, but you're much more likely to keep coming back than a pessimist would. You'll remember me telling you that I work in many different psychological fields. No matter where I'm working, I frequently teach people to be more optimistic. This is the core of today's most effective psychotherapies. Psychologists call it cognitive therapy. These techniques work whether my clients are long-term unemployed, or sports stars who are millionaires.

What follows in the rest of this chapter is the core of a seminar that's very close to my heart. I've been refining it over many years, and this has helped me to be a more skilful therapist, a better parent, and a more caring per-son. Look forward to some big changes in your life!

Let's do a quick three-part self-analysis. Would you describe yourself as a sceptic? I'm proud to call myself a sceptic because a sceptic wants evidence before making decisions. They're rational thinkers. A sceptic tries not to jump to conclusions. Next, do you think you're a cynic? No, I'm not a cynic, but back in the 1980s, if there was a club for cynics, I would have probably been its president. In my view, a cynic is a sceptic who is drowning in negativity. I was certainly drowning. Even when I was given overwhelming evidence about some topic, I kept trying to shoot holes in it. I was the 'king of the nitpickers' and I was often painful to be around. I'll give you a picture of how cynical I was. Over my desk where I used to work, I pinned up a cartoon. It showed a group of people lined up outside a caravan, like those Red Cross vans where you can donate blood. The sign outside the caravan said, 'Cynicism — Early Detection Mobile Unit'. I wrote my name over one of the people going into the caravan. In those days, I was proud to be a cynic, and I wanted people to know it.

What happened to me since then? Well, I talked myself out of being a cynic. How? That leads me to my last request for you to analyse yourself. Do you feel you're an optimist. I used to be a cynic and a pessimist. They go hand-in-hand. I was so depressed I had to do something. I did what a lot of men do when they face their mid-life crisis. I quit my job! I'd been a science teacher for 17 years, but I wanted to do different things with my life. So I went back to university to retrain as a psychologist. I got a lot more grey hairs, but I was enjoying life a lot more.

Then came what I love calling a blinding flash of common sense. Do you know the Bible story about God blinding Paul on the road to Damascus? God wanted to smarten up Paul, quickly. My blinding light came from the television. Late one night, back in 1991, I tuned in to watch an interview with Martin Seligman, an American psychology professor from the University of Pennsylvania, who is one of the most influential psychologists in the world today. He was the President of the American Psychological Association, but I like telling sports groups he's the Michael Jordan of psychology. Seligman was talking about optimism. Whammo! I was hooked. I discovered that psychologists had been investigating optimism, and they'd found the more optimistic you are, the more likely you will be successful in life, not for a year or so, but your whole life. This message destroyed my cynicism and pessimism. It was a case of goodbye pessimism, hello optimism.

I would rather be an optimist and a fool, than a pessimist and right.
Albert Einstein (My favourite genius)

If you want to become an expert on optimism, you should get hold of two of Seligman's books. I recommend both of them to nearly all of my clients and I think so much of these books, I've given away lots of copies to friends as presents. I've also loaned copies of these books to captains of different Australian sports teams, and never saw the books again. I'm confident both players digested everything as they both went on to even greater success. I've read some best selling books that are so flimsy they disappear after a year. *Learned Optimism* came out in 1990, *The Optimistic Child* was published in 1995, and you can still find them in bookstores as well as in most libraries.

Seligman began his career working with people with psychological problems such as depression and anxiety. He realised that the techniques he used to help people overcome their problems, might also be helpful for healthy people. He soon found out that he was right. How did he find out he was right? Well, he headed a large team of researchers that strove to answer another question: What's so special about the thinking of successful people? After studying thousands of people — businesspeople, elite athletes, West Point military cadets, politicians — Seligman came to the conclusion that optimistic thinking is an important ingredient in success. It's not absolutely necessary, but if you're an optimist, your chances of being successful are far greater than the average person. To put it in a nutshell, optimism leads to success. Most people think the reverse is far more common, that is, the more successful you are, the more optimistic you become. However, research doesn't support this popular view. This was a real eye-opener for me. It's also great news for anyone who wants to be more successful.

Optimism triangle

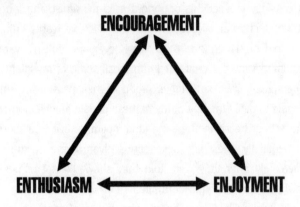

Seligman's team has measured the optimism levels of more than a million people. This group includes US presidents, Olympic gold medalists and some of the most successful salespeople in the world. The list is constantly growing. Later on I'll show you some of the overwhelming evidence on the benefits of optimistic thinking, but I do think it all comes down to the three corners of my optimism triangle.

How do you look at optimism?

People want to be seen as optimists, but what is optimism? Before I tell you my answer, listen to this story that Ronald Reagan, the former US President, used to devastating effect. There were two children, each about five years old. One was an optimist, the other was a pessimist. The pessimist was left alone in a room full of toys, but the optimist was put into a room full of manure. After a few minutes, the pessimist was sitting in the middle of all the toys, crying. There were tears running down his cheeks. The pessimist had broken one of the toys and was worried sick that he was going to get into trouble. The optimist was having a great time digging through the manure, throwing it everywhere. When asked about his strange behaviour, the optimist replied, 'There's so much manure here, there's got to be a pony underneath somewhere'.

Reagan's story says a lot about what the general public feels about optimism. Reagan successfully ridiculed his political opponent who was making a lot of negative comments about the economy of the United States. Reagan successfully labelled his opponent as a pessimist. The label stuck throughout the election and Reagan won easily. No-one wants to be called a pessimist. Hold on, I'll change that. Nearly everyone doesn't want to be called a pessimist. Why the change? I can recall some of my clients, those who were depressed, were sometimes proud of their pessimism. This gave them a loophole to avoid therapy. Some of these people made comments like 'optimists have their heads in the sand' and 'optimists live in a fool's paradise'. That's negativity! These are descriptions given to me by some of my clients immediately after they were told they showed a lot of pessimistic thinking on a psychological questionnaire.

Most people say optimists are happy, cheerful, confident, positive, look forward to the future and always look on the bright side. However, there's a more revealing and more rewarding way of spotlighting optimism. My favourite assessment comes from Wilson, the backyard philosopher in the television series *Home Improvement*. He once described the two easiest ways to go through life. First, you can believe everything you're told. This is what gullible people do. Second, you believe nothing you're told. This approach belongs to my former clubmates, the cynics. Both approaches mean you can go through life not having to think. I expand Wilson's philosophy by claiming that optimists are in the middle. Optimists are sceptics, rational thinkers, which means they make the extra effort to look at the evidence, especially when they're considering problems. Most of the time they reap the rewards of their extra thinking time and their decisions hit the bullseye. Sometimes they don't. When you think about optimists, remember two words. Optimists are very likely to be successful and healthy!

All right, I can feel your tension and your excitement. You're like a sprinter waiting for the starting gun, and you're asking, 'How can I be more optimistic?' I've got some great instructions for you. There are signposts that are so easy to follow. But where can you find them? If you want to be a champion optimist, a champion thinker, then you should study the thinking of champions. Most champions in sport, and in business, have one major advantage over their opposition. They give optimistic explanations for negative events, when things go wrong. Being optimistic gives them extra strength to bounce back quickly. It's all about thinking more clearly, so that you explain your problems, mistakes and losses more accurately. Optimism is not about putting your head in the sand and hoping and praying everything will get better. Champions are champions because they are determined, resilient and they persevere more than their opponents.

In all situations in life, we give explanations when we come across problems. However, often in life, things are happening so quickly, we're not even aware of the decisions we have made. Negative emotions such as anger, frustration and guilt are very often due to pessimistic explanations. These explanations are called automatic negative thoughts. On the other hand, champion optimists are skilful at giving rational alternative thoughts. With a bit of practice, using the following guidelines, it'll be easy for you to give optimistic explanations.

Before we get going, attempt the exercise 'Optimism at work' below. Then after you've digested the next few pages, come back to your answers and check to see whether you would give exactly the same ratings. My assessments of the optimism levels of the work explanations are at the end of the book.

Optimism at work

Analyse each group of explanations and then rate each explanation from 1 (most positive) to 5 (most negative).

1. A customer makes an angry complaint about your service.

_____ There are some people who are never satisfied.

_____ It was an unreasonable complaint as no-one can guarantee their service will be perfect.

_____ The customer was irritable and tired from a hectic day.

_____ It was a legitimate problem that rarely occurs.

_____ Australia is full of whingers.

2. Survey shows that staff morale is low.

_____ Everyone is anxious about future downsizing.

_____ Some of the staff are going through mid-life crises.

_____ The international economy looks gloomy.

_____ Recently there have been a few personality clashes.

_____ Many staff have been hit with the flu over the last month.

Swing your optimism bat at every problem you face!

I want to introduce you to my best teaching aid — a baseball bat. I've cured a lot of pessimism with my old wooden bat. Remember this baseball bat, and you too can be a champion optimist and you'll know exactly how to teach others to be optimists as well.

Here's my number one bit of encouragement I give to clients who feel it's impossible to change their pessimism into optimism. It's as simple as this — if you can count to three — one … two … three — you can learn how to be an optimist. There are three important questions we ask ourselves when something goes wrong, and each question is just like swinging your bat at a baseball. Remember, you get three swings at every single problem you'll ever face in your whole life! When you swing and miss, you've thought more like a pessimist. Hit the ball, and that's optimism in action.

What I'm about to say unsettles some people. Some people even feel threatened. It goes against what many Australians think. Some people have got angry at me for what I'm about to tell you in the next few minutes. You have to take total responsibility for your life, for everything that happens to you. Only losers blame others. Do you agree? I don't! In fact, I think this is one of the worst myths of today, because it's harmful, because it's a major reason for Australia having such high rates of depression and suicide. Let me explain exactly what I'm talking about.

Question 1: Who is responsible for the problem?

This is your first swing. You have a choice between an external or an internal cause. When you blame yourself, this is an internal cause. If you think that other people or circumstances were responsible, these are external causes. What do you automatically think when you hear someone is making an excuse? A cop out? A lie? Optimists aren't worried about this. Champion optimists look more broadly than pessimists, they're more rational than pessimists.

What percentage of life's problems are exclusively due to ourselves? My guess is about 30 per cent. Another 30–40 per cent is due to a mixture of internal and external causes, and those problems left over, have nothing to do with us. Visit a mental hospital and listen to the patients with suicidal depression. Who do they overwhelmingly blame for their problems in life? Themselves! You'll hear statements like, 'I can't do a thing right'. Many people in sport, competitors, coaches and commentators, only rely on one answer. They blame themselves or their own team. This habit is especially common in Australian sport. Those who give external causes are sometimes described as whingers, looking for excuses, avoiding their responsibilities and blaming others for their own mistakes. Champions see the external causes when things go wrong, as well as accurately seeing their own mistakes. They put their own performance into its proper perspective. Look at each of the explanations given by six champions on the next page. Who do they blame? Get the blinkers off and look outwards before you immediately look at yourself.

In my early days as a counsellor, I met a lot of resistance from clients who saw blaming others as sign of weakness. It shouldn't surprise you that I'm still meeting that antagonism, right now. In between, I even encountered hostility from a minister of religion. He evidently saw me preaching a message from Satan, a message to encourage young people never to take responsibility for their own actions. However, I've converted many non-believers by saying they were worried about being infected by the 'Fonzie phenomenon'. This is the complete inability to say you're wrong. I named it after the cult hero in the TV series, *Happy Days*. Fonzie always choked when he had to say he was wr-wr-wrong. In the series, this was humorous. In real life, people like this are painful. Optimists maintain a healthy balance between excusing and blaming themselves. Recently I've introduced a new label to show the illogical consequences of not being able to recognise your own mistakes. It's named after an Australian prime minister. A moderate dose of the 'Howard syndrome', the ability to brush off criticisms, is a healthy thing. Too much of it, and you show full-blown arrogance.

Many object to the practice of blaming others, but it has been accepted with open arms by the legal profession. Litigation rules. Liability insurance has skyrocketed. You'll hear distressed victims saying, 'Somebody has to pay for this'. It's interesting that the Australian community and politicians are now calling for legal changes to reduce payouts. They argue we have developed a culture of blaming others. Superficially they're right, when you hear about some outrageous claims for compensation. Deeper down, we have a generation of young people who regularly blame themselves, when they shouldn't.

This first question, and the first swing, is usually the least important of your three questions. Remember in baseball, if you swing and miss on the first pitch, it's no big deal. You still have two more chances to get a hit. You only need a single hit to be an optimist!

How sports champions explain negative situations

John Bertrand (Skipper of *Australia II*, the first non-American yacht to win the America's Cup in 132 years. Won final series 4–3.)

They might have a 3–1 lead, but they've been in a yacht race, and they know it. We're not done for yet, not by a long way. We've thrashed them twice, once when we ran out of time and once for real. We've suffered two diabolical gear failures, and we've made one ridiculous mistake at the start. Or, rather, I have, and the result is that we are 3–1. But it's a narrow 3–1, if you know what I mean. No-one in either boat thinks we are being thrashed.

Analysis: Internal and external, but very temporary and specific
Optimism rating: Very high

Martina Navratilova (After losing Wimbledon final.)

'I was trying to figure out if I should serve-and-volley or stay back. I wasn't concentrating enough on the toss, and I just gave it away. I gave it everything I had, but she played better on the big points.'

Analysis: Internal and external, fairly temporary and specific
Optimism rating: Above average

Roberto Baggio (Voted world's best soccer player in 1993. Missed his kick in the penalty shoot-out to decide the 1994 World Cup final. Played with a major leg injury.)

'Normally I side-foot them but I had so little energy left that I tried to blast it.'

Analysis: Internal, but very temporary and specific
Optimism rating: Very high

Mark Waugh (Dismissed in a test match playing a very unusual shot.)

'I tried to be a smart arse and late cut, but I picked the wrong ball. That one turned more than any ball he bowled that day.'

Analysis: Internal and external, extremely temporary, very specific
Optimism rating: Very high

Carl Lewis (Winner of 9 Olympic golds. Came 4th in Goodwill Games 100 metres.)

'The other guys have run a lot more races than I have this year and they're more confident than I am right now. But I still have a lot of races to run. I'm not going to win every race, but I'll be ready and sharp in August. I didn't drive out early and I popped my head up, which I don't usually do.'

Analysis: Internal and external, fairly temporary and specific
Optimism rating: Above average

Wayne Bennett (Coach of the Brisbane Broncos. His team made the semi-finals even though it looked impossible for them to do so after this loss against Illawarra.)

'We haven't played against a better side this season. It was one of the best performances I've seen from an Illawarra side. Our ball control was pretty ordinary. The effort was there from us, but we didn't execute it as well as the other team.'

Analysis: Mostly external, very temporary and fairly specific
Optimism rating: Very high

Question 2: How long-lasting is the problem?

Now for the second swing: You can choose between a temporary or a long-lasting cause in your explanation. To be an optimist, squeeze the length of the problem down to as brief as possible. There are two danger words to listen for when anybody is talking about a problem. Remember? We got up close and personal with these words in the last chapter. Actually, they're not danger words for me as a psychologist, because I know as soon as I hear them and their close substitutes, I've been given a big opportunity to show clients what's wrong with their thinking.

I've got a huge example from some counselling I did with a father and his teenage daughter. I set a ground rule that each was initially restricted to a single sentence description of their problem. The father started with 'I can never talk to her any more without her getting angry with me'. The daughter immediately screamed back, 'So what, every time you talk to me you always pick on me!'

These two had obviously had many verbal battles. Both of them showed high level pessimism because each was able to use double-punch exaggerations. I took over the role of the rational optimist and went looking for evidence of their claims. I started with the daughter and asked her to recall how many times her father had spoken to her in the last week. She guessed at least a dozen times. So how many times had her father picked on her, out of these dozen times? She had said always, and if this were accurate, she should now say 12 out of 12. Instead, her answer was two or three times.

Her father sat there smirking, impressed that I had shown his daughter was not seeing the situation clearly. He had smirked too early. Now it was time for me to turn my attention on him. I asked him how many times he'd spoken to his daughter in the week. He also thought 12 was a fair estimate. And how many times had his daughter responded with anger. It was about twice! Questions and simple calculations had shown they were both exaggerating their problem, and making it so much harder to solve their simple problem, that sometimes they disagreed about things.

When you refer to a problem with the words and phrases like always and all of the time, you're really saying the problem is more than long-lasting, it's permanent. That is very rarely true. Optimists are far more realistic when they give explanations with phrases like — some of the time, occasionally, a few times, recently, and lately. Become an accurate time reader.

Question 3: How big is the cause of the problem?

Your third and last swing is the most important. You decide on a specific or a generalised explanation. Pessimists give vague unclear causes that are often just colourful exaggerations. Optimists try to stick to the specifics. Again, it's easy to detect pessimistic thinking by the words commonly used: everything, nothing, everyone, no-one, everybody, nobody, totally and completely. Pessimists in sport often rely on vague generalisations such as the team lacked commitment, there was no enthusiasm and they had the wrong attitude. Optimists can easily attack their problems because they pinpoint specific goals. Vague explanations produce vague goals, and vague goals produce uncertain actions. The big message for pessimists is that success rarely comes from vague explanations.

I did an interview with the *Sydney Morning Herald* the day after a rugby league side was heavily beaten in the finals. The reporter said to me, 'Surely they'll be crushed and won't be able to bounce back next week.' I disagreed because their coach had a long history of giving specific explanations. I tipped them to surprise the pessimists and win their next game, and they won … 30–0.

In all codes of football, and lots of poor parenting, there's one word that keeps popping up when things go wrong. No, I don't mean the F-word. It's worse. It's 'lazy'. It's also a very popular description used by TV sports commentators. In cricket, a commentator said batsman got out with a lazy shot. His co-commentator then described it as half-hearted. I thought it was indecisive. The batsman lost his concentration due to some very good bowling. What's the difference in all these explanations? If you start calling yourself, or any one around you, lazy, it's a good way to destroy confidence. A football coach, famous for his temper and viciousness when he was a player, seemed to take great delight in publicly abusing his team after a loss early in the season. His summary, with plenty of venom in his voice, was that his players showed 'no pride'. Surprisingly, even though his team was full of stars, they never reached the finals that year. The coach's press-conference pessimism was probably just the tip of the iceberg. I'd expect to hear similar pessimistic abuse at most of his training sessions.

I have a huge collection of negative generalisations collected from clients in the world of professional sport. It doesn't matter what sport you look at. Choose a sport and the negative explanations will find you. Athletes will describe their own poor efforts as pathetic, insipid, gutless, disgraceful, laughable and spineless. They say they threw it away, dropped their bundle, showed no heart, choked, crashed, fell in a heap, gave it away on a platter, had a brain explosion. Ugh! These self put-downs are part of a vicious circle, as many athletes are brainwashed to accept abusive pessimism from their coaches.

This excessive negativity shouldn't surprise you, because there are more failures than successes when you reach the elite levels of sport. So many pessimists fall by the wayside. In my work with young sports stars, 14- and 15-year-olds, I look into their faces and know that only one in a thousand will reach the top. My files are full of optimism questionnaires completed by young champions who were pessimists, who then disappeared when they reached higher levels of competition.

It's not just the pessimistic athletes who are most likely to fail. It's also the pessimistic coaches. I enjoy a game I play every morning when I scan the sports pages of the major newspapers. Explanations from losing coaches attract me like a bee to honey. You can play the same game. It's just like putting the coach on the couch. These explanations will let you get into the minds of coaches and then you can predict the likely long-term success of different teams. I'll now show you how easy it is to become an expert at optimistic explanations. Take over my role as a psychologist and pull apart the explanations in the exercise 'Find the winners among the losers'.

Find the winners among the losers

Study the following post-game comments from senior football coaches in the nationwide AFL competition. Each is an explanation why they lost. All comments were made in the early part of the same season. Find the two most successful coaches. Then identify the coach who was sacked at the end of the season. The year after, his team went on to win the competition with a different coach.

Coach 1 'History tells us that we aren't mature, that we don't have the mental strength, that we aren't tough enough to come up week after week as the good teams do.'

Coach 2 'I thought we were a chance all night but they've got blokes who just decide to win it. The fact we are playing well but not winning is a good sign in one aspect, but also a worrying one.'

Coach 3 'Our whole midfield has been struggling pretty much all year.'

Coach 4 'We're really playing reactive football. We're second to move and guys are concerned about making a mistake.'

Coach 5 There was one quarter where they got away from us but I thought our blokes were pretty good because, as you know, we were a bit depleted and if we play with that intensity we'll win more than we lose.'

Coach 6 'I think the game will do us a world of good. We needed a game like that to let ourselves know about big-match footy again.'

Coach 7 'We were slow to come out of the blocks and took the first half to get any semblance of play going. We just frittered away and wasted opportunities when it mattered, mostly 30 or 40 metres from goal.'

Coach 8 'They had the commitment to be first to the ball. They took that from us. That was the most important ingredient of their win.'

Coach 9 'We've gone from the best team in the competition to the worst team in the competition in two weeks. That creates some sort of record we're going to have to deal with.'

Coach 10 'We obviously over-used the footy. We had 100-something handballs. We were just getting ourselves into trouble.'

The day optimism fixed a car and stopped a suicide

You know how passionate I am about teaching the fundamentals of optimistic thinking. This is psychology at its best. Listen to how easily you might be able to save someone's life. This is how I once did it.

I was in my office waiting for a client who was 30 minutes late for the start of our appointment. He eventually appeared and banged fiercely on the door. This was a very angry young man. To get a feel of the tension, realise that he was using expletives in every sentence. He burst out with, 'My life is stuffed! I'm going to end it.' I knew from his history that he was serious. I didn't throw any petrol by asking what his problem was. That word sets the wrong tone. Instead I asked what had happened in the last half hour. He immediately spat back, 'I can't depend on my car. It's a heap of crap.' Can you see I used a question based on the length of his problem, the second swing of my baseball bat? In less than 20 seconds he'd reduced his problem from his life to his car. I asked whether he had driven his car for our previous two appointments. He had, so the car was dependable, sometimes.

That word is so much better than never or always. In fact, I soon learnt his car only broke down, rarely, about once every few months. Here comes the third swing of my baseball bat: What exactly was wrong with the car? He knew immediately he needed to get the carburettor reconditioned, but he had no money. That was another incorrect generalisation. He had money but it went on cigarettes. It took another hour to work out he could save enough in the next two months. He was still alive 10 years later.

What would an optimist say right here and now?

An optimist would say show me the evidence. A good way of simplifying all this research is to use the three Cs — Competition, Commitment and Cooperation. Optimism helps you when you are competing against others — in business, education, and especially in sport.

Let's look at the role of optimism in business success. Think about the amount of rejection that insurance agents come across. 'No thanks, not interested', 'Sorry, I've got enough insurance' and so on. Optimists don't see these knock-backs as failures. They see them as challenges, where perseverance will eventually pay off. Seligman and his team of researchers have put together an impressive scorecard for optimism in so many areas of business. Very quickly, they found that optimists outsell pessimists, usually by 20 to 40 per cent in car sales, insurance, office products and real estate. Another big bonus with optimistic employees, they're far less likely to quit. Can you see why I get wound up when I'm talking about optimism?

Besides the business world, there's plenty of competition in education and politics, and not surprisingly, being optimistic helps you be a winner in both of these areas. Have you heard of West Point Military Academy? It's one of the most elite colleges in the world. They train the officers of the US Army. The discipline is incredible and plenty of the new recruits can't take it. They admit 1,200 and lose 100 within a month. Dropouts continue for the three years of the course. The military wanted to know what separates the stayers from the dropouts. So, all of the recruits undertook an optimism questionnaire, and they were followed for the next three years. Sure enough, the pessimists were far more likely to quit. Think about this. The 15-minute questionnaire gave more reliable predictions than the results from high school final exams.

Americans love their politics, so it didn't take long before Seligman and his team of researchers measured the optimism of politicians, especially US presidents. It's impossible to get a president to do an optimism questionnaire, but there's an excellent alternative. We can use a technique called CAVE — that's short for Content Analysis of Verbatim Explanations. When somebody gives an explanation, you can give it an optimism score. Collect enough explanations, and you have a substitute questionnaire. These explanations can be in speeches, newspaper reports or TV interviews. You find them, then you can score them. If optimism can be used to pick the successes in business and education, can it pick the winners of presidential elections? Yes, it can! The more optimistic candidate was the winner in 19 out of the 23 elections. Better still, on every occasion when an underdog won, he was more optimistic than his opponent.

Some more politics has been put under the optimism microscope. In the first Gulf War, if George Bush senior or Saddam Hussein gave optimistic explanations, this was a good sign to head for the air-raid shelter. Optimism predicted aggression, whilst pessimistic statements predicted caution and military inactivity. This example shows how optimism, in the wrong hands, can have tragic consequences.

I've got plenty of stories about optimism in sport, but I'll restrict myself to just one. Matt Biondi became an Olympic champion in Seoul in 1988, but before that, he had already shown he was a champion optimist. Several months before the Olympics, Biondi and the rest of his team-mates completed optimism questionnaires. He got one of the highest scores. Then, they all were part of a clever little experiment. At training, they were all given fake times. These times meant poor or disappointing performances. After a rest, they swam again. All the pessimists got worse. Two of the stars, who were nonetheless pessimists, swam much worse, two seconds slower than before. The optimists swam as well as before, and some like Biondi, swam even faster. Some were five seconds faster. Biondi was optimistic at training, he was optimistic at the Olympics. The media expected he would win seven golds. In his first race, he came third. In his second race he improved to take the silver. It looked like Biondi couldn't cope with the pressure. But this was an optimist. Optimism helps you to come to the front in times of adversity. Biondi then won his last five races. Optimism doesn't guarantee you're always a winner, but it certainly increases your chances.

My studies of Australian sportspeople have also found that most champions are boosted by high levels of optimism. Study the details of my results in 'Optimism and success in sport'. The moral of all these stories? If you're in any form of competition, optimism will give you a boost.

Optimism and success in sport

Over 2000 Australian sportspeople have completed the *Sports Explanatory Style Questionnaire*. This questionnaire measures optimism in sport.

Aussie rules

The footballers were all in the nationwide AFL competition. In the three seasons after being tested, 60 per cent of optimists regularly played the senior competition. However, only 34 per cent of pessimists were successful at doing so.

Basketball

All those tested were involved in the NBL either as players or coaches. Seventy-nine per cent of this group were rated as optimists and 42 per cent showed very high levels of optimism.

Cricket

All cricketers were members of the NSW state squad. Forty per cent of these elite cricketers achieved optimism scores that placed them in the top 20 per cent of all the sportspeople tested. Nearly all of the cricketers who were rated as extremely optimistic had competed at state level for more than five seasons.

Rugby league

All footballers played in the senior nationwide competition. Sixty-one per cent of optimists continued their careers by signing new contracts. Only 18 per cent of pessimists had their contracts renewed. This means optimistic footballers are three times more likely to be successful than pessimistic footballers.

Rugby league referees

Seventy-four per cent of referees who officiated in the higher competitions were rated as optimists. Only 38 per cent of referees who officiated at the lower levels were optimistic.

Okay, competition was the first 'C'. The next is commitment or, more specifically, personal commitment. Here's what you get at no extra cost when you're an optimist! You get massive long-term benefits. If you want to remain healthy, both physically and mentally, then take a huge dose of optimism. Several hundred men who were students at Harvard University in the 1940s, have been studied for the last 60 years. They've undergone thorough medical examinations every five years during this time. Initially the men were all very similar, both physically and psychologically. They were fit and healthy. However, they weren't tested for optimism. This was done later by analysing their diaries, and a questionnaire they completed in 1946 about their wartime experiences. Here's what they found. If you're a pessimist in your 20s, this is an accurate predictor of poor health when you reach middle age in your 40s, and right through to old age. I'll be a bit blunt. What I'm about to say often shakes up sports people that I work with. Because they're so healthy and fit, they think they'll have healthy futures. This study with the Harvard students shows otherwise. You can have a great body and good health at 25, but if you have a cynical attitude, a pessimistic way of thinking, it is likely that your health will fall apart 20 years down the track. That stuns a lot of sports people.

No pessimist ever sailed to an uncharted land …
Helen Keller (Educator who was deaf and blind)

Besides Martin Seligman's team at the University of Pennsylvania, other groups of psychologists have put optimism under the microscope. One group is led by Michael Scheier who, by coincidence, is based at another university in Pennsylvania, and Charles Carver at the University of Miami. When you read their reports, their enthusiasm and dedication leaps off the page at you. Scheier dedicated one article to the fighting spirit and optimism of his mother who was lying critically injured in the hospital at the time.

Here's a brief summary of some of their remarkable findings. Optimistic mothers are far less likely to suffer post-partum depression. In another investigation with patients who underwent coronary bypass surgery, the optimists showed lower levels of hostility and depression after surgery and were sitting up in bed and walking around the room a lot earlier than the pessimists. More importantly, when the patients were studied five years after surgery, the optimists were more likely to be sleeping better, eating healthier meals and showing greater satisfaction with their jobs and friends than the pessimists did. There was plenty of excitement when it was discovered the optimists also had important physiological differences from the pessimists, before and after surgery. Optimists were less likely to develop new Q waves in their EKGs and less likely to release the enzyme AST. Like me, you probably have no idea of the relevance of these two observations. Apparently both of these are excellent predictors of myocardial infarctions. That means the optimists were less likely to have heart attacks on the operating table!

Then there were studies of women who underwent surgery for breast cancer. Optimism scores on a questionnaire were able to predict the amount of distress these women would have in the first year after surgery. In another study, women with abnormal PAP smears completed the questionnaire before surgery. None of the women knew how far the cancer had developed. Those women who got the lowest scores, the pessimists, had the greatest amount of abnormal growth in the cervix. Does this mean that cancer might grow more quickly if you're a pessimist. Possibly it does!

Medical researchers at other universities have found more thought-provoking results about the link between optimism and physical health. If you're an optimist, you're going to save on doctor's bills. Pessimists made twice as many visits to doctors as the optimists did. Maybe this only means pessimists are more likely to be hypochondriacs. Possibly, but the same group of pessimists had twice as many infectious illnesses as the optimists. That's not due to being a hypochondriac. It appears that optimism gives you greater immunity. Our immune systems are based on T-cells in our blood, and when we grieve, say when someone close has died, these cells don't multiply as fast. However, T-cell activity in pessimists is normally low. The immunity levels of pessimists are like they're in a constant state of grief.

Harvard researchers studied 1,300 men for 10 years to discover that optimists were about 50 per cent less likely to develop heart disease. In a 23-year-long study carried out by Yale University, psychologists showed that being afraid of aging shortens your life, by around seven years. This sounds very familiar to the results from the *Nun Study* we previously looked at. A positive attitude about growing old had a bigger effect on lifespan than smoking, exercise, weight or blood pressure.

Now for the other important part of personal commitment — your mental health. It amazes me how many people I meet who are taking antidepressants. Psychiatrists and GPs commonly prescribe these drugs because they work. They help depressed people to be less depressed. However, I'm not alone when I say too many people rely on antidepressant drugs. Some people definitely need them, most of us don't. Researchers at the University of Connecticut, led by Dr Irving Kirsch, found the mood-lifting effect of the most popular antidepressants was little better than the placebo, a sugar pill. Needless to say, this report was attacked by some psychiatrists. However, it was also supported by a leading Australian psychiatrist, Professor Gavin Andrews at St Vincent's Hospital in Sydney. You can build up your own non-chemical barrier to depression by developing your optimism.

We've covered competition and commitment. My last 'C' is cooperation, and I'll discuss this very briefly. Unfortunately, the role of optimism in cooperation has not been studied as thoroughly as the other two areas. There's a lot of evidence, but instead of big research studies, it comes from everyday observations, made by people like me. When I did a lot of marriage and relationship counselling I saw, first-hand, the connection between pessimism and unhappy relationships.

Here's a quick sketch of what I've found when I measured the optimism of couples. If both partners have high levels, their relationship can quickly recover from various problems, even major ones. When you spend a lot of time working with couples who are in unhappy marriages or relationships, you don't meet a lot of optimistic people. You do meet couples who rarely cooperate with each other. I discovered this usually happens when both partners have low levels of optimism. However, problems also occur when there is a large difference in optimism levels, that is, one partner is very optimistic, while the other is pessimistic. This leads to a lot of frustration, for both partners. When you change the pessimism into optimistic thinking, the amount of cooperation increases, and when couples start to cooperate with each other, you can see life coming back into their relationship. I get a tremendous buzz when this happens with my clients.

That wraps up my quick discussion on optimism research … nearly. When I was a young boy in Queensland, I used to listen to a lot of serials on the radio. (Yes, there was no television around then.) As the announcer would say, 'Stay tuned for even more exciting adventures'. You'll find more excitement about optimism in a small book called *The Power of Optimism*. It inspires me a lot because it's written by a passionate therapist and speaker named Alan McGinnis. He runs a family counselling centre in California and his book is full of stories of how optimism has enriched the lives of so many people, both famous and anonymous. Join them.

Where does pessimism come from?

A quick checklist for you to think about: I believe these are four of the most likely causes of pessimistic thinking. Do any apply to you?

1. Early death of a parent. This is a strong indicator that a child will grow up to be a pessimist. It's hard to have an optimistic view of the world when you've had such a tragic loss. You tend to see

problems as long-lasting or even permanent. You see problems as big with lots of negative consequences.

2. Growing up in a family where your parents are frequently fighting. It doesn't have to be physical. Regular verbal abuse is just as bad. You know your parents are unhappy. Maybe they're staying together for the sake of the kids. Again, you are likely to lean toward pessimism, instead of optimism.

3. Parental unemployment. We can all see the gloomy picture this could produce for children.

4. Someone leaving the family. For example, an older brother or sister goes away to boarding school, or migrates to another country. The separation can also be temporary, but still create pessimism. Parents who are in the military, forced to be away for months, know what I'm talking about.

There are many more likely causes but these look like they're the most important. What's your checklist look like? Right about now you might be scratching your head. I'm now talking more about pessimism instead of optimism. There's an excellent reason for this. To increase optimism, we often directly attack pessimism.

Life wasn't meant to be easy. But take courage — for it can be delightful.

George Bernard Shaw (Brilliant author and playwright)

I hope you've enjoyed all the language detective work I've been throwing at you. I love it, it's like jogging — the more you do it, the easier it gets and it can even be addictive. Analysing your own language is the first step to becoming an optimist. Rational positive talk comes from rational positive thinking. The second step is to analyse the language of those around you. If they're being swept away with a flow of pessimistic thinking, you'll be less likely to be caught up in it. Others, I should add, includes the media. 'Bad news sells' seems fairly accurate.

These two steps are targeting the main goal of cognitive therapy. We want you to increase your awareness of how you and others think. Extra awareness means you're more likely to recognise your mistakes and, therefore, you'll be less likely to repeat them in the future. Another major goal of cognitive therapy also leads to optimism. Try to slow down your reaction when you hit a problem in everyday life. Realise that your first response, your first explanation, could often be based on faulty detective work. If there are more possible answers out there, don't be so quick to attack yourself and others. Encourage yourself to use words like maybe and possibly in some of your explanations.

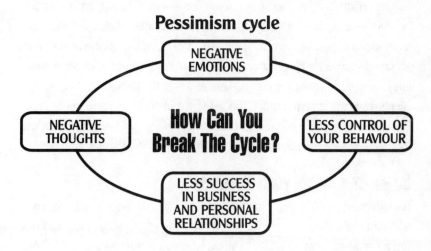

Pessimism cycle

I've given you some pessimistic key words to look for, but there's another way of increasing your awareness. Look at the 'Pessimism cycle'. Your emotions don't magically appear from nothing. You know they come from your thoughts, your explanations. Besides listening for negative language, be on the lookout for negative emotions. When you're in one of these states, go backwards and work out what you were thinking. Do this, and the RATs, the rational alternative thoughts, will be easier to find.

One very effective way of doing this is to keep a record of some of your thoughts. You can use something like the 'Weekly thinking record'. Use it for at least a week. How regularly you use it is up to you. But here are some guidelines. Like learning all new skills, start off with frequent practice. Maybe record at least five examples of negative thinking per day. I've had clients tell me, 'You're kidding. I'm not that negative!' Another said, 'If I wrote down every negative thought I had during one week, I'd run out of paper'. When clients follow this strategy many are surprised how often they have big irrational thoughts. These are the explanations that are like three strikes in baseball.

Many of our pessimistic thoughts are so brief there's a good chance you might miss them. We give numerous silent explanations: when you're driving and someone nearly hits you as they change lanes, when you forget someone's name, when you're watching a great program on TV and they keep putting on lots of commercials, when you feel like making love and your partner falls asleep. These little situations can lead to big problems if there are faulty explanations. Watch out for big explanations as well as the many small explanations you make every day. A Canadian psychologist uses an interesting technique to make his clients more aware of their negativity. Each of his clients carries a small counter. You press a button to increase your count. Probably they're like the counters cricket umpires use. At first, the clients get incredible scores. Then as they learn optimism skills, their scores drop rapidly.

Be positive, count your negatives

I've designed the 'Weekly thinking record' exercise to help my clients, so if you start to feel like a criminal under a spotlight, relax, and try to enjoy finding more about how you tick. I'll share with you a discovery I made about myself when I used this sheet. I realised I often suffered from Sunday neurosis. This is a term to describe a mild form of depression that occurs when the rush of a busy week is over and you feel you're in a void. This most commonly happens on a Sunday morning. When I analysed my written records, I saw that I fitted this pattern. That's why I recommend you fill in the first two columns as well. Initially you might think it's unnecessary, but all the clues you collect will help you reduce your pessimism.

The various techniques I've discussed appear simple. They are, but they work and they work well! At first, when you practise them, you might feel that it's a very forced process, and you might think it'll never become natural. If this thought crops up, focus on those champion optimists who are lucky enough not to need special training. They're relaxed and fully comfortable with how they think. Regularly remind yourself you have a fabulous computer inside your head, and it's there to help you think clearly, and rationally, and optimistically. When you put the right instructions, the right program, in your brain, optimistic thinking comes naturally, and you will benefit, and so will everyone who comes in contact with you.

Let me finish by telling you why scientists believe that all humans, our whole species, were designed to be optimists. Can you imagine hundreds of thousands of years ago when our ancestors were trying to survive in harsh environments in different places around the world? Think how optimistic they were to go hunting with only a few sticks and stones as weapons. What drove them was their belief that they could be successful. That's optimism. They were optimistic enough to leave behind other members of the group. Those who stayed behind also needed strong resources of optimism.

Weekly thinking record

Be on the lookout for situations where you have negative emotions. For example, when you feel angry, frustrated, annoyed, nervous, ashamed, disappointed, scared, embarrassed, lonely, hopeless, guilty, etc. Complete the following details for each situation.

TIME AND DATE	PLACE	NEGATIVE EMOTIONS	AUTOMATIC NEGATIVE THOUGHTS	RATIONAL ALTERNATIVE THOUGHTS

Think how optimistic you had to be if you were one of the first farmers, thousands of years ago. Imagine planting seeds for the first time. It took a lot of optimism to believe that these seeds would germinate, and grow so they would be able to be harvested, several months away! This theory explains the success of our species on this planet. It says we are all born to be optimists. Every religion is based on optimism, for a better life on this planet or after we die. All of us have optimism inside of us, and you now know how to find it. Enjoy the success and happiness it brings you.

Optimism is as necessary as air.
Lionel Tiger (Distinguished anthropologist)

Chapter 7
Inoculate Against Depression

I have a dream. I dream that one day, in every high school in the world, every teenager will receive training to learn the skills of optimistic thinking. It will be a compulsory subject that students look forward to doing because they know it will yield only success. No-one will fail. When my dream comes true you will feel the mental health of this planet rise. Professor Seligman and his team have shown us the way by condensing the wisdom of hundreds of books written on cognitive therapy. You've seen how I've continued to condense this wisdom, blending it with the excitement of sport.

My sense of achievement always grows when I stand in front of young people, with my baseball bat, teaching them how easy it is to be an optimistic thinker. I scan the audience, studying eyes, looking for something very special. I frequently see extra-intense staring. This tells me that my message has reached someone, someone who has probably come face to face with the pain and suffering that can come from depression. These eyes tell me, maybe, I've saved a life.

Seligman begins his magnificent book, *The Optimistic Child,* with a very moving account of the baseball season that was cancelled because of a polio epidemic. (Both Seligman and I grew up in a time when some of our classmates had leg braces due to polio. I remember it vividly. The polio vaccine changed all that.) Seligman's illustrious career as a clinical psychologist was driven by his dream to be able to inoculate people against a modern epidemic — depression. This is such an important goal because depression is the main pathway to suicidal thoughts.

Like baseball, cricket provides a rich supply of statistics. However, there's one cricket statistic I wish didn't exist. It's about the high frequency of suicides of cricketers. A book was written about this bizarre relationship, *By Their Own Hand.* One cricket coach who was startled by this observation reacted by joking about cricket being too much of a cerebral game. Even in

Australia's greatest ever cricket team, the 1948 Invincibles, one of them would later take his own life. The author of the book, David Frith, has updated and renamed the book, *Silence of the Heart*. He has included stories of suicides of sports stars away from cricket. It should be a text book in schools.

Old men go to death; and death comes to young men.

Sir Francis Bacon

What do the following sports stars have in common: six-time world surfing champion Layne Beachley, former Wimbledon champion Pat Cash and Olympic swimming legend Jon Konrads? They have all revealed that they had considered suicide. Obviously, this tragic problem is much bigger than any sport. In Australia, we have one of the highest rates of teenage suicides in the world. At a conference I heard an expert on suicide prevention state that these levels would be much higher if we recognised another unspoken source of suicides — autocides. This hit home hard as I had long known the death of one of my friends, back in the 1970s, was a deliberate self-inflicted motor cycle smash.

FEELING DOWN?

DISSATISFIED?   DISAPPOINTED?
DISCOURAGED?   DISILLUSIONED?
DISHEARTENED?   DESPONDENT?
DEFEATED?   DEJECTED?
DISTRESSED?   DESPERATE?

DEPRESSED?

The World Health Organisation released some worrying findings in 2002. They calculated that we humans are directly responsible, by various forms of violence, for the deaths of 1.6 million people every year. It gets worse … half of these deaths are suicides. That means we have a death by suicide on this planet every 40 seconds. It's estimated that every death by suicide represents anywhere from five to 20 attempts. I loathe calling these unsuccessful attempts. The attempts were not completed. Jerry Seinfeld told a joke about these attempts, ridiculing those who couldn't get their act together. If I ever meet him it will be the first thing I mention. I hope he never sees his two children suffering from depression. Those who thought he was funny probably would have joined in with the crowd in Seattle chanting jump, bitch, jump. One country stands out for its massive desire for self-destruction. It's China. That surprises every audience. They expect the United States, Britain, or Sweden would be more likely to be suicide prone. About 290,000 Chinese suicide every year, which means one death every two minutes. There is another concern about China. It's the only country in the world where more women than men die by suicide.

Do you know what happened in Australia yesterday? About seven Australians killed themselves. And today? Another seven will suicide. And tomorrow? Another seven deaths. And so it goes, every day of the year. I'll make this image even more devastating. Approximately 130,000 Australians die in a year, from all causes. Divide this number by the annual number of suicides, and you see that one in every 50 deaths around us is due to a person losing all hope, and self-destructing. If they died in war, there would be an outcry, there would be street marches.

There's another question that my audiences answer incorrectly. Which group of Australians are most likely to end their lives? Like road rage, everyone suspects male teenagers. Their figures are disturbing — at least 5,000 teenagers attempt suicide each year. A survey of 15–24-year-olds carried out by the Australian Democrats, showed that 53 per cent of those interviewed knew someone that has attempted or died from suicide. However, the worst group for suicides, a group that often ignores help, is middle aged men. About 1,000 men aged 25 to 44 kill themselves every year. Here's a horrendous statistic — the total number of suicides per year is higher than all the deaths from road accidents: 2,500 versus 1,800. Far too many people believe this haunting message from a popular song.

Nothing really matters to me.

Bohemian Rhapsody sung by Queen

All depressed people need help, many want help, but only some ask for help. We need to be skilful when we hear these requests for help. A long time ago I heard a crude attempt at counselling by the president of a sporting club. He brutally told a young man who had been sexually abused, 'Just get over it, and get on with your life. Grow up. We all have problems.' The president truly thought he was helping. However, you could see the pain on the young man's face after the comment. This sort of advice is common and is based on the belief that if you say something bluntly, and often very loudly, you can shake anyone out of their problems. A far better approach is to skilfully put problems into a better perspective. We've already done this a few times, but you can do some extra fine-tuning with the exercise 'Losses — Big and small'.

Losses — Big and small

Our lives are full of losses. Many we don't even recognise. Some of these are natural losses which result from normal body changes as we age. We have other losses due to many relationship changes. Some losses are sudden and traumatic.

Decide how difficult it would be for you to cope with each of the following losses. Number the situations from 1 (least difficult) to 20 (most difficult).

_____ You spend a week in jail.

_____ The most important person in your life is permanently hospitalised.

_____ Your car breaks down in heavy traffic.

_____ An injury prevents you playing your favourite sport.

_____ You are rejected by someone you love.

_____ You forget about a very important appointment.

_____ You miss out on a job you want badly.

_____ A friend attempts suicide.

_____ Your home is destroyed by fire.

_____ Someone close to you is murdered.

_____ You miss your favourite television program.

_____ A member of your family has a drug problem.

_____Your car is badly damaged in an accident.

_____You are sexually assaulted.

_____You lose the final of a sporting competition.

_____You are robbed in the street.

_____You lose your sight in one eye.

_____One of your parents dies.

_____You have a toothache.

_____Someone ridicules you in public.

Change your glasses and change your life

There's a very useful metaphor used by successful therapists and motivators. They say that when you've learnt how to deal with a problem, it's because you've put on new glasses. Your mental vision of the world has changed. Your vision has improved. It's a good image and I've often used it. However, when we talk about depression and suicide, I think we need to go a step higher.

Arthur Koestler, the great philosopher of science, said that every creative act involves the removal of 'the cataract of accepted belief'. He's so right. People who suffer from depression, in all its many shades, see the world through cloudy cataracts, and worse still, their cataracts are of their own creation. Irrational thoughts, pessimistic thoughts, negative thoughts, shallow thoughts, all build long-term mental cataracts. It's great to know you don't need a skilful surgeon to remove this problem. Mental cataracts can be removed far more easily and I've witnessed wonderful transformations right in front of me. Outwardly, these changes don't appear as spectacular as returning sight to the blind, but inwardly, the transformations are very similar.

One of the joys of being a psychologist is to help others heal themselves and eliminate the self-inflicted pain of depression. When I hear any descriptions of this pain, my determination to help goes even higher. However, the most vivid and moving description of depression I have ever come across, was written nearly 3,000 years ago! It's a masterpiece of pessimism from a man wallowing in misery. It's in the Bible. Go look up the Book of Job in the Old Testament, Chapter 3. I read it with some of my clients, not to depress them even further, but to show that depression is not just a problem of modern life. It's not a compulsory curse from present day living. We've been making ourselves depressed for thousands of years, and we have the ability to stop that, within ourselves. Many depressed clients have smiled after listening to Job's whining.

There are many unhelpful images of depression, bleak images that strengthen the grip, the stranglehold of depression, bleak images that thicken those mental cataracts. I'm certain this didn't cheer you up. How could it, but this is the way many people talk to themselves, constantly, about their depressed thoughts. Winston Churchill referred to his ongoing problem as his black dog. It bewilders me why an Australian institute set up to help combat depression has taken this name. Then there's the picture of depression being a thief that creeps up on you in the night. The same person then described his future as being 'condemned to be in the back of the photograph of life!' Another client also showed how negative images build in momentum once you get the ball rolling. When he was depressed, he said his brain crashed. He was an executive who had been retrenched. Later he repeatedly said he had been 'thrown on the scrap heap'. The image I saw was a man who was using himself as a punching bag.

Depression can sometimes be seen in romantic connotations. It is definitely connected with many creative people, and even regarded by some as providing inspiration. This is best summed up by Canadian singer and songwriter Joni Mitchell who claimed, 'Depression can be the sand that makes the pearl.' That's unhealthy thinking!

How can you find meaning in pain?

Austrian psychiatrist, Viktor Frankl, liked to sum up his successful school of therapy with the following gem from the German philosopher Nietzsche, 'He who has a why to live for, can bear almost any how'. You can find many more on Frankl's insights in his book *Man's Search for Meaning*. I rate it as one of the most important books written in the 20th century. Search it out and be rewarded. Frankl began writing while he was imprisoned in concentration camps during World War II. He survived, after his wife and family were killed, by helping other prisoners. A wonderful human being!

You can find positives, benefits, in the most unexpected places — even in illnesses and injuries. An important part of my work in sports psychology is helping athletes cope with injuries, especially if their career is ending. When I suggest there are many possible benefits from major injuries, I stand back quickly because I'm often hit with lots of hot comments, all with the flavour of, 'You've got to be kidding!' Most of my injured clients see things differently when they hear the next list of comments.

Reflection 'It gave me time to slow down and think about other important things in life.' 'I stepped back and looked at my life.' 'It helped open up my eyes a lot.'

Greater appreciation of life 'It showed me how much I love being active.' 'I realised I was so lucky I've never been so sick before.' 'My roommate in the hospital was much worse off — his career was finished.' 'I'm on crutches but I can still get out and about.'

Character development 'I grew a lot, more mature, in just a few months.' 'I learned to be patient.' 'Little problems don't worry me anymore.' 'I don't get so angry as quickly as before.' 'My pain tolerance is a lot higher.'

Increased empathy 'I'm closer to those with injuries.' 'I got a lot of help, so I try to help others with their rehab.'

Better time management 'I was determined to come back quicker than anyone thought possible.' 'I got so good at planning, I don't waste time any more.'

Improved confidence 'I beat this, so I can do anything.' 'I'm the comeback queen!'

Greater fitness 'I proved I could be super fit.' 'My recovery taught me how to make my body stronger.'

Closer relationships 'I found out I have a lot of good friends.' 'I saw how much my family cared for me.'

Increased motivation 'I've got a stronger work ethic.' 'I'm determined to be even better than before.'

Mishaps and misfortune are unavoidable in life. Misery is optional.
                                    Anonymous (Overheard on a train)

Some athletes show incredibly negative reactions when they suffer major injuries. Some use words like tragedy, disaster and nightmare, and sincerely believe what they're saying. In the days just after the horrific terrorist attacks in New York, several sports stars and commentators observed how inappropriate such descriptions seemed when talking about difficulties in sport. Just a few years later, the tragedies and disasters in sport had returned.

I love listening to those healers who are magicians with words. I heard a counsellor quietly tell a young woman, 'This isn't a me-thing! It's a we-thing!' This counsellor was a real wizard. You saw the power in his words from the look on the woman's face. Immediately she realised she had problems, but so do all of us. Immediately she realised by helping each other, you strengthen yourself and others against depression. Helping others, as Frankl practised, inside and outside of concentration camps, is the best way to find meaning in our pain, and then grow from it.

Hazel Hawke, former wife of Prime Minister Bob Hawke, showed she practises this principle. Recently she was diagnosed with Alzheimer's disease, what she calls 'the bloody A thing'. Instead of hiding, she let millions see her problem on the ABC TV program *Australian Story*. The Australian Medical Association praised her because 'her honesty and bravery would inspire others to seek help and help to better educate the public and the medical profession about early detection, treatment and care'. I've always been a fan of Hazel's and she's just outshone her husband's whole political career. Hazel's daughter said this was her mother's 'big final gift in the sense of sharingness'.

I hope I'm remembered like that. Follow Viktor Frankl and Hazel Hawke. You're well on your way out of depression, when you set out to help others, anybody. After you decide to help others, like the movie *Field of Dreams* says, they will come.

Don't talk about it, and it won't go away!

A winner of the Nobel Prize in medicine called psychologists the poets of biology. That's a beautiful description. Poets turn words into beauty, psychologists help people enrich their everyday lives. Drawing and drama are used in therapy with great results but the power of poetry is still largely untouched in psychology. Wayne Dyer is a psychologist who is an exception in many ways, including his enchantment with poems. Much of the incredible appeal of his book *Wisdom of the Ages* comes from his continuous use of poems to highlight powerful psychological themes. I'm following his example. The following poem is about a major problem in Australia — young Aboriginal men killing themselves. It was written by Darren Garvey from the Centre for Aboriginal Studies at Curtin University, Perth.

This is for the boy who never got to 21.
This is for the boy whose race had only just begun.
This is for the boy whose tight rope necklace fit too well
And his wick ran out of hope enough to light his private hell.
Now left with questions for the ones his actions left behind.
It's only memories now that keeps his spirit in our minds,
The wailing and wondering won't answer why he had to go.
We cannot ask him now so now we'll never get to know.
His leaving leaves a gap, a hole that no-one else can fill.
There's so many holes around now when our children start to kill.
So look around to see if there's a boy whose life you'll save.
I know I'd rather see a life than see another young man's grave.

This poem unites the pain of those who die and those who are left behind. It speaks for people of all colours and all ages. In every large crowd, there is a person who is, or will be, depressed and suicidal. This is a point I try to make with all coaches. At conferences, I tell coaches that they can be successful in a range of ways. They can coach athletes to improve their sporting performances, they can coach to win competitions, but most importantly they can coach young people to see their lives are precious, and not to be thrown away.

Sometimes I'm confronted by coaches who aggressively argue that they don't want to know about the personal problems of those they coach. They often say they are unskilled to help or they fear litigation. Some believe they will create suicidal thoughts if they try to discuss the topic. They prefer the 'head-in-the-sand' policy. My response is short. Listen more, and ask directly if you're worried about any athlete in your care. These two simple skills save lives. They are skills we should all practise. The next story hammers home how important they are.

I will long remember the massacre of 10 students and one teacher at Columbine High School in Colorado. I'll remember it mostly for what happened a year later. One 17-year-old student who survived, and who was one of the best basketballers in the state, hanged himself in his home. There's a common misconception that suicidal kids stand out because they must be losers, not sports stars. There's another big message in this story. The young man visited his coach almost every day, but the coach never detected any hints of the player's depression.

Be aware when you're frequently approached by someone, young or old. It's not being pessimistic to consider there might be an underlying problem. Also be alert for the sounds of silence. Silence can be a beautiful healing force or like Simon and Garfunkel sang, it can grow like a cancer. Many who are suicidal seek the company of others, but stay silent about their fears. They find it impossible to share their thoughts and feelings. We all say things we later regret, but it's what we don't say that often causes more problems, for ourselves and others. Silence is often promoted as a sign of inner strength, but it's also the same silence that can lead to tragic consequences.

This principle hit home again recently. I spoke about this topic to a large business group and after my talk I was told about a middle-aged man who attended church one Sunday. He lived in a large country town, but the rest of the congregation knew him well, and they were very surprised at his attendance because he hadn't been anywhere near the church for years. A few days later he killed himself, leaving a young family without a father. What prevents us from reaching out? We have resistance to making certain statements because saying these things are seen as signs of weakness. I started building a list that always produces a lot of intense discussion.

Five hardest things to say?

'I was wrong.'
'I'm sorry.'
'I don't know.'
'I need help.'
'I lied.'

A couple of American presidents paid the penalty for not having the strength to say the last one. The selection of these statements receive a lot of support from my audiences. Here are some of the many other nominations: 'I forgive you', 'Forgive me', 'I love you', 'I don't love you', 'I'm leaving you', 'I quit', 'I did it', 'I'll help you', 'I let you down', 'You let me down', 'I'll do it', 'I'll stop' and 'Thanks'.

Be on the lookout for the sounds of silence, those times when you become silent, unable to say things. Be on the lookout for times when others are subdued and distant. Encourage yourself and others to be strong enough to share any problems that are hidden beneath the silence. This won't create a burden. Instead, you'll feel like an oasis.

Do you tell stories, great stories?

I love telling stories and I'm not talking about gossiping. I'm talking about the skill that's been at the core of human communities for thousands of years. Unfortunately, today we mostly rely on electronic storytellers. Some of my most successful counselling sessions are due to my ability to share inspirational stories. The benefits of telling stories shouldn't be surprising as

Christianity is largely built around some short punchy stories, the parables told by Jesus.

We all need to be storytellers because it's a great way to deal with depression. I'm constantly sharing true stories with others, and whether I'm involved in one-on-one counselling, or I'm talking to an audience of hundreds, I always include a message. The message has a double effect. When I share it, I'm lifted as well. I'm constantly expanding my repertoire of stories. Many are snapshots, short and sharp.

Join in a very special storytelling session. Imagine you're with a group of friends, huddled around a fire on a dark cold night, with brilliant constellations of stars above you. Everyone there has come to help one of you, who is depressed. All of you want to hear stories to make you think.

Here's a handful of five stories from me. Discover the message in each, and then do something incredibly important. Decide what stories you would tell when it is your turn.

1. Have you heard of Arnold Palmer, one of the greatest golfers of all time? Very few people know when he embarked on his professional career in 1955, his first six months were a bitter disappointment. He was terrible! He was on the verge of quitting. Then he found a powerful message in a small best-selling book called *The Power of Positive Thinking*. The book talks about a golfer who became pessimistic after hitting his ball into the rough. After reaching the ball, something really strange happened. His partner handed him a blade of grass and told him to chew on it. After proving how soft it was, the partner then said, 'Well, an easy swing of your number five iron will cut through that grass like a knife. The rough is only mental'. Free of his pessimism, the golfer then hit the ball sweetly to the green. So did Arnold Palmer, for the next 40 years.

2. Depression is many things, too many things, but I often hear anger in the voices of my depressed clients. Worst of all, they're angry at themselves. They should listen to the ancient Greek,

Aristotle. About 2,300 years ago he said, 'Anyone can become angry — that's easy. But to be angry with the right person, to the right degree, at the right time, for the right purpose, and in the right way — that's not easy'. That's awesome!

3. In the year after President Kennedy's assassination in Dallas, the suicide rate in the United States went up one per cent. However, the suicide rate in Dallas jumped 20 per cent! I haven't been able to discover whether the jump in suicides was higher with teenagers, but what do you think? The youth of America embraced Kennedy as he showed them a bright future. With his death, pessimism and cynicism could grow in plenty of disillusioned young minds. Suicide does sometimes spread like a quick growing cancer. When we lose our heroes, we need others to replace them, quickly. We can all be heroes.

4. I'd like to visit two mountains. World travellers have said both mountains have a spiritual feel about them. One mountain is Mount Olympus in Greece, the legendary home of Zeus and the other ancient gods. The other mountain is Mount Fuji in Japan. There's a sign at the entrance to the forest at the base of this mountain. It was put there to dissuade the large numbers who come to the forest to kill themselves. The sign says, 'Your life is something precious that was given to you by your parents. Meditate on your parents, siblings and your children once more. Do not be troubled alone.' What would you put on a sign to stop all suicides?

5. My home is surrounded by masses of trees, and these trees are magnets for birds. For several weeks of every year, we're bombarded by the calls and squawks of young birds as they follow, chase and pester their parents for food. Nature has given all animals, including humans, a built-in persistence to survive. What happens to this magnificent gift? Birds learn to feed themselves. That's healthy growth. But many humans let depression grow and that stifles that wondrous persistence we should use to beat any of life's problems.

Time doesn't heal all wounds!

This piece of wisdom isn't from someone who is depressed, it's from me. Time heals physical injuries but not our mental wounds. We heal these important invisible wounds in our lives. That's great news because you can always help to heal yourself and others. It's up to you, and that's not a burden. It's a gift from life.

Chapter 8
Switch On the Right Side of Your Brain

Are you brave enough to do something silly, something that will show you exactly where you can tap into an incredible supply of mental energy? This could be one of the most important exercises you ever do in your life. Stand up and slowly lift your left leg up and down. As you do that, also swing your left arm around in a figure 8. At the same time, block your right nostril and breathe deeply through your left nostril. Keep going for at least 10 seconds and then sit back down.

What did you look like? Ridiculous? A bigger and more important question: What were you doing? The answer is that you stimulated some serious electrical activity on right side of your brain. The ancient Greeks knew about this reverse connection thousands of years ago. When a warrior had the right side of his brain damaged in battle, the left side of the body was affected. And they knew the left side of the brain controls the right side of the body.

Learning with different brains

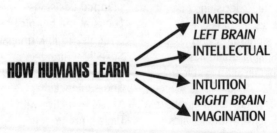

How important is the right side of our brains at work, in sport, and in the rest of our lives? Let me give you a hint of the enormous potential by first looking at sport. Was that such a surprise?

Any cricket fan knows the preponderance of left-handed batsmen in Australian cricket sides, as well as teams from other countries. Sometimes left-handers make up more than 50 per cent of the top batsmen. You can get the same pattern in baseball. Doesn't this tell us something very important? Only 15 to 20 per cent of men are left-handed.

What's going on? Study the summary 'Right brain versus left brain'. The right side of the brain is so important in sport because it has a major role in depth perception and automatic decision-making. Think of those two characteristics in any sport. It's highly likely that great sports champions like Don Bradman, Michael Jordan and Martina Navratilova got a lot of help from the right side of the brain. That might also be true for Tiger Woods. Even though Tiger is right-handed we know he is left-eye dominant.

Right brain versus left brain

Right brain

· Controls the left side of the body
· Stimulated by movement on the left side the body
· Generates creative ideas via imagination and fantasy
· Helps to solve problems by intuition and guesses
· Complex thinking — can cope with contradictions
· Produces spontaneous and automatic decisions
· Concentrates on details
· Identifies similarities and solutions using analogies
· Site for visualisation — pictures and images
· Language — creates metaphors
· Music — active without lyrics
· Writing — prefers running writing
· Major role in depth perception
· Active in interpreting symbols
· Involved mostly in the present

Left brain

· Controls the right side of the body
· Stimulated by movement on the right side of the body
· More involved when thinking requires facts and evidence
· Solves problems by logical analysis
· Step by step thinking — this must be followed by this
· Involved in slow planned decisions
· Looks at the big picture
· Struggles to link unrelated areas
· Speech centre
· Language — creates words and sentences
· Music — active with lyrics
· Prefers printing
· Small role in depth perception
· Active in mathematical calculations
· Gives an ordered sense of time

I heard tennis champ Pete Sampras clearly describe a right-brain perform-ance at the press conference after he easily won a Davis Cup semi-final. His description might have offended his beaten opponent, Mark Philippoussis. Sampras described his own game as effortless, he didn't have to think. For some listeners, the implication was that he had little opposition. I don't think so because I can't recall a time when Sampras ever derided an opponent. I'm certain he was describing one of those memorable days when his right brain was fully firing, helping his decisions and actions to feel like they were auto-matic, and so easy that time appears to stretch out.

Listen to post-match comments and you'll pick up clues when other ath-letes have just had right-brain-dominated performances. They use phrases like: in the zone, had a purple patch, could do no wrong, everything clicked, ran hot, had a blinder, everything turned to gold, so easy. Can you imagine how great you'd feel, how successful you'd be, if you had these feelings in your life, not just in sport?

Be an expert daydreamer like Einstein!

Daydreaming has received a lot of bad reviews. You don't see teachers writ-ing on student reports, 'Excellent at daydreaming. Keep up the good work.' Many feel daydreaming is only a short step away from being lazy. Here's a dramatic update. Daydreaming is a healthy activity and it can also be a very productive activity. It has been responsible for some major scientific discoveries, some of the biggest of all time! When you daydream, using your imagination for no particular purpose, your right brain is having fun!

Albert Einstein had a lot of fun in his life and he was a big fan of the power of the right brain. My collection of his thoughts on thinking all lean toward the right side of the brain. Einstein, a physicist and philosopher, pointed us in the right direction. Later on, neuroscientists were able to give us strong evidence that the right side of your brain plays a huge role in creativity and problem solving. There was always something suspicious about the high percentage of left-handers in professions like architects, engineers, dancers, musicians and comedians. One neuroscientist summed it up beautifully when he said your right brain helps you to think in three dimensions. Yes, I like that!

Einstein's thoughts on thinking

Everything has changed except our way of thinking.

Imagination is more important than knowledge. The really valuable thing is intuition.

Education is that which remains after you have forgotten everything you learned at school.

The gift of fantasy has meant more to me than my talent for absorbing positive knowledge.

The most incomprehensible thing about the world is that it is comprehensible.

Great spirits have always encountered violent opposition from mediocre minds.

The important thing is not to stop questioning. Curiosity has its own reason for existing.

Where am I and where am I meant to be?

Back in the 17th century, Sir Isaac Newton was on his mother's farm trying to avoid the plague sweeping London. Resting and relaxing, he saw an apple fall from a tree. His mind was fully prepared for creative thinking. The dropping apple inspired Newton to give a mathematical explanation of how the universe was controlled by gravity. His ideas became the foundations of science for the next 300 hundred years, until they were challenged by Einstein. Again the inspiration came from daydreaming. Einstein imagined what would happen if he travelled on a particle of light. His imagination was responsible for another revolution in science. He solved other complicated mathematical problems after he went sailing, spending most of his time fascinated by the colours and shapes of clouds and waves.

Einstein and Newton both tapped into the power of the right side of the brain. Over the last three decades, neuroscientists have discovered marvellous things about the human brain. In a nutshell, they found the left half of the human brain is the language and analytic side and the right side is the images and creative side.

When Einstein died in 1955, his brain was preserved and it quickly became one of science's most valuable objects of research. After much analysis, a single discovery stood out. Only a small part of Einstein's brain was abnormally enlarged — the area dealing with mathematical ability and spatial perception was 15 per cent wider than normal. This discovery was not made until 1999. That's why I think that someday we'll be able to find some anatomical evidence that Einstein's brilliance also came from his right brain. He certainly left us enough clues in his thoughts and actions.

I get a lot of inspiration from a giant picture I have in my office. It shows Einstein, or as I like to call him, my mate Albert, celebrating his 70th birthday in his own special way. He's poking out his tongue. Being silly and having a strange sense of humour were essential parts of Einstein's personality and his success. You can add humour to the list of right brain strengths. An accidental discovery made in 2000 by doctors working at a New York Medical School, pinpointed the main area for humour. Brain scans showed that when you have a good laugh, the electrical activity in the area of the brain just behind your right eye, just lights up.

Even though I'm often like a fanatic preaching the benefits of the right brain, I must add some words of caution. Several over-generalisations appeared back in the 1970s.

Some argued the cultures of the East and West were due to the use of the right and left sides of the brain. In the mystical and philosophical East, right-brain thinking is more common. On the other hand, the materialistic West makes greater use of the left brain. This simplistic explanation of cultural diversity didn't last long.

There's another thing to keep in mind. The summary showing the differences between the left and right brain is not rigid. Many tasks are attacked by both sides of the brain, even though one side is frequently far more dominant. The brain is very adaptable and has been able to compensate for damage to one side by activating the other side to do tasks that were previously out of its realm.

However, we really do have two brains. We have a left and right hemispheres connected by a narrow bridge of connecting tissue called the *corpus callosum.* I make a lot of friends with women when I emphasise in my seminars that the *corpus callosum* in women is thicker than that found in men's brains. Being thicker, it's richer in connections between the two halves of the brain. More connections mean more communication between each side of the brain. Maybe that explains that mysterious characteristic called women's intuition. Women may have been given a big advantage in brain design.

Back in the 1970s the *corpus callosum* was surgically separated to help some patients who were suffering from nearly constant epileptic seizures. When the hemispheres were completely separated, the frequency of seizures dropped markedly. Complete separation also allowed the two sides to function independently and show their special qualities.

Today, we don't need to rely on this surgery to reveal the special qualities of each hemisphere. Instead, there are technical marvels such as the EEG which records the brain's electrical activity, CAT scans which give detailed x-rays of the brain and MRIs which pinpoint electromagnetic activity in different regions of the brain.

Are you ready to make this far more personal? Put your hands on the top of your head. What do you feel? Nothing? If your fingers were like an EEG machine, you would feel constant vibrations coming from the immense number of electrical waves going in all directions from your brain. Your brain is like a miniature television transmission tower. That's a double WOW!!

Most of your brainwaves are the rapid beta waves. They bounce up and down at about 25 per second. Less common are the slower alpha waves that leave your brain around 10 per second. There are even slower waves but let's stick to these two as they will help you understand how you can tap into the strengths of your right brain.

The up/down relationship between beta and alpha waves was beautifully shown in a study of champion pistol and rifle shooters, and Olympic archers. These athletes are concentration experts for two reasons. First, they show cardiac deceleration. Sorry, I meant to say their heart rates decrease just before they shoot. This happens in elite golfers as well. However, the second reason is brainwave related. In the last five seconds before shooting, there is a lot more alpha wave activity on the left side of the brain. This helps to switch off this side of the brain. The right side becomes more in control and, hey presto, depth perception will be more accurate.

These shooters are not from Mars, with extra special powers. Everyone can use these powers, and not just for sport. Your right brain has so many strengths to help you in so many areas of your life. And the steps are so simple and easy to follow. That's a triple WOW!!!

Hypnotise yourself into healthy hallucinations

Thousands of years ago, a Taoist philosopher wrote that even the longest journey begins with a single step. Great advice. Daydreaming is your very first step along the pathway to fully use your right brain.

The next step is visualisation. This is a term frequently used by sports-people, and frequently used incorrectly. Visualisation is just like watching yourself on a video recording, with the sound turned off. When most sports-people talk about visualisation they're really referring to imagery. It involves a lot more action than visualisation because you add in your other senses. The big one is the kinesthetic sense, a mixture of touch and movement. There's also sound and even taste.

Up one level from imagery is self-hypnosis. It's more intense, vivid and life-like than imagery. The number one way of using and stimulating your right brain is self-hypnosis. Basically, it's a very smart form of daydreaming. It's so simple, it works with all ages. I've taught it to 9-year-olds and an elderly woman who wouldn't reveal her age, but I knew she was in her 80s.

Alpha waves give you the key to change imagery into self-hypnosis. There is a multitude of simple ways to replace the rapid beta brainwaves with the slower alpha waves. You can do this within a few minutes and it's very similar to locating and fine-tuning television stations on a new TV. This is the essential ingredient of self-hypnosis, and it's such a simple step, but it's often ignored.

Expect to feel amazing sensations during self-hypnosis. Some of my swimming clients have told me they even tasted chlorine during their self-hypnosis sessions. Your body might also react during these sessions. I've seen fingers and feet twitching, heads shaking slightly and rapid eye movement (REM). What's that? When you feel your eye lids flickering, it's due to REM. Normally this only happens in deep sleep, when you're dreaming and normally it takes several hours to reach this REM sleep. When you experience REM after a few minutes of self-hypnosis, it shows you how quickly you can enter a dreamlike state.

After self-hypnosis? If you have the time you will enjoy meditation. If you don't want to invest the considerable time needed for meditation, you'll still get big rewards from 10-minute sessions of self-hypnosis.

Grab hold of this next image. When you use self-hypnosis you're standing alongside Steven Spielberg as a movie director. He's made movies about the past, the present and the future. So can you, except you get to be the main actor.

I teach athletes to use self-hypnosis in four major roles. First, and most importantly, it allows you to mentally rehearse your next game or event. Second, you can replay previous successful performances. Third, you will relax more and sleep better on the night before you compete. Lastly, self-hypnosis can quicken the healing of injuries.

I know you're a rational sceptic, so you must be thinking, how does self-hypnosis do all these things. Why does it work? At the deep level, it works because self-hypnosis produces electrical impulses in your muscles, similar to the real thing. You get lots of extra hours of practice like flight simulators for pilots and astronauts. Practising is so important. Irish sports psychologist, Aidan Moran, believes 10,000 hours or 10 years of practice is needed to become a world-class achiever in any skill, whether it's chess or gymnastics, sculpture or cricket, pistol shooting or public speaking. Your right brain lets you squeeze in large amounts of practise into short self-hypnosis sessions.

When you rehearse, replay and relax, you lift your confidence and concentration. What do you get when you mix confidence and concentration? Hint — it's another 'C' word, a huge one. You get commitment!

These three mental strengths go a long way to covering all the bases of success, not only in sport, but in business and personal relationships as well.

Here are just a few scenarios where my non-sport clients have used self-hypnosis to be more successful — studying and then doing an exam, written or practical; speaking in public; being interviewed for a job; making a sales presentation at a meeting; cold-calling a prospective client by phone; going on a date; and giving evidence in a court case. Nick Faldo, the golfer, used it to learn how to land a helicopter!

Basic training in self-hypnosis

Exercise 1

Sit comfortably in a chair and have a close friend sit in a chair in front of you. Stare at the other person's face, study every detail. Then look at the rest of the body — clothes, body shape as well as the positions of arms, hands, legs, feet. Close your eyes for a minute, and try to visualise the person's face and body. Open your eyes and pick up on the details you missed. Close your eyes again to repeat this process. Then try to visualise the person walking up to you and talking to you. Imagine how you feel about your friend — tune into the emotions you have for this person. This exercise will be effective if it lasts 5 to 10 minutes.

Exercise 2

Place a single raisin or peanut, or both, in your mouth and chew and swallow very slowly. Be aware of every sensation, every movement. Repeat this process without the food. In your mind, relive everything, from using your fingers, moving your hands to your mouth, opening your mouth, moving your jaw, teeth, tongue, tasting the food as it mixes with saliva. Then swallow and feel the energy of the food particles being carried to every part of your body. When you become extremely skilful at this exercise, you can easily mentally rehearse anything.

Exercise 3

Select a specific event you wish to prepare for. Select an object that will play some part, even very minor, in your event. Maybe it is a pen you will use in an exam; maybe the notes for a speech you will give; or some a piece of equipment used in your sport, such as a golf club, tennis racquet, cricket ball, running spikes, or even swimming goggles.

Hold whatever object you select in both hands. Close your eyes and slowly explore all its fine details with both your hands. Concentrate on its outline and texture. Continue for at least a minute. Repeat this process without holding the object. With your eyes still closed, imagine yourself using this object. See yourself from your mind's eye, that is, see yourself succeeding from behind your own eyes. Visualise colour and hear any sounds that will be there in the real situation. Imagine the movements of your body. Have a break of about 15 minutes and then repeat all the steps of this exercise.

Begin this final part of the exercise only after you are comfortable with the previous part. Step out of your body and see yourself as if you were watching yourself on a TV screen or how a spectator would see you. Visualise close-ups, long-shots, see yourself from different angles. Finally, go back to seeing yourself from your mind's eye.

Sounds great, doesn't it? It will sound even greater when you hear some of the testimonials from a bunch of champions from several different sports. First up is golf. Are you a golfer? If you are, I'd like to apologise. I'm on the side of those who regard golf as a good walk spoiled. I can also see the flip side — a game of golf is a good metaphor for life and, therefore, it's good practice for life, a combination of the smooth and the rough. Whilst I have no desire to ever pick up a golf club, I greatly admire the champions of golf. My top two golfing heroes are Jack Nicklaus and Gary Player. Both of them have told the world how important self-hypnosis was in helping them to be two of the most successful golfers of all time.

Jack Nicklaus was asked what was the most important part of his preparation for a tournament. His answer bewildered the interviewer. It was what he did on the plane, while he was flying to the tournament. High in the skies, he mentally rehearsed playing each hole on the course. Fully aware of the course layout, he had heaps of practice even before he arrived at the golf course. Up there, he was doing self-hypnosis. Down on the real course he used to 'go to the movies', as he describes in his book, *Golf My Way*.

> First I 'see' the ball where I want it to finish, nice and white sitting up high on the bright green grass. Then the scene quickly changes and I 'see' the ball going there: its path, trajectory, and shape, even its behavior on landing. Then there is a sort of fade-out, and the next scene shows me making the kind of swing that will turn the previous images into reality.

This is vision, vision and more vision. It's pure visualisation without tapping into those other senses that are used in imagery. Nicklaus' choice of visualisation whilst in the thick of the action is obviously logical as he couldn't completely switch off to do a self-hypnosis session out on the green. There's another big reason. I've found you need at least 30 to 60 minutes recovery time after a session before you should compete.

Gary Player, one of Nicklaus' great rivals, became the youngest player to win the prestigious grand slam of golf. Player was a deeply religious man who combined prayer and meditation. Thirty-four years after winning the US Open to complete his grand slam, he clearly recalled an important part of his preparation.

> And I used to go down the scoreboard that listed the names of the champions through the years — 1965 was vacant. I'd stand there for a few minutes everyday and I meditated. I saw my name up there. Gary Player, 1965 Open Champion. It was almost a self-hypnosis.

When I meet Gary Player, I plan to tell him that it was self-hypnosis. I'm looking forward to meeting him.

Let's move onto other sports. A few years ago, a handful of athletes were voted to be the best of the 20th century. Jean Claude Killy, winner of three gold medals in Olympic alpine skiing, was chosen for the honour of *Skier of the Century*. One of his championships was remarkable because he was injured and unable to train before the event. Instead, all his practice was done mentally, thanks to the lifelike sessions that came from his right brain. Imagination rules!

We can move away from the snow and dive into the warm water of a pool. During his fabulous diving career Greg Louganis won an incredible 47 US championships and five world titles on top of blitzing his opposition in the 1984 and 1988 Olympics. To achieve record scores in the springboard and platform events he rehearsed each dive mentally as well as setting all his dives to music that no-one else could hear.

Back in Australia, Greg Chappell led the national cricket team and was truly a batting maestro. However, in the 1980s he descended into a major slump. Even though he averaged over 50 runs every time he batted, he was unable to score a run in six consecutive innings. This was a shock to every follower of cricket. Chappell later revealed to Dr Rudi Webster, the manager of the West Indian cricket team, that it was mental action rather than physical practice that helped him break out of his chains. Imagery and self-hypnosis again came to the rescue.

Want to break out of your prison?

I've given you a collage to show you how images from the right brain have been translated into extraordinary levels of success for sportspeople. There's another group of people, a very special group, who have used the powers of the right brain to help them stay strong and hold onto their hopes for the future. I'm talking about prisoners of war, captives and hostages. Listen to the next three stories of courage.

When the American hostages were detained in Iran, one hostage went on an incredible train trip, courtesy of his imagination, all around Europe. The trip lasted the full 444 days of his captivity. During World War II, Austrian psychiatrist Viktor Frankl survived four years in a concentration camp. He strengthened himself by helping others and doing something quite strange. He regularly imagined he was climbing mountains! When he was released, you know what he did? That's right, he went mountain climbing.

An acclaimed Chinese piano player was imprisoned during the Chinese Cultural Revolution. Held for seven years, he never played a piano until his release in 1965. To the astonishment of music judges, his playing ability had improved. Like the Iranian hostage and Viktor Frankl, he had used self-hypnosis to travel outside of the prison bars.

Self-hypnosis is so effective but so simple. I've put together a wide menu of self-hypnosis recipes that you can sample. However, whenever I cook, I love making my own inspired variations. I recommend you follow the same philosophy with self-hypnosis techniques. Feel free to change or create brand new versions.

Before I let you loose to become a self-hypnosis expert, I'd like to share a few special moments I've had as a psychologist.

A woman had recovered physically from a major operation, surgery to remove a cancer. The surgery was rated a complete success. However, she became severely depressed even though she had wonderful support from her husband and family. I asked her where she would see herself being happy, anywhere in the world, at any time. She replied very quickly, automatically. (I know I'm on the right track when the subconscious responds like this.) She said she would be back in Ireland, in the little town where she grew up over 50 years ago. She hadn't been able to visit her birthplace for over a decade. After learning self-hypnosis, she not only travelled via her imagination to that Irish town on the other side of the world, she went back half a century in the past to visit the people who she had grown up with, but were no longer living. During our last session together, a few months later, she hugged me and thanked me for giving her a never-ending supply of Qantas tickets, plus a time machine to travel backwards. She no longer had any depressed thoughts.

Meditation eliminates medication.
                    Zig Ziglar (Stunning American speaker)

Another client was a CEO who frequently dealt with problems by spraying abuse, criticism and swear words. His new release valve became an imaginary high speed trip on a super-powerful motor bike. His staff all reported a wonderful transformation in his behaviour at work.

A third client was a sportswoman who had suffered a career-ending injury. She wasn't keen to attempt self-hypnosis until her partner asked to join the session. They lay head to head, stretched out in opposite directions, on their lounge room floor. No part of their bodies touched, but they vividly sensed they were spiritually as one. Later I read that Buddhist monks say they are in *Noble Company* when they meditate in a group.

This couple enjoyed that experience and so have I when I've lead groups through sessions. A Sydney newspaper printed an article about my work with a photo of me in action. Surrounded by a dressing room full of footballers stretched out on the floor, I was standing with my hands in a praying position. I had no memory of doing this. That feeling of peace and harmony comes when you are in *Noble Company*. Share your sessions with those you love. The best way to become an expert at anything is to teach it and share it.

Top 10 essential self-hypnosis techniques

Complete Steps 1, 2 and 3 before each self-hypnosis technique.

Step 1 — Preparation

It is strongly recommended that you keep your eyes closed in all exercises. Try to breathe only through your nostrils. Sit comfortably or lie on the floor. If you are on the floor, place a small pillow or rolled up towel underneath your head. Make your body symmetrical, that is, position your arms and legs so that both sides of your body are the same. Also, keep your arms, hands, legs and feet uncrossed.

Step 2 — Counting backwards

Begin with a couple of deep breaths, and then silently count backwards from 10 to 1. Count as you breathe out.

Step 3 — Silent chant

As you breathe out, silently repeat a short word. If you want to relax, effective words are 'calm', 'peace' and 'quiet'. If you want to be highly focused, some great words to use are 'strength' or 'sharp'. As you say either of these words, think of all your personal strengths and skills that have helped you to be successful. Another powerful word is 'sacrifice'. As you repeat this word think of all the effort and hard work you have done to reach where you are today. You could also think of the sacrifices made by others to help you.

Exercises to relax and heal your body

Exercise 1 — Walking down stairs

Imagine there are 10 steps in front of you. Look down at the bottom of the steps to see a very peaceful place, a wonderful place where you know you'll be totally relaxed. Feel your body move as you slowly start to walk down the steps. Feel your feet lift, your knees and legs rise and your arms moving.

When you reach the bottom, feel yourself walking into your special place. Allow all your senses to come alive. Hear the sounds, see all the colours, smell the fragrances and feel sensations on your skin. Enjoy every moment as you completely relax.

Exercise 2 — White light

Feel an intense beam of white light enter your body through the top of your head. This light enriches your whole body, every muscle, bone, every particle of your body. You can feel this light healing any part of you that is injured or hurt. Let the light leave your body through your feet as it takes away your problems.

Exercise 3 — Lying on warm sand

Imagine you're lying on the warm sand of a beach. Someone you enjoy being with starts to cover your feet with a thin layer of the golden sand. As the sand touches your skin you feel so relaxed and comfortable. Feel the sand gently falling on your legs and spreading up to your neck. The warmth and tingle of the sand helps to revitalise your whole body.

Exercise 4 — Problems in a balloon

Place your problems in the basket beneath a large balloon. Look upwards as the balloon rises and your problems disappear. Without any problems, you feel so calm and relaxed.

Exercise 5 — Soaring like an eagle

See an eagle gracefully flying, patiently gliding, waiting to find a column of rising air. Become that eagle. Then feel the freedom as you soar on a rising thermal. Let yourself rise higher and higher. Enjoy the exhilaration.

Exercises to lift confidence and concentration

Exercise 6 — Climbing up stairs

There are 10 steps in front of you. They're just one step away from you, so real and so clear. Feel your body move as you slowly start to climb the steps. Feel your feet lift, your knees and legs rise and your arms moving. As you go up each step you get stronger, filled with extra energy. Your confidence keeps growing and at the top step you know you have a total commitment to excel. See yourself, totally focused, enjoying every moment as you succeed in doing everything you want to do.

Exercise 7 — Blue sky

Imagine you are looking up at the brightest blue sky you have ever seen. It's so bright, it's blinding, and you have to squeeze your eyelids tighter to keep out the light. But this light is so pure and powerful you feel it being absorbed through every part of your body. As it enters your body, you feel its warmth and you feel stronger. This boost of energy will help you do anything you want to do. For example, it can give you incredible powers of concentration.

Exercise 8 — A silent place

Imagine you're in a very isolated place. Maybe you're in a desert or high on a mountain. In this place, there are no other people or animals. Nothing moves. There is total silence. Everything is perfectly quiet. In this silence it's so easy for you to concentrate on the things you want achieve.

Exercise 9 — Flow of confidence and commitment

All your confidence and commitment grows in your mind. Imagine it's flowing from your mind, down into your neck muscles. It's a warm feeling, a tingling sensation that spreads down your arms and into your hands. Squeeze your fists tightly to force the feeling further around your body. Let the flow of confidence and commitment go down your shoulders, chest, stomach, legs to your feet.

Exercise 10 — Double video screens

Imagine you're sitting in front of two gigantic video screens. On the left screen, see yourself having a problem. Make this screen go black, and then turn on the right screen. Now see yourself being completely successful.

Finish all sessions by counting slowly from 1 to 5. Spend a few minutes stretching. Your body might feel slightly strange. Your mind has been highly active whilst your muscles have been inactive.

Some very special self-hypnosis exercises

There's some subterfuge surrounding this title. I think every self-hypnosis is very special. Why? Because every self-hypnosis exercise, whether it's simple or complicated, whether it lasts a few minutes or hours, makes you feel more alive, makes you feel special. But ... the next nine exercises are some of my favourites. They have given me, and many of my clients, plenty of enjoyment plus personal insights. Each exercise will take you to some very special places and situations. Expect to be excited!

Coming home

Imagine you're walking down the street where you live. You look around in all directions as you notice all the details of your neighbourhood. As you try to see your home in the distance it seems hazy. It becomes clearer and clearer as you get closer and closer to the door of your home. You enjoy this feeling of coming home, coming home where you feel relaxed and comfortable. As you reach to open the door, you are surprised, very surprised, as it opens in front of you. Standing there, smiling, is a member of your family, or maybe it is a very close friend. You smile as you are happy to see this person. You hear the noises of many other people talking and laughing. Your home is filled with your strongest supporters — family and friends. Everyone starts to notice that you have entered, and one by one they turn towards you, smiling and welcoming you home. As you look at each happy face you absorb their good wishes. Everyone here cares for you and wants you to achieve your dreams. As you walk around the room you receive hugs, kisses, pats on your back and warm handshakes. People thank you for all the times you have helped them.

Now for another surprise, your biggest and best surprise. Everyone slowly moves into another room to watch a gigantic television screen. You follow and decide to stand at the back of everyone else. The dark screen comes alive. On the screen are images of you, achieving many incredible things, your dreams. The room is filled with cheering. When the screen goes dark again, everyone turns around to look at you, and one by one they start to clap. Your home is alive with the rich sounds of applause for you. With all this praise and support, you know you can achieve whatever you have set your heart on.

Nature calls, nature roars

Ancient hunters and warriors often tried to tap into the strengths of the animals around them. This theme is the basis of a powerful exercise. It has been successfully used to boost confidence. Take your time at each step. Begin by seeing an elephant rampaging, unstoppable.

Feel yourself absorbing the strength of the elephant. You feel stronger in your body, you feel stronger in your mind. Now see a snake such as a cobra attacking its prey at lightning speed. Feel yourself using the speed of the cobra — you have lightning quick thoughts and responses. Then see an eagle gracefully flying, patiently rising on the hot thermals. Let your body fill with the patience of an eagle, patience that is needed to succeed, patience to grow and improve. Lastly, select an animal that combines all these characteristics — strength, speed and patience. Let this animal represent you being successful. The tiger, wolf, dragon and shark are popular symbols.

Enter your doorway to peace and tranquility

Collect five blank sheets of paper and a thick coloured pen. Red is a popular choice. Slowly draw a large 5 on the first sheet. Stare at the number for about 10 seconds and then turn the page over. On the second sheet slowly draw the number 4. Repeat the process. On the next sheet draw a 3. Repeat again. Then draw a 2 and repeat. On the final sheet draw a 1, but this time stare and imagine the number is a door. On the other side of the door is any place you desire to be.

Now you're fully prepared to close your eyes and repeat all of the above. However, this time you will imagine you're doing all the steps in your mind. Take as long as you need to see the numbers completely disappear. You might prefer to see each number crumble or shatter apart. When you reach the 1, feel yourself going through the door. Some sportspeople imagine they go through a large banner as they run onto the field. Wherever you are once you go through the doorway, let all your senses become highly alert. Remain on the other side of your door for 5 to 10 minutes. As in all self-hypnosis, many people enjoy stretching after the session.

Use a tiny bit of pain for a great gain!

The success of self-hypnosis springs from strong emotions. You can make your emotions grow even stronger using this simple technique.

It follows the same way your body reacts to hot and cold. If you first put your hand into warm water and then into cold water, what do you feel? The water probably feels much colder, maybe freezing. Put your hand back into the warm water and it will feel hotter than before. You can now add some heat to your emotions.

Close your eyes and silently repeat these three words: *succeed, achieve, win.* Say them slowly or quickly. Change your pace as you feel like it. You might like to emphasise a different word each time you repeat this awesome trio of words. You have now warmed your mind for the rest of the exercise.

Think of a person who you greatly admire or even love. Someone who is extremely important to you, someone who is connected to you in wonderful ways. Enjoy experiencing all of these thoughts, for at least 30 seconds. To cool down your emotions, think of a person you like much less. Stay here very briefly, for less than 10 seconds. Quickly return to your image of the person you greatly admire. Feel the increased power in your emotions and how much clearer you see this person.

Now swing your mind to a time in your own life, a time of success, a time of achieving, a time of winning. Relive this exciting time in your life for at least one minute. Then briefly, less than 10 seconds, relive a moment in your life when you were unsuccessful. Return to your time of great success and feel the extra energy in your body. You might even feel like smiling as a great feeling of success takes over your whole body.

Heal yourself with light

There are many different ways you can imagine light helping to heal or energise your body. The following three self-hypnosis techniques were all devised by professional sportspeople. Each technique has achieved spectacular results.

See yourself standing in a totally empty room. All the walls and ceiling are shining white. You are the only coloured object in the room. Make the part of your body that is damaged or hurt, a different colour. From all sides of the room come small pockets of light, like miniature glowing comets. They touch you and enter your body. As your body absorbs each ball of light, you feel a wonderful warm sensation as the light moves to heal any part of your body that is injured or in pain. Let the colour of the injury change, maybe from black to gold, or from red to white.

Shooting an injury away

The next technique was devised by one of my happiest clients. His doctors had shown him an X-ray of the major injury he had suffered. There were many dark spots on the X-ray that had to disappear for his injury to be healed. Several times a day, my client imagined he was staring at this X-ray. He used an imaginary laser gun to fire at each of the dark spots until they all disappeared. Within two months of using this technique, he returned to his sporting career. One doctor had given him no chance, whilst the other said he only had 50 per cent chance of ever playing his sport again.

Photocopy your body

This technique uses the image of a photocopying machine. Imagine the part of your body that is injured is under a very bright light. This light moves, something like the flash you can see on the glass surface of a photocopying machine. As the light moves along your body, it massages your injury from inside your body. Feel the light going backward and forward, over and over, deeper and deeper. When you finish, imagine the light has left a perfect copy, a copy without the injury.

What was the greatest day of your life?

Charles Dickens began one of his books by saying, 'It was the best of times, it was the worst of times, it was the age of wisdom, it was the age of foolishness'. Does that grab you like it grabs me? Dickens was describing the late 18th century, the time of the French Revolution, but I think he could be talking about any day in our lives.

Every day you enter could contain the best and the worst. Every day you could meet wisdom and foolishness. I knew a football coach who had a sign over his office door that said 'The best is yet to come'. This message is obviously optimistic, but it can still lead to frustration. At a deeper level, it can blind you to what is already in front of you. Look forward to the future, but also focus on the beauty and riches you have already found in your life. This self-hypnosis exercise will help you see this more clearly.

Begin by either sitting in a chair, or lying on the floor. Stare strongly at a point straight ahead of you for 10 seconds and then let your eyelids gently drop. Let your subconscious release images of some of the best days of your life. There are images with family or friends, images of you being successful working, images of enjoyment, pleasure and happiness. When you have found one of these days that you would like to revisit, and relive, open your eyes, look in all directions, and let yourself smile and nod. Return to this great day in your life. Close your eyes again and see a clear flat pond or lake. A single drop falls and creates a perfect expanding circle. Watch this circle grow. You can see it from any direction you wish, even from under the surface of the water. The water becomes perfectly still again ready for another drop. Let it all happen again, and again, if you wish. As your body and mind are perfectly relaxed and in tune with each other, become part of the images of your best day. Learn even more about yourself by doing it all again with a different day in your life.

The dinner party to end all dinner parties!

You have been given five wishes that will come true. Five fascinating people, heroes, champions, anyone you select, will soon visit you. All you have to do is think of them. Say each name, silently, knowing that each will come and share their lives with you. Every relationship grows stronger by sharing. So share your deepest thoughts and feelings with each of your guests. Remember what you said to your guests and what they said to you.

Keep away from the dark side of your right brain!

Your right brain is truly powerful. Unfortunately, it's so powerful it can not only help you, it can also hurt you, sometimes mildly, sometimes very badly. This happens when we indulge in negative self-hypnosis and this plays a big role in Post Traumatic Stress Disorder, or PTSD. Thankfully this neutral label has replaced battle fatigue and the terrible World War I term shell shock. PTSD is not just linked to war experiences, outward signs of wounds are not necessary. Any highly emotional event can stimulate it, events such as a car accident, rape, imprisonment and public humiliation. The French documentary called *The Unforgettable Experience,* described it perfectly. There are several probable culprits in the brain and one of them is the right frontal lobe. It doesn't appear to function properly in PTSD sufferers. A disturbing emotional image gets too strong in the right hemisphere. Today, many therapies such as Eye Movement Desensitization and Reprocessing, EMDR, have been able to help with PTSD.

I've side-tracked into the world of neuropsychiatry to highlight the worst possible effects of the right brain's dark side. In everyday life, there are other ways we feel its negative power. I saw the potential of some of this power in a hospital. It was a large modern, efficiently run private hospital. What would you like to look at while you're waiting to go into the operating room? How about large vividly coloured pictures of dissected human bodies? All the pictures, along one wall in a busy corridor, were the same posters used for teaching anatomy. I was in the hospital for several hours and watched in amazement as patients were wheeled down the corridor and then left for several minutes, with the posters in full view. Dr Patch Adams and his sidekick Dr John Graham-Pole have shown drawings and pictures, mixed with imagination, and lots of laughter, are potent preventive medicine. The hospital posters, if not hurting, weren't helping. I also heard a doctor in his pre-operation rounds, ask every patient, 'Do you have any major worries?' Surely he was encouraging the negative side of the right brain to get active.

Laughter is hazardous to your illness.

Dr John Graham-Pole

Do you know what's stronger than willpower? It's 'don'tpower'. Never heard of it? It's a term I invented for something terrible that we use over and over again. It leads to negative self-hypnosis. I frequently hear it when I'm working with sportspeople as it's probably the number one teaching tool used by many coaches. I swear 'don't' is the second most commonly used 'word' in all the sports I've been connected to.

One prominent AFL coach gave a 40-minute speech at a pre-season camp. He had just joined the club and was trying to clearly set out his coaching philosophy. After his talk, I asked him how many times he thought he had used 'don't'. He guessed about a handful, no more than six times was his very confident prediction. I sat at the back of the room throughout his speech and I had kept a far more accurate score. His total was 43! After I gave a talk on 'don'tpower' at a coaching course, I was approached by rugby league coach, Wayne Bennett. With a broad smile on his face he told me that I had just thrown away most of his coaching instructions.

'Don'tpower' also has a strong grip on everyday life. One estimate has been made that by age 18, the average teenager has been hit with 'don't' about 150,000 times. One place to hear it in action is the supermarket. I always enjoy going to a supermarket because it's like entering a giant psychological laboratory. They remind me of rat mazes, but it's human behavior on display. Up front comes 'don'tpower' especially when you mix frustrated parents with tired and bored children. There are repeated choruses of 'Don't!' as children are threatened, grabbed, pulled and sometimes slapped. 'Don't touch that!' and 'Don't hit your brother!' are some of my favourites. But the list is endless.

Any instruction containing 'don't' is built on the premise that the best way to teach something is to describe the total opposite scenario. But guess what? 'Don'tpower' often produces results that are the opposite of what was hoped for. It's so easy to use but so unreliable. You can get a backflip when you asked for a forward somersault. Why does this happen? Blame the right side of the brain again. It's guilty because it works so well creating images, even negative images.

Do this quick exercise for me. Don't think of a tiger. Don't, don't think of a tiger. I don't want you to think of any part of a tiger! What happened? If you are like every other person on this planet, you're right brain produced an image of a tiger before you could do anything about it. Let's continue. Think about a kangaroo. See a kangaroo hopping, a kangaroo taking huge bounds. What happened to your images of the tiger. They disappeared quickly, immediately, didn't they?

> *Some supporters come up and say 'good luck' but most will say 'don't let us down.'*
>
> Reuben Thorne (New Zealand captain, before losing to Australia in 2003 Rugby World Cup.)

Whenever we hear any instruction beginning with 'don't', the right brain automatically comes into action and forms the negative image, the image you don't want to see, the dark side of the original instruction. Then there is a delay as the whole brain tries to change that image. Possibly, the more logical left side of the brain tries to assert more control. It's at this point we often get ourselves into trouble. We try to follow the 'don't' part of the message but the original image dominates. This drives coaches mad when they see their teams apparently ignoring or disobeying their instructions. I try to tell them that they're asking for trouble, literally, when they use 'don'tpower'. I think it's close to being a disease of negativity. I've built up a collection of over 100 'don't' instructions commonly heard in various sports. Skilful sports coaches, business managers and parents, should use them as often as they use quotes in Latin.

The most effective way of destroying 'don'tpower' is to flood your mind with more direct instructions that don't require the right side of the brain to reverse and backflip. You can start doing this in the exercise 'Willpower versus "don'tpower"'.

Willpower versus 'don'tpower'

What is a more effective way of saying each of the following instructions.

· Don't worry about it. Don't get nervous. Don't panic.

· Don't think about the audience.

· Don't make any mistakes. Don't stuff it up. Don't lose the plot.

· Don't be disappointed. Don't get frustrated.

· Don't say anything controversial.

· Don't feel angry about it. Don't be so upset.

· Don't do anything undisciplined.

· Don't get lazy. Don't get complacent. Don't relax.

· Don't be overconfident. Don't be too cocky.

· Don't let me down.

· Don't read too much into what they said.

· Don't argue with me.

· Don't be afraid to speak up.

Other examples

How I make some people uncomfortable

Self-hypnosis, meditation, as well as prayer, can all help tap into our inner-most strengths. I sometimes tell my audiences that I'm not religious. I clarify my position by saying I'm not a follower of any single religion. Why do I feel it necessary to make these public declarations? Religion and psychology have a great deal in common, but religion is a very personal thing. As a psychologist I sometimes find that a message or skill I want to teach can be shown by using an example from a religion. I refer to lots of different religions. Comments and looks I get from audiences tell me some people feel uneasy when I refer to these examples. Some might suspect I'm trying to convert them away from their religion. Others are sometimes offended because they've rejected all forms of religion. Both groups feel threatened. Those in-between these groups enjoy my references to religions, religious people and religious experiences. Prayer is one of those experiences.

As I said earlier, prayer is in close company to self-hypnosis and meditation. All three are enriching and enlightening. The right side of your brain is the driving force behind healing achieved through self-hypnosis and meditation. Does it play a part in the success of prayer? I don't know the answer to that mind-boggling question.

All I can do is sit back and marvel at the power of prayer when I hear stories like Peter Doyle's. He's a famous restaurant owner in Sydney who was diagnosed with melanoma. The cancer was so severe it attacked the entire right side of his body. Doctors told him how long he was likely to survive, but he proved them wrong. They now say he is cured. He combined radiation therapy with plenty of prayer. I regularly hear similar powerful stories from those who attend my seminars on the right brain. This makes me appreciate even more the beauty and mystery of life.

> *A message for life*
> *Our deepest fear is not that we are inadequate. Our deepest fear is that we are powerful beyond measure. It is our light, not our dark-ness, that most frightens us. We ask ourselves, who am I to be brilliant, gorgeous, talented, and fabulous? Actually, who are you not*

to be? You are a child of God, your playing small does not serve the world. There is nothing enlightened about shrinking so that other people won't feel insecure around you. We are all meant to shine, as children do. We were born to make manifest the glory of God that is within us. It's not just in some of us, it's in everyone. And as we let our own light shine, we unconsciously give other people permission to do the same. As we are liberated from our own fear, our presence automatically liberates others.

From *A Return to Love: Reflections on the Principles of a Course of Miracles*, Marianne Williamson

Chapter 9
Beyond Your Wildest Dreams

I've learnt a lot by writing this book. I learnt that Nelson Mandela wasn't the author of this inspiring passage that I call 'A Message for Life'. Plenty of people, including some high flying motivators, think Mandela used it in his 1994 inauguration speech. I thought so too, until a wonderful editor reviewed my manuscript. The passage was actually written by the American author Marianne Williamson in 1992. It's not surprising I was wrong, giving credit to Mandela. Marianne's words have the same level of insight and power of any of his pearls of wisdom.

If you want to help others by lifting their self-esteem or self-confidence, let them read Marianne's message. She's telling us to think big … really big. She's telling us to achieve, accomplish, succeed. Above all, she's saying we should let our imaginations loose and discover our dreams. Some people do have clear visions of their dreams, but they do nothing to achieve them. What stops them? The thought of taking a risk drops on them and squashes those dreams. Splat! We can all take more risks in life. More risks might mean more mistakes, but it definitely means more success.

I'm now going to give you verbal whiplash. That's what happens when I quickly jump from one topic to another. From Mandela to Homer Simpson! You either love or hate *The Simpsons* cartoon series. I love it. Blended into the bizarre scenarios are many gems of wisdom. Sometimes they stand out and sparkle, often they're carefully disguised as brief throwaway lines. One of my favourites came from Homer, 'Trying is the first step toward failure'.

You know Homer's on the right track, for two big reasons. When you try, you accept that failure lives in the shadow of success. You head toward both of them when you try to do something new. Without trying you will never reach one of them — success. You can always fail by doing nothing. The other reason why Homer was on target? What do you think when you hear someone say, 'I'll try to do it' or 'I'll try to be there'? It's extremely unlikely the person will do it or be there. Right? When you mix the word 'try' into your promises, you're releasing all the commitment. You end up with the conviction of a Kamikaze pilot who has been on 50 missions.

Instead of trying, take risks, take more of them because it's impossible not to take risks in life. It's time for some more awareness lifting. I've got a couple of quick exercises that will shine the light on you and the risks you take.

First up, we're heading into your subconscious. Did you know we all carry around with us a gigantic library and an immense video collection? Your library contains every bit of information, knowledge and wisdom you've encountered in your life so far. Your video collection contains perfect copies of everything you have ever seen. Everything! I'd like to reintroduce you to your subconscious. Can you recall a time when you did or said something and you had no idea why you did it or said it? The answer is simple. Your subconscious was pulling some of its long tangled strings. If you want to be more aware of the signals being sent by your subconscious, have a look at the exercise 'Taking risks'. This will let you open several doors. Close your eyes, take slow deep breaths and silently say, 'taking risks'. What message immediately popped into your consciousness? It could be a word, an image, a memory, a phrase, a place, whatever it was, write it down in one of the rectangular boxes. Repeat the process until all the boxes form an eight-piece profile of how your subconscious reacts to taking risks.

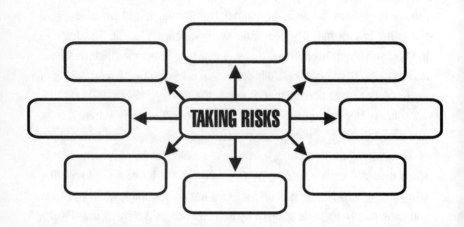

STOP! Only read forward after you have completed your risk profile. How many of your associations would you rate as negative? A common answer is at least half. Sometimes it's eight out of eight. This fits in with a headline I recently saw. It said, 'Watch it: the dream can be a nightmare.' It was on the top of an article detailing the problems facing those starting new businesses. Unfortunately the connection between dream and nightmare is widespread.

Look at the poem 'Unseen Risks' and it will wipe away negative reviews of taking risks. Someone gave me this poem decades ago and I've treasured it ever since. Read the poem slowly. Let it refresh you. This poem touches something deep inside of me every time I read it.

Unseen Risks

To laugh is to risk appearing the fool.
To cry is to risk appearing sentimental.
To reach for another is to risk involvement.
To place your ideas, your dreams before others is to risk their loss.
To love is to risk not being loved in return.
To live is to risk dying.
To believe is to risk despair.
To try is to risk failure.
But risks must be taken, because the
  greatest hazard in life is to risk nothing.
Those who risk nothing, do nothing.
Without risks, you cannot learn, feel,
  change, grow, love and live.

I always look forward to doing the next exercise with my seminar audiences. You can feel an emotional awareness spreading. Let's do it now. Give yourself 5 to 10 minutes to list all the risks you've taken over the last year. Well done, you're finished, aren't you? Were you surprised how your list kept growing? Now, this next step will tell you so much about your life. Put a tick against any of your risks that gave you any amount of success, yes, any amount of success. What have you discovered? I bet the scales weighing your risks are tilted heavily, very heavily, toward the success side. Risk and success go hand in hand. It's so obvious when your eyes are open. When you keep your eyes closed it's so easy to be apathetic. Be on the alert for apathy-linked statements because they're risk killers. One of my most provocative business-training sessions is based on a negative collection that I introduce as the *Best Statements to Prevent Progress*. What amazes me is that this list constantly keeps expanding.

Best statements to prevent progress
or Top 10 risk-killing statements

1. If it ain't broke, don't fix it.
2. We tried something like that once and it didn't work.
3. Don't rock the boat.
4. I wish it were that easy.
5. It's always been like that.
6. You're asking for trouble if you change too many things.
7. It will take too much time to do that.
8. We've never had any complaints before.
9. Get used to it.
10. Why are you never satisfied?

Here's two more, maybe they're the worst: Why bother? Who cares? Make sure you bother and care. You'll do this when you embrace the opportunities found in risks. Right around the corner you'll find your dreams that lead to success.

> *It's better to be a pirate than join the navy.*
> Steve Jobs (Co-founder of Apple Computers)

What's the word dreamers ignore?

There's one word I want to warn you about. It's realistic. This one word has probably stopped more risk taking and killed more dreams than any other word in the dictionary. Listen to this profile of a woman who ignored that constant warning, 'Be realistic!' Her mother was only 13 years old when she was born, and the cycle continued when she was sexually abused and also became pregnant when only 13! Surely no-one could become an international celebrity with a background like this. She proved the realistic thinkers wrong.

The woman is Oprah Winfrey. Whenever I watch her program I see why she has succeeded. She loves life and she loves people. It's so obvious in her face, her eyes and her voice. Non-dreaming critics and cynics are irritated by her enthusiasm, but her gigantic worldwide audiences are lifted by her spirit. So are her employees. It's been reported that all new employees are asked to list their dreams when they join her company, and then Oprah helps to fulfil these dreams as they continue working for her. She lives a life according to the principle that caring is not a sometime thing, it's an all-the-time thing. I'm going to give her a hug when I meet her. One of my dreams is to meet Oprah Winfrey. I'll let you in on a secret: I rarely watch her program. That doesn't stop me from believing she certainly is an extraordinary woman, a dreamer.

The world admired Christopher Reeve, the actor who showed he was a real superman after he became a quadriplegic. And there is another quadriplegic who offends and disgusts nearly everyone, except for all those who love his biting humour. His fans include Bill Clinton, Bob Dylan, Robin Williams and me. His admirers now stretch worldwide thanks to the television version of his humour, *Quads!* Cartoonist John Callahan, now in his fifties, has been in a wheelchair for more than 30 years after his spinal cord was severed in a car accident. Both he and the uninjured driver were drunk, and the six years after his accident were an alcoholic blur. After his decision to stop drinking, he started drawing his unforgettable cartoons. To do so, he has to hold both hands together, which requires great willpower and effort. Callahan's cartoons are deliberately confrontational, not from bitterness, but from a desire to disrupt ignorance and apathy. Those who see giant realistic obstacles between them and their dreams should share some of Callahan's humour.

Congratulations or criticisms?

Sometimes after a speech, I receive very special heartfelt thanks. I never forget these occasions. A careers advisor told me I had made him aware of the thousands, yes thousands of times, he had told students to be realistic in their choice of careers. He was going to stop saying it.

There are also times when I need to duck for cover after I finish a speech. Giving lots of talks and seminars has taught me that sometimes my message can be misinterpreted. A teacher at a high school targeted me after one of my talks on dreams and risks, accusing me of encouraging his students to take stupid risks, from drugs to unsafe sex. I realised he had a point and since then I've added a discussion of smart versus dumb risks.

A smart risk can involve a low chance of success, while a dumb risk is often very likely to be successful. Confused? Consider two big examples of taking dumb risks. One depressed client I counselled had managed to lose his job, his home and his wife after one day of intensive gambling. It was a near certainty that this combination of consequences was going to happen when you heard the details of the risks he took. Another dumb risk involved a friend of mine who is a surfer and believed he could conquer any waves. He went into the surf on a stormy day, and I still cheekily remind him that he was half way to New Zealand before he was rescued. Plenty of smart risks never pay off, but they never endanger your life or hurt others. Dumb risks do!

Three dreams — from Brazil, India and Canada

One of my favourite authors is a Brazilian writer named Paulo Coelho. Every teenager should read his short story *The Alchemist*. Like several of his other books it's built around a powerful theme — dare to go after your dream and you will receive unexpected help. He sums this up when he writes, 'When you want something, all the universe conspires in helping you to achieve it'. I totally agree with Coelho's belief, totally. It's happened in my life and many other people have told me how they have enjoyed the same fabulous experience. When your dream is right, when it involves enriching your life and others, help and guidance will appear out of nowhere.

Ever been at the right place, at the right time? When you are, expect a big dream to inspire you. In 1998, the Australian cricket team was in India, being convincingly beaten by India. This meant the match finished a day early. Steve Waugh had received a note from Shamula Dujeda, a persuasive woman who works with charities in Kolkata. She wrote:

Sorry you are losing the match and by the time this gets to you, you will have lost. But that's life. Maybe God has influenced you to come and visit my projects instead of playing the fifth day. Instead of drinking beer with your mates, come with me.

He did, and now he is the patron of a mission for 80 young girls whose parents have Hansen's disease — leprosy. Since his first visit there, Steve has raised more than $120,000 for the Udayan Mission. *Udayan* means resurrection. When our dreams lift the lives of others, that's what religion should be all about.

There's another thing I strongly believe about dreams. They can touch and inspire others in many unexpected directions. I want you to take another look at the movie, *Field of Dreams*. It's much more than a syrupy homage to baseball. It's a movie that gets to me every time I see it, because it's about the special bond between men and their fathers. Lots of men have told me how the message in the movie also hits them. Do you know how the movie was born? Its conception was in the mind of a Canadian writer who built a novel around a dream — an Iowa corn farmer ploughs up his field to build a baseball field to meet his dead father for a unique game of baseball. The book captivated an American movie director who then hooked Kevin Costner with his dream of making a movie based on the book. Costner helped to get the money to make the movie which was nominated for an Academy Award. The farm in the movie has since been visited by thousands of people who come to show they believe in the beauty of dreams.

The power of the dream behind the movie took a very unexpected turn when the owner of the farm received a heart-wrenching letter. You can read a copy of it in the book, *Life 101*. The letter came from a man whose base-ball-loving son had died in a plane crash … which happened in a corn field in Iowa. The boy had seen, and greatly enjoyed, the movie. The father thought the baseball field in the film had returned to a corn field, until he accidentally discovered a newspaper article about the field, and all its visi-tors. In the letter, he told how he and his family were about to visit the field and 'have the chance to walk with my son one more time'. The father soon received a letter from Kevin Costner, saying, 'If the movie means anything to me now it's that you get that chance to walk with your son. I am with you in spirit. Love, Kevin'. That's class!

Are you a big dreamer or a great pretender?

When I was a teenager I wrote a poem about a small group of people. They were all dreamers. I mentioned John Lennon, John Kennedy, and included myself in the group. When I showed my poem to a friend, he laughed at me. I was deeply hurt and I vividly remember him asking, 'Do you really think you're like them?' I'm certain I said nothing, but my silent answer was 'Yes!' Today, I'm a bigger dreamer than I ever was and I'm proud of it. Dreamers can expect a lot of flak. Dreamers challenge, unsettle, even scare non-dreamers. Sometimes the whole world can be aware of your dreams. That's great. But sometimes no-one else is aware of your dreams. That's still great. Because without dreams, our lives are bland and sterile.

Ever heard of the McDonald brothers, Dick and Maurice? You've probably guessed they must have something to do with McDonald's, the hamburger restaurants. In fact, Dick and Maurice were the founders, who set up their first restaurant in 1937. They refined a 'speedy service system' and by the 1950s they were so successful, they sold franchises for 10 new restaurants. Did Dick and Maurice have a huge dream of success? When a new owner wanted to name his restaurant, McDonald's, Dick responded, 'What for? McDonald's means nothing in Phoenix'. Does that sound like a great dreamer? Along came Ray Kroc who opened up 100 restaurants between 1955 to 1959, and in 1961 bought the exclusive rights to McDonald's. Now, that's a great dreamer!

You can find great dreamers who have been successful, anywhere, and at any age. How about starting a thesis for your PhD at the age of 85? Ron Fitch did, and received his doctorate from the University of NSW at the sprightly age of 92. He's believed to be the oldest student in the world to receive a PhD. Non-dreamers should listen closely to Ron, 'Too many of my old mates retired and vegetated. But there's always something you can do with your mind. It kept me occupied and it kept me young.'

Ron and Ray share the same spirit. Do you?

Everyone is capable of some greatness in their lives and this is why I get annoyed at a comment that politicians like to say about education, especially when they're making election promises. They will introduce programs for gifted and talented students. Every single student is gifted and talented in some way! Everyone should be encouraged to dream big. Academically successful students won't change the future as much as dreamers will.

There are plenty of great dreamers and there are also lots more superficial dreamers. This sort of dreaming shouldn't be rated as dreaming. When you surround yourself with shallow dreams, you're just pretending you're serious about real success. Early in the book, I hit you with some of my views on gambling. It stifles, and often extinguishes, that commitment, that effort, the action you need to truly go after your dreams.

Millions of South Africans are dreaming about finding their road to riches, every week. They think they've found a rainbow that leads to a pot of gold, in the state lottery, called *Uthingo*. That's Zulu for rainbow. It sells 28 million tickets a week, collecting \$US 500 million a year. The company running the lottery says it has created 10,000 jobs and made around 300 millionaires. It also helps most of the ticket buyers to stay in poverty and daily despair.

Experts on the social consequences of gambling agree that it can cause an artificial euphoria, through the short-term achieving of dreams. Gambling also does something else, in the opposite direction. Talking about this is a guaranteed way to offend gamblers. One of the attractions of gambling is that it can produce a numbness, an anaesthetic effect, whether you live in a shanty town in Johannesburg, or you're a high roller in a casino in Melbourne. Gambling is a poor substitute for the commitment needed to reach your dreams.

What's the difference between a dream and a fantasy?

Besides superficial dreaming, there is also surrogate dreaming. It's a form of fantasising. This happens when we make idols of sport, movie, rock stars. Fans can become devoted, fanatical and obsessed. Television competitions across the world offer opportunities for unknown singers to become new pop idols.

Have another think about that word, idol. In some minds, it leads to unhealthy worshipping, even building shrines from vast collections of memorabilia. The Elvis and Michael Jackson collections could fill museums. We need to remember all present day idols are like all of the gods worshipped by the ancient Greeks, they have flaws. For those blinded by the light from their idols, the message from Billy Connolly and me is *Get a life!*

However, fantasies do definitely spice up life. There are those remarkable personalities who take their greatest fantasies and run with them, literally. They're often running from the law. Karl Power is an international sports star impostor. His list of achievements thus far — he has lined up in a team photograph with Manchester United, one of the world's greatest soccer teams; he went out to bat for England in a test match against Australia but walked off the field to answer a mobile phone call before his ruse was discovered. That effort even got him smiles and applause from the police. Lastly, maybe, was his performance on the centre court at Wimbledon. For several minutes he and a friend hit the ball in what appeared to be a warm-up by the real players. At all three risk-taking events, he got plenty of laughs from the crowds, but always received condemnation from officials. At Wimbledon they labelled him as an extremely irresponsible show-off. Something happens when some people become officials — they lose their sense of humour.

If you follow all the rules, you miss all the fun.

Katherine Hepburn

Ahmad Ali Rida is an Australian who has taken on many false identities and many professional careers, without any qualifications, except for a cunning mind. He posed as a barrister, a naval officer, a member of the Australian Medical Association, and he fooled the Prime Minister, John Howard. He's now on the run.

Then there was Oxford engineering student, 23-year-old Matthew Richardson. He has the same name as a US professor who is a leading authority on finance. The student version was wrongly invited to Beijing to present a series of lectures on global economics. He went, ad-libbed and learnt a lot from an introductory finance textbook. In China, they thought he was a child prodigy, and everyone called him 'professor'. Young Matthew was complimented for his lectures, before he decided to escape. Real life can often be far more fun than fiction.

In 1999, a group of 41 Romanians tricked their way into Ireland pretending to be a folk choir. It was a con and a scam, mixed with the charm of a prank and a hoax. Some harsh critics might rant and rave that these Romanians were cheating queue jumpers, who were nothing but illegal immigrants. Thankfully, the scam has so impressed the Irish, they're making a film about it. The Irish saw the same qualities that helped generations of their own ancestors search for their dreams around the word, from Boston to Brisbane. I'm so glad I have some Irish blood in me.

There's a part of me that would love to settle down and have a white picket fence, a couple of kids, a wife and a goldfish. But another part of me somehow needs to go roll around in the mud.

Johnny Depp (Eccentric actor)

Dreams can lead to many things, including many excesses. Rolling in the mud can help develop a creativity, an eccentricity, that leads to success. However, it sometimes leads to rolling and dying in the gutter like actor River Phoenix. Beware of achieving dreams too easily. Consider two young men who have reached star status in movies and television. The *Terminator* trilogy of movies helped Arnold Schwarzenegger to become the governor of California. However, the life of one actor nose-dived after having a lead role in the second movie. Edward Furlong, now in his mid-twenties, spent $2 million on drugs, and twice booked himself into rehabilitation clinics. He escaped the deadly killer in the movie, and hopefully he's escaped a more constant danger.

Another star's face is familiar around the world — he's known for his television and movie roles including *Malcolm in the Middle* and *Agent Cody Banks*. In real life, Frankie Muniz could have been hurtling toward a James Dean finale. Only 16 years old, he was caught driving his $US 100,000 nitro-charged car at 225 kilometres per hour. Another case of too much, too soon.

What are you doing? Nothing much?

From the outside, it sometimes looks like dreamers are standing still. However, when you look closer, you find they're following our secret formula for success. Their dream links their vision and passion, and they follow this up with plenty of action, activity and work that often is never recognised by others. In a television interview, Sylvester Stallone talked about Rocky being a metaphor for his life, his long struggle for success. His mother told him, 'Be patient for seven years'. His response was that he would be on food stamps by then. However, his mother's prediction was remarkably accurate. Stallone's success came within weeks of the seven year time limit. Obviously, the encouragement from Stallone's mother sank in, and helped her son to remain committed to his dream of writing and starring in his own movie. A few wonderfully chosen words can work wonders. In those seven years, Sly was very, very busy.

It was, and still is, a disgrace that Layne Beachley had to win so many world championships before she received her proper recognition from the Australian sporting media and public. She was the best female surfer in the world, for six years, before the awards came. She referred to this, with her typical humour, when she received a Best Sportswoman award. Her ability to keep her standards at the very highest is not surprising when you know of her workload and determination away from the waves. Before sponsors arrived, she worked at every store in a shopping complex near her home in Sydney's north. She struggled for years to find the money to allow her to take part in events around the world. She summed up her success, 'I'm prepared to work hard, to get my hands dirty'. This is the fuel that makes dreams come true. Layne is an exceptional champion because she also overcame two bouts of chronic fatigue syndrome.

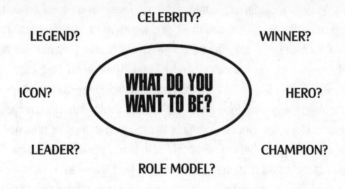

CELEBRITY?

LEGEND?   WINNER?

ICON?   **WHAT DO YOU WANT TO BE?**   HERO?

LEADER?   CHAMPION?

ROLE MODEL?

Champions who chased and caught their dreams!

Look at any comedian and you're looking at a brave person, a constant risk taker and dreamer. Chris Rock has a reputation for joking about issues that other comedians avoid. Recently voted as America's best comedian by *Time* magazine, he sharply dissected the difference between conforming and being different. He said, 'If you don't take a risk, you're Starbucks. You're 7-Eleven. You're just a corporate. You're buying a franchise if you're just doing jokes that have been done.' What he's saying about risk taking applies everywhere.

When Anthony Mundine won the World Boxing Association super-middleweight crown in 2003, he silenced many of his critics, but not all of them. That was not important because those who despise his confidence, will continue to do so. He has regularly been rubbished for modelling himself on Muhammad Ali, but he's a lot closer to Ali than any of his detractors. Both Anthony and Ali have strong convictions, about themselves and about helping other black people. Here was a young man who threw away a highly paid career as a rugby league footballer, to go after a dream that eluded his father. Anthony became the second Aborigine to be a world boxing champion. Smiling after his victory, even with a cracked rib, he spoke for dreamers, of all colours, everywhere, 'I'm going to set more goals now, more ridiculous goals that people think I won't achieve.'

Mary Moody, a gardening expert, author and television personality, twice chased her dreams all the way to France, leaving her husband and family back in Australia. Her story has certainly touched many, as her two books about her adventures, including a love affair, have been bestsellers. How many women, and men, are in marriages or long-term relationships and want to drop everything to run off and capture those unfulfilled dreams?

I want to share with you an image of a champion that sums up why I love sport and life. It's probably one of the best sports photos ever taken. Every member of the crowd is staring and smiling at Don Bradman as he strides out to bat. The eyes of young boys near him are so deeply focused on their hero. The faces of the adults show the same admiration for a champion. There's something extra special in this scene. The crowd is all English and they're applauding the captain of the Australian cricket team — England's arch rivals.

We need more respect like this in today's sport. The young boys in the crowd would now be at least 60 years old. If only we could ask them how that day affected the rest of their lives. I'm certain they were inspired and dreamed to also achieve great things. We can all be lifted when we see others achieve their dreams.

When Cathy Freeman won her gold medal at the Sydney Olympics, her success helped to pull a nation closer together. Her dream to be an Olympic champion inspired so many Australians. Her race stopped our country for at least 40 seconds. Dreams can have amazing effects on other people. Let's do something amazing!

Absorb the exciting message left for us by Michelangelo, painter, sculptor, architect, poet and dreamer.

The greater danger for most of us
is not that our aim is too high
and we miss it,
but that it is too low
and we reach it.

Champions

Champions grow by dreams, big dreams.

Champions are those who get back up when others say they can't.

Champions spread enthusiasm.

Champions have talent plus lots of discipline.

Champions prepare for the unexpected.

Champions use the right words instead of shouting and abusing.

Champions know the head is the most important part of the body.

Champions prefer to have a strong opponent than a weak one.

Champions have goals so they know where they're going.

Champions know they have to fail sometimes to keep growing.

Champions strive for excellence instead of perfection.

Champions are more concerned about character than reputation.

Champions love doing what others say they can't do.

Champions look for opportunities where others see obstacles.

Champions are willing to make mistakes.

Champions use more self-encouragement than self-criticism.

Champions are quick, but never in a hurry.

Champions might lose, but they never get beaten.

Champions make their own luck.

Champions have the will to win and the will to prepare to win.

Champions enjoy what they do.

Champions forgive others and themselves.

Champions look for the significant and ignore the insignificant.

Champions hit targets others don't see.

Champions are willing to listen to crazy ideas.

Champions _____

Champions _____

Champions _____

Champions _____

Complete the blank lines with insights from your own life.

Chapter 10
Turn Goals Into Gold, Gold, Gold

At the Moscow Olympics, an Australian television commentator, Norman 'Nugget' May, screamed 'It's gold, gold, gold' every time Australia won another gold medal in swimming. The expression has stuck in my mind ever since. One gold isn't enough. You can reach out for gold medals throughout your life, one after another. There are a huge number of life events you can enter and win. But, how, how, how? The simple answer is you have to have goals, goals, goals!

I once heard a soccer coach being interviewed by the press. He was asked, 'What are your goals for the upcoming season?' He smiled and replied, 'The only goals I think about are the ones that go in the back of the net'. A member of his team later told me the coach had very detailed goals planned for each part of the year. This coach surprised many by the results he was able to achieve. How can you plan your own goals? Listen to a superb comment that comes, second-hand, from American leadership guru, Warren Bennis.

I wake up every morning determined both to change the world and have one hell of a good time. Sometimes this makes planning the day a little difficult.

It's a great start to know what's important, what's significant in your life. I found a beautiful way to open up this question from the book, *Tuesdays With Morrie*. It's the true story about Morrie Schwartz, a psychology professor, who was dying from the painful Lou Gehrig's disease. Morrie was about to be interviewed on American television, but before agreeing to take part, he asked his distinguished interviewer, Ted Koppel, a question hidden within a surprising request, 'Tell me something close to your heart'. Ted and Morrie quickly went from complete strangers to close friends. What would you tell Morrie if he asked you?

Time can make a huge difference to what you think is important. What we felt was important when we were children, is now long forgotten. But your future? What will be important in your future? There's an exercise I learnt from an NLP trainer that I've used many times to help clients discover goals that weren't previously thought of. Interested? Read only the rest of this paragraph, and follow the simple steps, before you read onto the next paragraph. Stand up, eyes closed, think about your future, where you might be, what you're doing. After this becomes clearer and clearer, lift one of your hands and point to the direction of your future.

You had many possible directions to point to. Forward, over your shoulder, straight above your head, to your left or right, down to the ground. My clients have shown all these and many other in-between combinations. So, what's the point? (Sorry about the cheap pun.) When you're having difficulties identifying your goals, otherwise known as your possible future, it helps to stand up and repeat this exercise. If it does not initially help, slowly drop your hand and then again point in the direction of your future. This simple activity has loosened many minds.

Do you want to end up like a fossil?

Do you remember the first big, really big question I fired at you in this book? It was, 'How will you leave your mark on this planet?' I had just described the precious fossils I find on many of my runs, and each of these fossils has left a mark lasting more than 200 million years. The animals that left the fossils were brainless and spineless. So imagine what a great mark you can leave. I painted this scenario for a group of managers and one of them called out, 'That's scary!' I don't think so, do you? For me, it's always a truly eye-opening challenge.

Your goals are important signposts for where you're heading in life, but you need to discover more about yourself. What pathway are you on, right now? Where are you heading and, take a deep breath, do you really want to be heading in this direction? Will you be proud of the pathway you follow in your life? Will you be proud of the tracks you've left along your pathway? Many people find their answers too late in their lives. Let's dig deeper right now.

I encourage all my clients to do some time travel, to help them find answers to the challenge inspired by my fossils. Time travel is a lot easier than it sounds. Just look up in the night skies and you're seeing images of stars as they were hundreds of millions of years ago. It's also easy to jump into the future if you use your imagination the right way. I'm giving you three free tickets to visit your future.

Here's the first ticket. How would your career and life change if you were given a million dollars? The answer to this question immediately tells some people they have the wrong jobs. A few years ago I spoke at a high school, and the first five teachers who volunteered their answers to this question all said the same thing. What do you think they said? They all said they'd quit their jobs, immediately! The principal of the school didn't see anything wrong with their responses. This told me that this wasn't an outstanding school. The five teachers, and probably many more, had no passion for their careers. No passion, no success.

The afternoon knows what the morning never suspected.

Swedish proverb

Now for your second ticket. Imagine you're celebrating your 100th birthday! A businesswoman at one of my seminars said she absolutely dreaded the idea of being 100 years old. Her image involved being withered, frail and helpless. My image for you at 100 is healthy, alert and active. People have come from all over the world to celebrate with you. You're surrounded by the most important people in your life, many of whom you love. You can hear everything everyone is saying about you, privately and publicly. What would you like to hear them say? What are the highlights of your life, in your first 100 years?

This can be a very emotional exercise and I get far better results than talking about obituaries and what you want engraved on your gravestone. I have livened up groups with an exercise to dream up humorous gravestone messages. I start off the discussion with examples given by three celebrities.

Comedian Spike Milligan wanted 'I told you I was sick'. His family followed this request, but not his wish to be buried in a washing machine! Actor

Dustin Hoffman likes 'I knew this was going to happen' and billionaire Ted Turner's choice is 'I have nothing else to say'.

How would humour change the final summary of your life?

Three ways to look into your future

Imagine something **exciting.** You have become an instant millionaire. You've just been given one million dollars. What do you do?

1. _____
2. _____
3. _____
4. _____
5. _____

Imagine something **slightly bizarre.** You're celebrating your 100th birthday! You can hear everything everyone is saying about you. These are the most important people in your life. How would you like them to describe your life?

1. _____
2. _____
3. _____
4. _____
5. _____

Imagine something **dramatic.** You've just been told you have a year to live. What would you do in the next 12 months?

1. _____
2. _____
3. _____
4. _____
5. _____

I'll now hand you the third ticket to help you look into your future. What would you do if you were told you had one year to live? Or five, or 10 years?

Once I was working with a struggling team, and I asked them what they would do if they had one year to live. There were some great answers, but there also were a few terrible ones. These players said they'd get drunk nearly every day and seduce as many women as they could find. The coach stood alongside me at the end of the session and simply said, 'These are not quality people. These are the players who often don't follow my instructions.' He was so impressed that I could discover this group by just asking one question. The team came last in the competition that year, and most of the players who gave selfish answers soon left the club.

Be really smart with your goals!

All my questions might have left you slightly confused. That's okay, in fact, that's excellent because, the first step in learning is confusion. I borrowed those words of wisdom from John Dewey, the great American educator and philosopher. Let's get less confused by looking at the big picture, the basic components of all successful goal setting.

Smart people have goals, and the key word is SMART.

S stands for specific. Vague goals give vague results. It's as simple as that.

M gives you measured. If you can view your goal as something you can count, time or check off, you know exactly how successful you have been. It's not always possible, but with a bit of ingenuity, you can keep a score in many life events as well as sports events.

A equals affirmative. Some goals are headed in the wrong direction when they focus on reducing negative behaviour. Examples like 'I want to make less mistakes' and 'I want to be less nervous when I speak', paint the wrong pictures. Affirmative goals are those described in a positive way. Other alternatives for the A-component are 'achievable' and 'attainable'. I've scrubbed them from my vocabulary and so should you.

R in my system stands for recorded instead of a popular alternative 'realistic'. I'd like to shoot a lot of bullet holes in that word. Pessimists often defend themselves by arguing they are only being realistic. My position is summed up by the former Israeli Prime Minister, Ben-Gurion. He once said, 'Anyone who does not believe in miracles is not a realist'. I encourage my clients to reach for the sky and shoot for the stars. A beautiful photo I have in my office sums up my argument. It shows two people abseiling down one of the pylons of the Sydney Harbour Bridge. They're about 10 storeys from the ground. So what? The photo is special for me because one of the abseilers is in a wheelchair. People achieve goals that are often described by others as amazing, surprising and even miraculous. Throw the word 'realistic' out of your vocabulary.

Let's get back to **R** for recorded. Often the difference between first and second place in sport is only a few centimetres, or a tenth of a second. Such incredibly small amounts. Athletes train so hard to attack these small amounts. But there's a small very light object that many athletes have a phobia about using. They refuse to pick up a pen and use it. World champions like sprinter Michael Johnson, praise the power of the pen. Writing your goals down is like planting seeds of success. Make your goals germinate on paper, or on your computer screen.

The **T** in SMART is time-tabled. Set a completion date. Your subconscious will thank you and offer unexpected support when you do this. It's like knowing the exact day you will start your holidays. Have you ever found extra amounts of energy to complete everything before you took your well deserved break? The same principle works here. That's the full background to successful goal setting. Now you're ready for the step-by-step guidelines, what happens up front.

Why New Year resolutions rarely last till February

These guidelines are successful for the same reasons that new year resolutions usually end up in the garbage bin. Do you know the easiest place to find a parking space? It's outside a fitness centre in February. This is the time when so many new year resolutions often disappear due to lethargy. I can identify two major reasons why these resolutions normally lead to failure. First, they are based on a wipe the slate clean approach. Most people try to forget all of the previous year. Throw out all the failures, all the unsuccessful attempts. What else gets tossed out? There are mini successes mixed in with the big failures. It's hard to go forward when you're always starting from scratch.

The second reason for the quick fade-out for new year resolutions is due to their lack of balance. Most resolutions are solitary. I first recognised that goals are stronger in groups, groups that cover all areas of life, when I read Denis Waitley's *Seeds of Greatness*. Workaholics have very unbalanced goals. They sometimes use this term in a proud way, like a badge of courage. A different label grabs me a lot more. I encourage you to be a 'life-aholic'. That means you are addicted to all areas of your life! It's not just the business world where you find work addictions. Hobbies sometimes grow out of healthy proportions.

Look at the exercise 'My achievements'. This is your springboard to start bouncing on. You can fill in a lot of the spaces if you give yourself about an hour to put the last 12 months of your life on replay. Let the failures, problems and mistakes float away. Instead, grab onto your successes, no matter how small they are. Write all of them down. The next step is very important, so pay close attention. I don't like using 'don't' but this looks like an exception. Don't look at what you have written for at least two days. Let the dust settle. Let your mind sleep on it.

My achievements

In the last 12 months, I achieved the following:

Financial (Income and assets)

_____

_____

_____

_____

_____

Work and career

_____

_____

_____

_____

_____

Physical (Health and fitness)

_____
_____
_____
_____
_____

Relationships (Family and spouse/partner)

_____
_____
_____
_____
_____

Social (Friends and community)

_____
_____
_____
_____
_____

Internal (Educational, recreational and spiritual)

_____
_____
_____
_____
_____
_____

Are you sure you have a balanced view of life?

After you've had a good break, start filling in the exercise 'My future achievements'. I recommend you spend at least four weeks completing it.

One section causes problems for many of my clients. The three areas of internal improvement — educational, recreational and spiritual — are often not considered to be important. This problem doesn't arise if you dig deeper into each of these parts. Many, or maybe most, educational achievements happen away from structured courses in schools and colleges. You can learn plenty from hobbies, building and repairing, television documentaries, newspapers, libraries, the internet and so on. The list is truly endless. Bruce Springsteen was savage when he sang, 'We learnt more from a three minute record than we did at school'. I've worked with many young people who struggled and even suffered through school and, unfortunately, they share Springsteen's sentiments. Take a bigger look at your education and make sure it's a life-long process.

Education, the best you can get, can come from the most bizarre sources. Here's a personal example. I was driving through the outskirts of Sydney, through an industrial area, and by chance I got stuck behind one truck for several kilometres, before we headed off in different directions. Time spent together was less than five minutes. How did I get educated in such a short period of time? The truck was carrying a dirty, beaten up, rusty dumpster. At a set of lights, we stopped, and I read on the dumpster some graffiti that you could barely see. It said 'God is good'. As I've told you before, I consider myself religious, but I haven't found a single religion that fully satisfies my spiritual desires. This sign, which would probably soon disappear under more dirt and grime, told me so clearly what all religions are based on. It's simply, do good. Drop one 'o' from good and you have it. They're the same. How much good do you do? Be prepared to be educated anywhere and at any time, when you want it.

How can you have recreational achievements? You can, when you know the word is based on recreating yourself. In the Middle Ages only the wealthy could stop working. They went away to recharge inwardly. Recreation had a deeper value than holidays which were all religious festivals. How times have changed. It's not uncommon today to be exhausted after an extended holiday, and be proud of it.

Spiritual achievements can be found with or without religious inspiration. If you're truly inspired, you have achieved spiritual growth. Where can we find this inspiration? When you watch children playing, amusing them-selves, smiling, laughing about the simplest of everyday things, you have a big answer. American therapist, John Bradshaw, has helped millions, based on healing the inner child. Go read his book, *Home Coming,* if you think I'm exaggerating.

I think children can help us in many more ways, especially when we're chasing our goals as adults. When you look at a child, you see the best evi-dence that God hasn't given up on us. Every child tells us there is always hope for the future. The way children behave is very special, they tell us how we should behave, at least sometimes. I found the school that was definitely designed for me. The sign outside said 'Occasional Child Care Centre'. For greater fulfilment in our lives, we should all be occasional children. I can now see the picture of Albert Einstein, grinning from ear to ear, as he spins around on a bike, just for the fun of it. He was a very distinguished profes-sor of physics at the time. If it was good enough for Albert, it's …

My future achievements

In the next 12 months, I will do my best to achieve the following:
Financial (Income and assets)

_____

_____

_____

_____

_____

_____

Work and career

_____

_____

_____

_____

_____

_____

_____

Physical (Health and fitness)

_____

_____

_____

_____

_____

Relationships (Family and spouse/partner)

_____

_____

_____

_____

Social (Friends and community)

_____

_____

_____

_____

Internal (Educational, recreational and spiritual)

_____

_____

_____

_____

_____

_____ (Signature and date)

Finally, right at the bottom of the page is space for your signature and date. This sends a message to yourself that you are signing a very important contract, a contact with yourself!

Everything you've ever wanted to do with your goals!

What do you do now? Where do you go from here? You've got a page crammed with future achievements and there's a good chance you're confused or uncertain, again. I hope you are, because we'll replace any uncertainty with excitement. Plenty of others have been exactly where you are right now. Nearly everyone who does this exercise builds up a minimum of 60 achievements to target in 12 months. Having so many goals will give you far more successes than putting all your eggs in one basket, or even a handful of baskets. Having all these goals gives you plenty to think about.

To organise your thinking and add some high octane energy, I've got a simple six-step plan for you to follow. Use the exercise 'Goal attack plan' for each one of your future achievements.

Goal attack plan

Step 1: Clear picture of my goal

Step 2: Benefits, advantages and rewards when I reach my goal

Step 3: Obstacles to get around

Step 4: Everyone who will help me

Step 5: 10 pathways I'll take to reach my goal

Step 6: Celebration date

Let me explain why this plan is so successful.

Step 1: Clear picture of my goal. More details means greater clarity. An example I use a lot in my seminars is about the family home. Instead of simply thinking you want a comfortable home, you make this goal far more vivid and enticing with details like, 'a well built, energy efficient two-storey house in a quiet street, with solar heating, a short walk to a secluded beach or bushland, with three spacious bedrooms, a large garage with lots of room for messy hobbies, with a cosy fireplace'.

The detailed picture of your goal should give the same inspiration that you get when you discover a tremendous mission statement. These are popular with most businesses, and many have attracted criticism, sometimes deserved, because they can overflow with vague generalisations or can be cut to the bone. I found a collection of inspiring guidelines that skilfully mixes clarity with emotion. It's the gold standard given to employees at a hotel chain.

The Ritz-Carlton Hotel is a place where the genuine care and comfort of our guests is our highest mission. We pledge to provide the finest personal service and facilities for our guests who will always enjoy a warm, relaxed yet refined ambience. The Ritz-Carlton enlivens the senses, instils well-being, and fulfils even the unexpressed wishes and needs of our guests.

I think that's brilliant. You can find shorter summaries of goals that contain as much, or even more power. My favourite school motto belongs to a Catholic college in Sydney, 'Forming Strong Minds and Gentle Hearts'. Make sure each description of every one your goals contains a big dose of passion.

Step 2. This step is missing from most goal programs and that's exactly why many goal programs aren't successful. We all need encouragement and excitement to create perseverance to reach our goals. When you list your **Benefits, advantages and rewards** you're encouraging and exciting yourself. Give yourself lots of space and use it all.

Step 3. Spend a little time on the **Obstacles to get around**. Remember obstacles are easier to get past than barriers. Unfortunately, I've found too many people sink their goals by wallowing amongst their obstacles. Practise diving over them.

Step 4: Everyone who will help me. This step is another one to encourage and excite you. You'll be surprised how many people are ready to help you, everyone from long-term mentors to brief acquaintances. There will be many prospective helpers who you have never met. That means you have to find them and approach them. You might not know their names but you can get lots of clues from titles such as non-fiction editor, senior human resource manager, and one of my favourites, personal assistant. PAs are often very willing to listen to you and point you in valuable directions.

Step 5: 10 pathways I'll take to reach my goal. Like an athlete ready for a huge effort, you're now fully stretched and warmed up. You're ready for the action. However, there's an image you need to throw away before you start sprinting. Success is not like running along a single road. Instead, it's like you're travelling along a whole lot of pathways at the same time. I want you to plan 10 separate routes to travel along. Describe 10 separate courses of action that will guide you to your final destination, what you want to achieve. Maybe you won't get to the end of some of your pathways, but that doesn't matter. The combined effect of all these pathways will be success.

Step 6. Words can be like weapons, they can cut and wound. One of the least helpful words in goal setting is deadline. Think about it. Look at my uplifting alternative — **Celebration date**. Now go for it!

When you reach your first achievement using this 10-pathway model, something special happens. You become part of a much bigger process. There's a Zen poem that tells us what it's all about.

> *The great path has no gates.*
> *Thousands of roads enter it.*
> *When you pass through this gateless gate*
> *You walk freely between heaven and earth.*

Aaron McMillan is a young Australian pianist who is quite remarkable for several reasons. Two days after he had surgery to remove a brain tumour, he was playing beautifully on television. His neurosurgeon, Dr Charlie Teo, was then interviewed about this spectacular transformation. Dr Teo said something so profound, I couldn't get it out of my head. After describing Aaron's recovery as miraculous, Dr Teo passionately said about Aaron 'He's here for a purpose'. He is, so am I, and so are you! We're all here for a purpose, not to follow a fixed pathway set by fate, but any pathway we believe will satisfy our purpose in life. So many are lost, because they have given little or no time to study this word. I've written this chapter, and this book, to help you see your purpose. Keep looking at your purpose and how you're going to leave your mark that someone might find in 200 million years.

The purpose of life is to find out 'Who am I?', 'Why am I here?' and 'Where am I going?'

George Harrison (Musician and student of life)

Chapter 11
You're Already Outstanding!

Ever won a huge lottery? No? Well, I've got some great news. You have ... at least twice. The first time you won was in the first microsecond you were conceived, when your unique combination of genetics was created. The odds of that happening were astronomical. But you're here!

We have to come closer to the present for another exciting lottery win. I found a news item that seems to have slipped under nearly everyone's radar. As soon as I picked up this discovery I started sharing it with hundreds of amazed high school students. Here it is. In the very first week of 2002, an asteroid, a 300-metre-wide rock, travelling at 30 kilometres per second came flying at us, and as you've probably guessed, it missed us, but it was very, very close. It flew between us and the moon. If this asteroid had travelled in a slightly different direction for just five hours, it would have slammed into Earth. For astronomers, an asteroid coming that close is nearly regarded as a hit on Earth, and this only happens once in 100,000 years! In 2004, NASA scientists were very worried about a 500-metre-wide asteroid but it eventually missed us by 12 million kilometres, about 32 times the distance to the moon.

If you thought the asteroid crater in Arizona was huge, this will shake you. The asteroid that created the American crater was really a baby. It was only 40 metres across. Back in 1908, an asteroid that was about 100 metres wide wiped out 2,000 square kilometres in Siberia. If the 2002 rogue rock had hit us, it would have been goodbye to many cities, either through direct damage, flooding by tsunamis, or massive changes in our weather. Wherever you are right now, I'd like you to have a quick look at the sky. If it's blue, imagine it totally blackened with asteroid debris. Now, fully enjoy and appreciate the beauty of that blue sky. But, go a step further and let your appreciation expand, so that you realise your life is the most precious prize you have, or will ever win in any of life's many lotteries.

How precious life is became even clearer to me a couple of years ago. Synchronicity struck me again, separated by just three days. I met two remarkable people, two beautiful people, beautiful in a very special way. They are both cancer survivors, cancer beaters, celebrators of life.

I bumped into a woman I hadn't seen for at least a decade. She was dedicated to counselling other women with cancer. Her commitment had been recognised as she was given the honour of carrying the Olympic torch when it travelled around Australia prior to the 2000 Olympics. I'll not forget something from our meeting. Her eyes glowed with sincerity as she told me that cancer had helped her to see her life more clearly.

Three days later I was introduced to a man who had been told 12 years before our meeting, that he had three months to live. Instead of lying down and letting his life escape, he began a quest to learn how to beat cancer, using nature's gifts. Now he freely shares his vast knowledge. After our meeting I drove for three hours to return home. Even though I do a lot of long-distance driving, I often arrive home tired and sometimes drained. Not this time! I got home full of energy and excitement. What does that tell you? Enthusiasm for life is truly contagious.

Over the last few years, I've set out to spend more time with high school students who lack this enthusiasm. These young people are proud to say 'I'm bored'. Many are bored with school, but worse than that, many are bored with their lives. I regularly ask school groups to put up their hands if they're proud of themselves. Few hands go up. That's my cue to become energised and make the best use of the hour I'm given to lift their levels of personal pride. When that goes up, so does enthusiasm for life. I like to stir up these audiences with three insights, two are true, and the other one, I'll let you make up your mind.

One school subject that's usually high up on the unpopularity ratings is maths. Many hands shoot up when I ask, 'Who doesn't like maths?' Nearly all of those hands go up again when I enquire 'Who's not good at maths?' My reply is that they're all wrong, because everyone in the audience is a mathematical genius. By the way, so are you. I'll quickly prove it. Every morning you solve a super complicated puzzle. Count how many pieces of clothes you put on when you got dressed this morning. Include your watch or any jewellery you put on. What total did you get? A common answer is eight. If you counted eight, there are more than 40,000 combinations of getting dressed. If you got nine, there are over 360,000 possible ways of getting dressed. For 10, there are 3.6 million different combinations. For 11 items, you're faced with nearly 40 million different ways of getting dressed! My disenchanted students start to see that they should be proud of themselves. So, as you get dressed every day for the rest of your life, say to yourself … 'It's easy to be successful, because I'm a genius'.

The second surprise comes when I tell the students they're all multimillionaires, because they each own property worth millions of dollars. Where? The invaluable assets are our bodies. An Australian woman was awarded 13 million dollars for life-long injuries that occurred at her birth. What would you prefer? Thirteen million dollars in your bank account or a healthy body?

My next insight immediately receives a lot of snickering. A team of anthropologists has just finished an intensive 10-year study, looking at faces all around the world, and they came up with an amazing fact. They found that one out of every three people is either sensationally beautiful or incredibly handsome. Everyone in my audience is asked to look sideways and closely study the person sitting on the left, and then the person on the right. By now, there's considerable giggling, even when I do this exercise with business executives or rugged footballers. I now show my mind-reading skills, 'Some of you might be thinking you didn't see anyone sensationally beautiful or incredibly handsome. If that's true, then the one out of every three, must be … '

Accept the challenges I put to my student audiences. Realise and appreciate the gifts you've been given. First, you're very lucky to be alive. Second, you've been given a brain that helps you solve complicated problems every day of your life. Third, you have millions of dollars worth of assets. Lastly, and smile as you read this, you're so good looking!

Take a crazy look at your career

Those who are disgruntled, dejected and depressed at their jobs don't know about the outstanding things going on around them at their workplaces.

In my team-building seminar with business clients, I ask if anyone would be happier if their full-time occupation was in sport. Many eyes light up and a few heads usually nod. Then I hit them with the exercise 'Careers and sports'. See if you can find the same challenges of sport in the dozen careers I've selected.

Careers and sports

Match the following careers with the appropriate sport: Accountant, chef, cleaner, dentist, doctor, gardener, journalist, librarian, manager, politician, receptionist, salesperson.

1. Basketball _____
2. Orienteering _____
3. Bowling _____
4. Caving _____
5. Fencing _____
6. Cricket _____
7. Fishing _____
8. Synchronised swimming _____
9. Rock and roll wrestling _____
10. Soccer goalie _____
11. Surfing _____
12. Gymnastics _____

Like so many mind-stretching exercises, there is no rigid set of answers. Creativity gives the best answers. This is how I see the dozen careers have links with sports.

Basketballers get paid to pick up things and dump them. So do cleaners. When librarians go searching the aisles and shelves to find a book, they show plenty of orienteering skills. Bowlers and accountants have their heads down while they still keep a close eye on plenty of changing numbers. Doctors and caving enthusiasts spend a lot of time looking into holes, whereas fencers and dentists excel in prodding with sharp instruments. Managers do plenty of the ducking, weaving, running and chasing that cricketers do. A good salesperson can catch a client without a hidden fishing hook. Politicians like to champion individuality and free speech, but in parliament they often look and sound like synchronised swimmers. What you see and hear from some journalists can be twisted versions of reality, just like rock and roll wrestlers. A soccer goalie is constantly stopping and blocking things from going in and getting past, like a dedicated receptionist. Besides both being in the fresh air, surfers and gardeners also get tattooed by the sun. I know very little about gymnastics except that a complicated routine can be ruined in that last critical ending. A meal from a chef can suffer the same fate.

Now you know cleaners are really playing basketball, librarians don't need an orienteering compass to make their discoveries, accountants can be as excited as tenpin bowlers getting a strike, and on it goes. Maybe your career avoided this analysis, or roasting. Well, do something about.

What do you do for a living?

You meet someone for the first time, maybe at a party, and it's likely you'll be asked this quick ice-breaker. I get some strange looks when I answer. I look forward to the responses. My automatic reply is that I do so many things I can't keep track of them all. We all do lots of things, but many of these things are blurred because we often only look at our careers in the same old ways. There's a very quick way of looking differently at your job, your work or your business. You can look at yourself from all different directions at the one time. It's my own version of a 360 degree review. It will also tell you how important your job is to you.

The next diagram probably looks like a landing field for aliens in Peru. I call it a 'Work review wheel'. Close your eyes and ask yourself, 'What do I do?' Start your answer by saying 'I ...' and then let your subconscious mind send quick images. Listen for one- or two-word responses. Write your first answer at the end of any spoke and then go right around the circle, adding extra descriptions. To boost your perception you might need to regularly close your eyes. The words motivate, communicate, influence and improve are already there to give you a flying start. That's because we all fill these roles every day of our lives. Motivate means 'to move'. You get yourself going every day. If you didn't, you're not alive. You also help to get others going, whether you give someone instructions or just a brief smile. Humans are born to motivate. I hope you've guessed the next link. You have to communicate to motivate. On the other hand, you influence and improve whenever you motivate yourself or someone else. Go to it! Come back and I'll share some of the answers I've collected from others who have already done this exercise.

Work review wheel

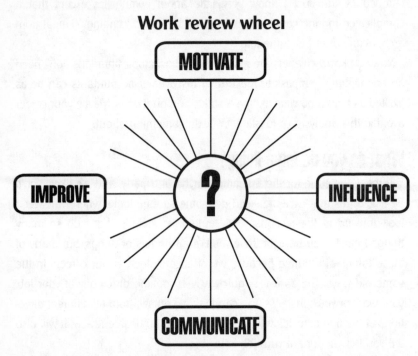

Here's a sample of the outstanding range of answers I've heard from my clients: guide, organise, change, inspire, analyse, experiment, empower, facilitate, evaluate, judge, develop, question, observe, help, provide opportunity, educate, extend, reflect, support, protect, mould, criticise, strengthen beliefs, demonstrate, instruct, explore, praise, lift awareness, counsel, enable, challenge, discipline, resolve conflicts, share, answer, learn, inform, show pride, mentor, listen, plan, lead, encourage, excite, sell ideas and dreams. Wow!

It's an impressive list, and it's even more impressive because I'm certain you've been involved in every one of these activities. If you don't think so, look again at your career. If you don't do these things with others, you do them with yourself! There's a third reason why this list is impressive. It was put together by sports coaches, from many different sports, when I asked them to identify what they did as coaches. Do you see where I'm heading? No matter what your career is, you have opportunities to do exactly the same activities as a sports coach.

You're a coach! What are the images in your mind right now as you think about the word 'coach'? Maybe you see a basketball coach screaming as he strides along the side of the court. Maybe it's a football coach spitting out instructions to his team through the microphone attached to a headset.

Look at the bigger picture. Don Shula holds the title of the most success-ful American football coach of all time. He won more games than any other coach in NFL history. Like all great sports coaches, he is a deep thinker about life, and he has shared many of his insights in his book, *Everyone's A Coach*. This title gives us a powerful message that I strongly support.

Get ready for a huge shake-up. We can do even more things that will put us in the same group with Buddha, Jesus, Muhammad, Mandela, Gandhi, Mother Teresa and John F. Kennedy. They were all great coaches. Are you a great coach?

Great coaching compilation

Great coaches show:
Commitment, Competence, Confidence,
Concentration, Concern, Compassion, Courage

Great coaches:
Communicate, Confer, Consult, Correspond,
Contact, Convene, Confide, Collect, Compare,
Consider, Comprehend, Compute, Confirm, Contribute,
Cooperate, Complement, Collaborate, Coordinate, Concur,
Compliment, Coax, Commend, Congratulate, Comfort, Counsel,
Consolidate, Construct, Correlate, Combine, Connect,

Correct, Confront, Control, Condemn,
Commence, Continue, Complete

Great coaches improve:
Colleagues, Cohorts, Compatriots,
Committees, Coalitions, Congregations, Consortiums,
Councils, Conferences, Congresses,
Companies, Corporations,
Communities

Stand out as a coach!

Isn't that an awesome review? I hope it makes you feel important. Why? You can do all of these things. You can be a coach in everything you do in your life, at work, with your family and friends, with strangers, even driving along a busy street. You have so many opportunities to become a great coach in so many different ways.

Have another close look at our 'Great coaching compilation'. I always tease my audiences by asking them whether they can add any more 'Co-words'. Can you? I've deliberately left off two descriptions. The first is command. This is a favourite of managers who see themselves more as cops than coaches. Yes, sometimes coaches do have to take full command and make people do things they don't want to do. However, 'cop managers' usually use this word in a different context. They argue that they have to command respect. I've never seen that as a logical combination of ideas. You earn respect by your actions. Sometimes I've heard the hidden message when managers tell staff and sport coaches tell teams, 'I demand respect'.

There was a high profile Australian coach who probably believed in the philosophy of commanding respect. This was his recorded greeting on his answering machine, 'Not available at the moment. Leave your name and number, and if you make the cut I'll get back to you. If you don't, well, you'll just have to lift your game'. How does that grab you? The coach had a long career with several peaks of success mixed with episodes of confrontation that preceded his resignations from different clubs. After one public revelation of discontent amongst his players he agreed with the description that he was not a diplomat and prided himself for calling a spade a spade. He then said, 'The flip side of being very direct is that you're also very honest. I like people who are straightforward and direct and honest. We're dealing with men in a tough, professional sport.' Some time later the coach was involved in a physical altercation with a journalist.

I know several coaches who have been praised for being 'brutally honest'. I loathe everything that fits into that description. Sometimes you'll hear the extended version, 'brutally honest, but fair'. One American footballer put this picture in a different frame when he assessed his coach, 'He's fair, all right. He treats us all like dirt.'

A cricketer gave what he thought was a glowing recommendation of his former coach, 'He's a good communicator. He loves winning and doesn't tolerate fools lightly. He's a very reasonable man but very hard at the same time.' Such an image seems rich in contradictions. Labelling others as fools is a habit I find in those who are abrupt and quick tempered. Maybe I'm more aware of some of these contradictions as I once counselled a woman who told me her husband was 'incredibly cruel, but he can be very loving'.

Unfortunately, many people automatically connect compassion with being soft. They should have another look at one of the greatest coaches of the 20th century. Nelson Mandela coached a nation to freedom with compassion and he earned respect from the world. Great coaches command with care, confront with understanding and communicate with sincerity.

I've already mentioned one coach who I admire greatly. Wayne Bennett has been the head coach of the Brisbane Broncos since the club was formed in 1988. In a very moving television documentary on Bennett's personal life, it was clear he was a true father figure to his players. The captain of the team summed up Bennett's coaching principles when he said any player who leaves the Broncos leaves as a better person. Wayne Bennett is a coach who deserves all the respect he receives. Live your life so you earn respect. I think respect is a very special form of love that strengthens everyone who gives and receives it.

I haven't forgotten about the other 'Co-word' missing from the list. Great coaches can improve countries. Mandela did it, so can we all. We're now talking about the wonderful benefits that can flow from improving your own life. My mother told me the following story a long, long time ago.

A small child was given a gigantic jigsaw puzzle based on the map of the world. The parent thought it would keep the child busy for hours. Within a short time, the grinning child proudly told the parent the puzzle was complete. How was it possible? The child had found the reverse side of the puzzle was a picture of a person. After putting the person together, the child flicked over the puzzle to find the map of the world was complete.

You've got courage!

For the first five years that I gave talks to sports groups, I would emphasise the importance of the three Cs in sports success: Confidence, Concentration and Commitment. However, the more I studied and thought about success in sport, as well as everyday life, I realised that this important trio had to be expanded. I saw that a far more emotional human characteristic linked these three concepts. This fourth concept is another C. It's Courage. I love saying this word. It's a great word.

You'll hear me often repeat the following message in my seminars: You can learn big things from little things. You only have to throw away two letters to completely reverse the word 'insignificant'. I had to watch an old movie classic many times before it became very significant to me. There was significance, wisdom, surrounded and hidden by humour, even silliness. Do you remember the cowardly lion from *The Wizard of Oz*? He desperately wanted some courage. Like his fellow travellers in the movie, he achieved his goal simply by learning about himself. He learnt, I've learnt, that courage exists within the spirit of every human being. Once you fully accept this, look out! You will be unstoppable.

This message was hammered home to me after I read two articles in the same newspaper. I confess that I belong to the 'Sports Addicts Club'. We always start reading a newspaper by first looking at the sports section. I was obeying this club rule back in 1998 when I discovered an article with the word courage in the title. Out came the scissors and it went into my file of stories that sports addicts live for. It was about a cricketer who became a temporary hero for all supporters of English cricket. He prevented England from being beaten by South Africa. He batted and batted for three hours, to achieve his career best score. Commentators said his performance was built on courage, it was gutsy and he showed character.

After the sports section was fully devoured I turned to the rest of the paper. There I found an incredibly moving story about more courage, but what a difference! Gabriella Mazzalli, a young English nurse living in Sydney, had 90 per cent of her body burnt when a former friend poured petrol over her and set her alight. She underwent 11 skin graft operations but still dreamed of returning to nursing in England so she could help other burns patients. This story has become a permanent symbol for me. I only have to glance at this story to be reminded of the rich source of courage that exists within all of us.

Gabriella and the cricketer both showed different forms of courage, but for the same reason. They were both placed in positions where courage usually appears — in problems, crises, tragedies. Are they any different from you and me? I don't think so. Imagine asking Gabriella the day before she was burnt, 'Could you cope with five months of agony in a burns unit?' I'm guessing her answer would have been the same as mine. But she did survive because that courage is within us all to help us, especially through terrible times.

One of Australia's greatest coaches taps into this theme when he wants to turn around some of his young players who are down in the dumps and feeling sorry for themselves. Kevin Sheedy, the record setting coach of Essendon Football Club in Melbourne, takes some of his players along to the local maternity hospital. They get a brilliant close-up look at courage. They see premature babies fighting for their lives. I ask my audiences to imagine they are there looking at these tiny babies. Could you pick the baby with the most courage? I bet you couldn't. We are all born with courage within us. I have made this belief the cornerstone of a powerful team-bonding session.

A person with outward courage dares to die.

A person with inward courage dares to live.

Lao-Tzu (Chinese philosopher, 6th century BC)

In the late 1990s there was a lot of controversy about team-bonding sessions in rugby league football. There were headlines screaming about the problems caused by some footballers whilst they were drunk, usually after team-bonding sessions. Some sports clubs, like many big corporations, try to build stronger teams by attacking a wide variety of wilderness survival tasks. They attempt mountain climbing, abseiling, rafting down rivers, riding horses. I've witnessed all of these, taken part in some of them, and I want to give you my personal guarantee. The next session has produced far more impressive results than any of these physically draining sessions. I won't describe it as emotionally draining, it's emotionally uplifting. It's so powerful, because unlike group therapy, you share your strengths, instead of your problems. Expect to shed a tear and get a lump in your throat.

I enjoyed molding this session as it was joint effort with rugby league legend Wayne Pearce. At the time he was coaching the Balmain Tigers who were suffering a string of losses. Their next game was against the best team in the competition, the Brisbane Broncos. We put our heads together and here's what happened.

At a team meeting the players read through the two newspaper articles on courage. Everyone, including Wayne and myself, then briefly described a time in our lives when we showed courage. It started slowly as players began to volunteer. The emotions quickly grew as we started to become aware of the unknown strengths of members of the team. There were a few teary eyes. There were also a lot of laughs. The team did not look like losers in their next game. The Broncos were considered very lucky to escape with a draw.

I soon repeated this session with a major soccer team and got the same results. Their coach was stunned when he told me he had learnt more about his players in the one-hour session than he had learnt over the previous 12 months.

This feeling has been repeated over and over, whether I do the session with sports or business teams. What can you do? Maybe you would prefer to keep your personal life to yourself. That's fine. You'll learn about your strengths by simply recalling your own examples of courage. You might be surprised what you have forgotten. I certainly was. If you want to build stronger bonds with those around you, go ahead and follow the same steps I've described above. Remember, it often takes courage to talk about your own courage. Whichever pathway you decide, you'll be rewarded.

Expect an amazing discovery if you do it with a group. I've found that about one person in 10 has shown courage while saving someone's life! A highlight of my career was the privilege to review the courage of a young team of champions. When I met them, they hadn't yet shown they were champions on the football field. All of us there in the session got an incredible insight into the character of the squad. Out of the group of 20 players, five had saved a life. These were 15-year-old boys who revealed they were special young men. The very next day, they went out and caused a gigantic upset, not just by beating the favourite team, but by flogging them. They won the Australian championship that year.

How smart do you really think you are?

Do you have to be intelligent to be successful, or outstanding? If you think, yes, I'll agree with you if you tell me what intelligence you're talking about. Most people link intelligence to IQ. Do you know what your IQ is? I don't know mine, and I've no interest in knowing what it is. Don't get me wrong, I've got nothing against psychological questionnaires. Psychological tests can be extremely revealing and helpful. I have to say that because I've designed 15 questionnaires myself. One of the most watched programs on Australian television in recent years was the *National IQ Test*. The ratings were huge, the first year it appeared. The second year, even though viewers could take part in a completely different test, interest was much lower. I hope one day we can finally put IQ on the shelf and leave it there as a relic of the 20th century.

Nowadays, at least seven different types of intelligence have been identified. The work of Howard Gardner, a highly respected psychologist at the

Harvard School of Education, has helped to put IQ into its proper place. He split the following seven forms of intelligence: logical-mathematical (that's what IQ mostly measures), linguistic (language smart, more than just knowing a lot of words, it's about being able to communicate), spatial (for art, sculpture, engineering and architecture), musical, kinesthetic (highlighted in sport, dancing and acting), interpersonal (people smart), intrapersonal (self smart).

One of the biggest and most valuable changes in psychology over the last 10 years is the study of emotional intelligence, or EQ. The way I look at EQ is that it's a mixture of people smart, self smart and word smart. There's also a touch of street smart, the ability to think on the run, when you're in difficult situations. Great leaders, whether they're in politics, military, business or sport, all have high levels of emotional intelligence. You quickly become aware that they are emotionally literate — they skilfully use words and actions to build winning relationships, they can win negotiations without dropping bombs on people.

Some are born great, some achieve greatness, and some have greatness thrust upon them.

William Shakespeare

Great leaders such as Gandhi, Mandela, Lincoln and Churchill, all used their emotional intelligence to carry out great changes. Their words and deeds helped them tap into something vast and usually unstoppable, people power. Each could have been described as 'a man of the people'. Each could feel the pulse of his nation.

Unfortunately, few women have been leaders of their countries. Elizabeth I, England's long reigning queen in the sixteenth century, was such a remarkable exception she has been used as a case study of what makes a successful CEO. Initially, she simply inherited enormous political power, but as her reign progressed it transformed into people power. She was not only respected, she was loved by her people. That's the ultimate bond between a leader and his or her followers. However, emotional intelligence can also have a dark side. It should be a measure of caring and understanding of others but sometimes experts at EQ can translate their skills into manipulation. Surely, Adolf Hitler had such incredibly high levels of EQ he was able to disguise many of his immoral motives. So do cult leaders.

What about your EQ? There are strict measures of IQ but EQ is still finding its feet when it comes to measurement. Not surprisingly, the Internet abounds with simplistic tests to measure EQ. On the other hand, there are only a few reputable tests that will tell you a lot about your EQ.

I've constructed my own questionnaire the 'Emotional skills review (ESR)'. When you complete the questionnaire accurately, that means as honestly as you can, you can calculate your own measurements of different components of EQ. They will give you insights that you can use to lift your emotional skills. Many of my clients have gone a step further and asked others to assess them with this questionnaire. Sometimes you have to be brave to learn more about yourself.

Before you head off to assess your emotional intelligence, join in a quick exercise. Take a deep breath and hold it for five seconds. Phew. What did that show you? Every second of your life is breathtaking! You can now add that to all your other outstanding characteristics.

Emotional skills review
Instructions

On the following pages are 60 self-descriptions given by people in a wide range of careers. Please read each statement carefully. Then decide how true each statement is about you. *Circle the number you select.*

Factor 1: Showing and controlling emotions

	Never			Sometimes			Always
1. I get angry with myself when I perform poorly.	7	6	5	4	3	2	1
2. I can talk about my strengths without being embarrassed.	1	2	3	4	5	6	7
3. I use criticisms to learn more about myself.	1	2	3	4	5	6	7
4. When I'm disappointed, I become moody and don't feel like talking.	7	6	5	4	3	2	1
5. I feel comfortable when I ask for help.	1	2	3	4	5	6	7
6. I ignore people when I'm annoyed with them.	7	6	5	4	3	2	1
7. I get frustrated when others don't approve of my work.	7	6	5	4	3	2	1
8. I stay calm and in control even in a crisis.	1	2	3	4	5	6	7
9. I become hostile when someone lets me down.	7	6	5	4	3	2	1
10. I don't like to discuss my failures.	7	6	5	4	3	2	1
11. If I get upset I can quickly identify the reasons why.	1	2	3	4	5	6	7
12. I enjoy talking to large groups.	1	2	3	4	5	6	7
13. I feel very nervous when I'm under pressure.	7	6	5	4	3	2	1
14. I only share my feelings with very few people.	7	6	5	4	3	2	1
15. Others can tell I'm passionate about what I do.	1	2	3	4	5	6	7

Factor 1   TOTAL = [   ]   AVERAGE = [   ]

Factor 2: Emotional thinking — optimism and perseverance

	Never		Sometimes				Always
16. I blame myself for problems before I look anywhere else.	7	6	5	4	3	2	1
17. I bounce back from setbacks.	1	2	3	4	5	6	7
18. I enjoy tough competition.	1	2	3	4	5	6	7
19. I adapt quickly when there are big changes in my life.	1	2	3	4	5	6	7
20. I remember my mistakes more clearly than my successes	7	6	5	4	3	2	1
21. If I say I'll do something, I follow it up.	1	2	3	4	5	6	7
22. I lose motivation when a project looks doomed.	7	6	5	4	3	2	1
23. I try to achieve small realistic goals instead of big dreams.	7	6	5	4	3	2	1
24. I'm willing to take risks to achieve big things.	1	2	3	4	5	6	7
25. I persist with problems after others have given up.	1	2	3	4	5	6	7
26. I worry about my future.	7	6	5	4	3	2	1
27. I can see the funny side of setbacks.	1	2	3	4	5	6	7
28. I am proud of what I'm doing with my life.	1	2	3	4	5	6	7
29. I push myself to do things that others can't do.	1	2	3	4	5	6	7
30. I quickly become bored.	7	6	5	4	3	2	1

Factor 2   TOTAL = ☐   AVERAGE = ☐

Factor 3: Emotional thinking — creativity and problem solving

	Never			Sometimes			Always
31. I jump to conclusions.	7	6	5	4	3	2	1
32. I find creative solutions for problems.	1	2	3	4	5	6	7
33. I make quick decisions that I later regret.	7	6	5	4	3	2	1
34. I like doing things differently.	1	2	3	4	5	6	7
35. I surprise people with my answers to problems.	1	2	3	4	5	6	7
36. I get confused when I'm faced with a lot of problems.	7	6	5	4	3	2	1
37. Daydreaming gives me useful ideas.	1	2	3	4	5	6	7
38. I like following routine procedures.	7	6	5	4	3	2	1
39. I benefit from using my intuition.	1	2	3	4	5	6	7
40. Problems have helped to build my character.	1	2	3	4	5	6	7
41. I can get a clear picture of how something will look long before it is finished.	1	2	3	4	5	6	7
42. I enjoy listening to different opinions.	1	2	3	4	5	6	7
43. I focus on one problem at a time.	7	6	5	4	3	2	1
44. I can get good ideas from a wide range of sources.	1	2	3	4	5	6	7
45. I love studying new and unusual discoveries.	1	2	3	4	5	6	7

Factor 3   TOTAL = ☐   AVERAGE = ☐

Factor 4: Emotional connections —
Caring, sharing and building relationships

	Never			Sometimes			Always
46. If I find an interesting idea, I share it with others.	1	2	3	4	5	6	7
47. I can easily turn strangers into friends.	1	2	3	4	5	6	7
48. I listen carefully to other people's problems.	1	2	3	4	5	6	7
49. I avoid trying to get others to do things differently.	7	6	5	4	3	2	1
50. People enjoy my sense of humour.	1	2	3	4	5	6	7
51. I help groups work more effectively.	1	2	3	4	5	6	7
52. I find it difficult to show affection to those close to me.	7	6	5	4	3	2	1
53. My enthusiasm rubs off on others.	1	2	3	4	5	6	7
54. I treat everyone equally.	1	2	3	4	5	6	7
55. I get poor results whenever I try to resolve conflicts.	7	6	5	4	3	2	1
56. I feel useless when someone cries in front of me.	7	6	5	4	3	2	1
57. I build relationships on trust and mutual respect.	1	2	3	4	5	6	7
58. I refuse to help anyone who seems to be lazy.	7	6	5	4	3	2	1
59. I give positive feedback when someone does a good job.	1	2	3	4	5	6	7
60. I feel uncomfortable when I receive compliments.	7	6	5	4	3	2	1

Factor 4   TOTAL = ☐   AVERAGE = ☐

Chapter 12
Leadership is Like Making Bread

Everyone can be a leader. I've seen faces tighten up when I've made this statement. Many prefer the safety of being a follower. But safety can be like a cocoon, nothing more than a restrictive invisible shell. Leadership is about experiencing the excitement of life at its fullest. Instead of being a burden, it rewards you. When I say this in my seminars my level of activity skyrockets, my pace quickens and hands start to wave. I want you to get excited about being a leader.

If you ask students why they're heading off to universities, chasing higher education degrees, you expect answers like, 'I want to be a doctor, an accountant, a teacher, an engineer', don't you? What if a student stared back at you and said with conviction, 'I want to learn how to be a leader'. We'd know immediately that student was likely to go on to great things. Why don't we hear our youth saying they want to be leaders? I'm blaming the myth of myths, that only the very selective few can be leaders.

I've put together the exercise 'Leaders are ...' to describe many of the different ways I look at leadership. Doesn't it give you a boost too? That's why we should teach our children to all strive to be leaders. That's why you should strive to be a leader. We need more leaders, true leaders. Study the questions I've placed under each view of leadership. Take plenty of time to answer each of them because your answers will tell you something very important. You might be surprised by what you learn. Your answers will tell you how much leadership you show in your life. Opportunities to lead are all around you. Find them!

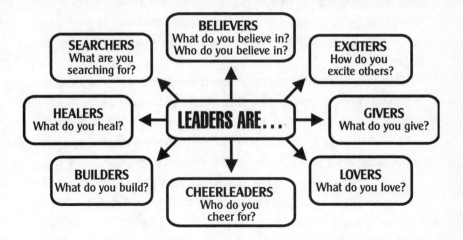

Healers, searchers, believers, exciters, givers, lovers, cheerleaders, builders. What a list! But wait, there's more. There's so much more to learn about leadership when your imagination is released. We can get a lot of help from a business mastermind. Tom Peters is a prolific author and a sensational speaker who finds business insights all over the world, and he frequently comes at you from unexpected directions.

Hold onto your seat, and get ready to be hit by a typical zinger from Tom Peters. He sees a strong link between the three main Hindu gods and business success. The gods are Brahma the Creator, Shiva the Destroyer and Vishnu the Preserver. Tom declares, 'This troika is all you need to know about business'.

I think these three also apply to leadership. Certainly, leaders are creators. Creators are the healers and builders on our list. Gandhi and Mandela were leaders who healed wounds and built new nations.

Can successful leaders also be destroyers? Pablo Picasso, one of the greatest painters of the 20th century, stated that 'Every act of creation is first of all an act of destruction'. I agree with Picasso. His paintings often shocked because he regularly broke conventions. He opened up new approaches to art by breaking old ones.

Maybe you think this image of destroying is too harsh to be linked to a picture of leadership. If you do, consider this. Leaders are definitely changers, internally and externally. They change things around them and they're also strong enough to change their own viewpoints. Sometimes these changes are revolutionary. Sometimes these changes are slow but they can still be powerful.

If leadership is about changing, how is it possible to also be a preserver? Yes, these qualities can co-exist. This frequently happens in the political arena. Australian Prime Minister, John Howard, showed a mixture of destroying and preserving in his political actions. He undertook radical economic restructuring when he turned the taxation system upside down. At the same time, he steadfastly defended his conservative stance on many social issues such as maintaining the English Queen as the Head of Australia.

You know you're in uncertain territory when many describe restructuring as reforms, whilst many others consider the same actions as regressive. British Prime Minister Margaret Thatcher and American President Ronald Reagan also followed dual pathways, mixing conservative and radical policies. Do you?

About now you might have noticed I've strayed into political leadership. I deliberately moved this way to make a big point. I don't admire many political leaders. In fact, I'm slightly uncomfortable using these two words together, political and leaders. I say this with disappointment, not bitterness.

Having power does not equate to being a true leader. Look at the spectrum of politics around the world. We have everything from brutal dictators to mere mouthpieces and figureheads. Someone once said we get the leaders we deserve. Not so! We usually get what we expect. Why do so many Americans not vote in presidential elections? It could be apathy due to ignorance or laziness, or the belief that the candidates are often so poor that little separates their policies. I go for this last explanation. I see another widespread problem in politics. Often, ethics has given way to economics. Balanced budgets are given a much higher priority than helping the poor and disadvantaged.

Before you start thinking I'm doing a good job spreading disillusionment and I'm demotivating you instead of motivating you, here's the good news. We can raise the level of political leadership by expecting more, a whole lot more. We can also do this in areas ranging from business leadership to leadership in families.

In my eyes, politicians and business executives lose their status as leaders when they are fixated on their positions. For them, position equals power. The manager who threatens, 'Do as you're told. I'm in charge' is no different from the parent who bellows, 'Do it because I told you' and the sports coach who declares, 'Don't argue with me. I'm running this show.'

Compare these with the politicians and CEOs who argue, 'We had to take these tough decisions. They were unavoidable.' They all belong in the same basket, and it's not the same basket that contains true leadership.

Power corrupts some. Promotions have produced personality transformations, for the worse. As one wit observed, promotions can be just like a monkey climbing up a rope. The higher it goes, the more you can see its backside.

> *Being in power is like being a lady. If you have to tell people you are, you aren't.*
>
> Margaret Thatcher

Leadership is like enthusiasm, it's contagious. However, so is apathy. Start now by killing some apathy around you by acting like a leader. It's easier than you think. Go back and re-read all the tremendous qualities of great coaches. Remember, you're a coach. You can't go past the high energy characteristics of passion — commitment, competence and confidence, but to be a great leader you need to combine these with the signs of caring leadership — concern, courage and compassion. Re-read your answers to the questions under the different perspectives of leadership, 'What do you give?', 'What do you heal?' and so on. You've already got a lot to work with. Someone will quickly copy you and if that someone is in your family, you will immediately receive rich rewards.

How many teams would want you to lead them?

Failures can still have good, even great, ideas. I learnt a huge idea from an unsuccessful coach. You read that right, he was unsuccessful. He shared this pearl with his team and with me.

Ask yourself, are you the sort of person that everyone wants in their team? I've taken this a step higher with the question above.

Leadership can be seen everywhere because teams are everywhere. They make up families, rock bands, church choirs, street gangs and boards of directors. They connect nurses with doctors, TV reporters with camera crews, pilots with baggage handlers. They're the basis for the police, all branches of the military, as well as political parties and governments. They've also been in the animal kingdom for millions, billions of years. Teams, teams and more teams.

You're a rare person, a hermit, if you don't take part in a team somewhere, sometime. Teams are responsible for our success on this planet and are essential for the survival of our species. So is leadership! You can't have one without the other. Like love, you can't have too much leadership, good leadership. You can be a leader in different teams, all at the same time.

At its best, leadership is a loving act. It is about inspiring others with
the idea that you and they, together, could make this a better world.
Hugh Mackay (Social psychologist and a great Australian)

Why don't we have more great leaders? The first step towards changing this situation is to start using the word leader more often. It's usually hidden under other titles, like manager, and even mum and dad. All three of these titles describe very important leaders. How often are they recognised as leaders?

Some think there's a giant step from management up to leadership? I don't, but one of America's best known investigator of leadership, does! Warren Bennis is a very thoughtful author who has produced a stream of books on leadership. From his interviews with 96 prominent leaders he wrote *Leadership: Strategies for Taking Charge* which became an instant bestseller when it was originally published in 1985. It's recently been updated and republished. Besides being a prolific author, Bennis has been a close adviser to four US presidents. This is someone we can learn something from. You're also allowed to disagree with him. Bennis produced his famous 12-point 'Leadership checklist' that put a huge gap between leadership and management. I believe we are all leaders at different times. A poor manager is a poor leader. Great managers are great leaders, as well as being great coaches. Decide how much you agree with each of Bennis' points.

Leadership checklist

The manager administers; the leader innovates.

The manager is a copy; the leader is an original.

The manager maintains; the leader develops.

The manager focuses on systems and structure; the leader focuses on people.

The manager relies on control; the leader inspires trust.

The manager has a short-range view; the leader has a long-range perspective.

The manager asks how and when; the leader asks what and why.

The manager has his eye always on the bottom line; the leader has his eye on the horizon.

The manager imitates; the leader originates.

The manager accepts the status quo; the leader challenges it.

The manager is the classic good soldier; the leader is his own person.

The manager does things right; the leader does the right thing.

From *Managing People Is Like Herding Cats,* Warren Bennis

How did we get so confused about leadership?

Bennis has summed up a common perception, a misconception, that goes back hundreds of years. You can discover where it started by studying the origin of words. All around the world, managers gain MBAs to lift their qualifications and credibility. However, this qualification still has one foot fixed in the past because it retains the outdated term administration.

Before I go on, I want to digress. Why don't universities take a giant step forward and replace the MBA with an MBL — a Master of Business Leadership? I'd like to see that! Now let's get back to my passion for word analysis. Administration was the dominant word in business before it was replaced by management. Do you know when and why this happened?

Business analyst, John Adair, put leadership into a new light for me when he explained the origin of the words management and its offshoot, manager. The word management is derived from the Latin word *manus*, meaning hand, and entered the English language in the mid-17th century, thanks purely to the military. English soldiers who learned to handle horses at Italian riding schools, brought the word back and it was soon used to deal with a wide variety of things — swords, ships, money, machines. Its first reference to humans applied to soldiers in the English Civil War. It took another 200 years before management also covered employees. So, those managers who like to think of themselves as ruling with an iron fist are certainly rekindling the original spirit of managing powerful war horses.

Studying the origin of words reveals more about the leader at the top of the management tree — chief executive officer or CEO. The word chief simply comes from the Latin word for head, whereas leader comes from a Germanic word meaning 'one who can make someone walk'. I know what I think sounds better. The word officer clearly shows links to the military and it also throws away the sound of passion needed to be a great leader. The term CEO has a permanent footing in business-speak and managers strive to reach this ultimate goal.

That's a massive paradox because the tenure of CEOs is so uncertain and brief. The Business Council of Australia says the average CEO lifespan is around four years. Would CEOs have such a rapid turnover, if they were renamed *chief executive leaders*? Maybe the poor achievements of many CEOs is linked to their salaries. Australian chief executives are the third highest paid in the world and they constantly receive golden handshakes even when they have glorious failures.

Look all around you to discover leadership!

I want you to use your imagination to see many new images of leadership. Imagination and images, that's a powerful combination! Warren Bennis frequently uses this combination. As I've said before, leadership is everywhere, sometimes obvious, sometimes hidden. You will now look for it in some strange places. Your right brain is ready to give you spectacular, maybe even crazy, but always helpful ways of looking at leadership.

Leadership is like making bread. Great leaders can skilfully mix dissimilar ingredients to produce a spectacular transformation. Consider what goes into bread — flour, yeast, sugar, salt and water. Separately, each is fairly bland, even repulsive. Taste some yeast sometime! The ingredients need time to combine, for the yeast to grow. But what results! Nothing can compare to the enchanting smell of bread baking in a home. It's a sign of love and happiness.

Unfortunately, in some hands, leadership is like smoking cigarettes. When leadership becomes a bland addictive habit, it's damaging to your health, and those around you.

Leadership should be like herding cats. Unlike dogs, cats don't respond to threats. You have to approach them with kindness and patience. Why not lead humans this way? Leadership is also like a dictionary. Your leadership can be a valuable resource for others, by providing insights for them to use and develop. Leadership is even connected to body piercing. Leadership can be painful, especially when it's based on temporary fads. Leadership is often negative when it's like a waterfall. Sometimes leaders look and sound impressive, when they're surrounded by lots of fury and spray, but that only diverts attention from a sharp fall in their principles.

Ready for a final shock? Leadership is like pornography. What! It's difficult to paint a clear picture of leadership, to talk about and describe it accurately, but when you see it, you know what it is!

From great, to good, to downright ugly!

Feel dizzy with all these images in your head? No matter how you feel, I know you've been enjoying yourself. That's what mind stretching is all about. I've got a third layer of the leadership cake ready for you to digest. This is a smorgasbord of contemporary leaders, many I admire, some I don't. There's a great deal to be learned by knowing fully why you don't like someone or something.

Let's begin our leadership smorgasbord. Do you want to hear a great story about trust? When Bill Gates, the world's richest man, set up a new Microsoft research centre, he selected a professor of computing to head the massive new project. Here comes the trust. Gates simply gave the professor three lines of instructions:

1. Hire the best people you can find and let them do what they want.
2. If all your projects succeed, you've failed.
3. Get staff from far and wide, not just from around the corner.

Gates' glasses might say 'nerd' or 'geek' to those who are jealous of his achievements but his words say 'leader'. They certainly do! There's something else that says he's a leader. By age 44, he had given away $US 22 billion to help solve some of the world's biggest problems.

Inseparable from trust is telling the truth. Tom Peters puts it at the top of leadership qualities. The whole world is now aware that President Bill Clinton did some semantic side-stepping when he wanted to keep his private life private. In Australian politics, Prime Minister Howard did some word distorting when he introduced the concept of a core promise. He proposed that promises are not binding unless they are a core promise. That's true verbal gymnastics! Many commentators felt his honesty barometer dropped.

Early in the book I introduced you to several Australians who have soared to the highest levels of business success. You can't ignore a CEO named Daft who likes watching the bizarre comedy series, *Fawlty Towers*. It gets even better. When Douglas Daft was in charge of Coca-Cola's operations in Asia, he made *Fawlty Towers* videos compulsory viewing for his staff. This is a great 'Daft Idea' from a very different leader.

He explained, 'If you want to understand life, that's wonderful viewing. You shouldn't take yourself too seriously. If you do, you'll end up like Basil Fawlty.'

That's not daft. Sorry, it's hard to stop the puns when they're so obvious. I would like to meet Doug Daft. He sounds like a very interesting CEO. He also showed he is capable of doing something some leaders can't. He expressed regret for the past actions of his company. Under his guidance Coca-Cola gave over $US 200 million to black employees to settle a racial discrimination lawsuit. Daft sent a memo to Coke employees, 'Today we are closing a painful chapter in our company's history.' I'm looking forward to meeting Doug someday.

Jac Nasser, the Australian who was CEO of Ford Motor Company until his resignation in 2001, had been on the wrong end of some stinging criticism during his leadership tenure. He was grilled by the US Congress about Ford's slow reaction time to respond to a large number of accidents and deaths in one of Ford's most popular models. Defective tyres were blamed. However, he personally answered many phone calls from irate customers about the largest recall in the history of the motor industry. That took guts.

There's a huge distance between tough and brutal. Unfortunately, some leaders act in the brutal end of the spectrum and defend their actions by proudly declaring they were simply being tough. Al 'Chainsaw' Dunlap is a business leader who preaches and practised a philosophy summed up in the title of his autobiography, *Mean Business*. He has commented that if you want a friend, get a dog. He has two dogs. I don't think I'd want him to be a neighbour of mine. When he came to Australia he gave the following advice to the young media mogul, James Packer, 'If you worry about those whose feelings you hurt, you will fail'. Dunlap is now paying off millions of dollars in corporate fines in the United States for his illegal behaviour throughout the 1990s.

Back in Australia, I saw a seminar promoted as *Leading Women: Insights Into the Careers of High Achievers*. One of the speakers revealed her secret for success — 'It's more important to be respected when you lead a company than to be liked'.

This is an insight I don't like hearing. I've also heard this message from other corporate heads but I still believe it's shallow advice. It seems they're trying to split invisible hairs. I've never met anyone who I respected and didn't like as well. Have you?

I'll back my viewpoint with a sports anecdote. Read the following inscription on a plaque given to Tom Landry, after his retirement as the long-time coach of the Dallas Cowboys football team.

> We cherished the victories, we down-played the defeats but we always admired the Cowboys' coach for his pursuit of excellence, and his uncommon grace, both on and off the field.

Impressed? You should be. The plaque came from the Washington Redskins, the greatest rivals of the Dallas Cowboys. When you admire your main adversary for his 'uncommon grace', of course you're going to like the man.

Those who subscribe to the philosophy that being liked is an unnecessary part of leadership are very likely to be frequent users of the line, 'Nothing personal'. You can absolve yourself of any contemptible action with this sure fire defence. Not really. It only works if you don't care about being disliked. It only works if you don't care about the personal consequences of your actions, you don't care that others might be hurt.

Leadership and learning are indispensable to one another.

John F. Kennedy

Fortune magazine gave Jack Welch an outstanding tag when they called him the *Manager of the Twentieth Century*. It's easy to pinpoint the reason for the long-term success of Welch, Chairman and CEO of General Electric, an organisation with 350,000 employees. He had the courage to change his outlook to life when he left his bitter 'Neutron' Jack face back in the 1980s. His nickname came from the bomb that killed all life and left buildings empty and completely untouched. It seemed an appropriate name for someone who cut 100,000 workers at GE.

However, he became famous for getting out of the ivory tower and even taught classes to thousands of his GE employees. Finally, he did something often unheard of amongst leaders. Instead of hiding his mistakes, he highlighted them. He argued, 'It's great for me because I can talk to employees all the time and say if your chief executive can make the biggest mistake the company has ever made, you shouldn't be too frightened to have a swing'.

That word honesty keeps appearing when you talk about successful leaders, doesn't it? As you might expect I prefer a more accurate version for Welch's award from *Fortune* magazine. It would be *Business Leader of the Twentieth Century.*

However, there are many other serious contenders and my nomination would be Akio Morita. When you read about his philosophy and his achievements I'm certain you'll be captivated like I was when I first became aware of this remarkable man.

Ricardo Semler is an extremely successful businessman, a multimillionaire in Brazil, and he's put together his own formula for leadership in his latest book, *The Seven-Day Weekend*. I think he's on the right track.

His formula is:

$$\text{Leadership} = IQ + EQ + SQ - Ego$$

I'd replace IQ with JQ, the technical knowledge and skills of a particular job. We've previously talked about EQ, emotional intelligence. Semler invented SQ for spiritual intelligence or awareness.

Ego, the concept attributed to Sigmund Freud, has many negative connotations. How we normally look at ego can be summed up by a single observation. Brian Gilbertson, the ex-CEO of BHP Billiton lasted only six months in his job. Before transferring from South Africa to run the worldwide company, he had a reputation for abrasiveness, which is often a sign of low EQ. Whenever his helicopter landed at his head office in Johannesburg, the staff catch cry was 'The ego has landed'. The ego quickly crashed.

There's another CEO who proudly declared, 'I don't get stressed. I give stress.' His ego hasn't crashed — yet.

Kill my boss? Do I dare live out the American dream?

Homer Simpson

What makes a great leader?

Look closely at each of the following important human qualities. Select the top 10 characteristics that you think are necessary to be a great leader.

AMBITIOUS	CREDIBLE	INDEPENDENT
APPROACHABLE	DEPENDABLE	INSPIRING
BROAD-MINDED	DETERMINED	INTELLIGENT
CARING	ECCENTRIC	LOYAL
CHEERFUL	FAIR-MINDED	MATURE
COMPETENT	FORWARD-LOOKING	OPTIMISTIC

CONFIDENT	FRIENDLY	SELF-CONTROLLED
COOPERATIVE	HELPFUL	SINCERE
COURAGEOUS	HONEST	STRAIGHTFORWARD
CREATIVE	IMAGINATIVE	SUPPORTIVE

TOP 10 CHARACTERISTICS	SELF-RATING (Poor/Fair/Good/Excellent)
1	
2	
3	
4	
5	
6	
7	
8	
9	
10	

Leaders need to have extra awareness, or to be surrounded by those who can provide important insights, into anything, from boots to weapons of mass destruction. In 1989, President George Bush gave a gift of cowboy boots to Chinese Premier Li Peng. That was a bad idea, an uniformed idea.

On one boot was the flag of the USA, and on the other was the flag of China. In China, anything connected or associated with the feet is considered unclean.

Then in 2003, President George W Bush didn't sample any *matooke* on his whirlwind tour of Africa. *Matooke* is the east-African word for food. The president brought his own chefs, and therefore missed several opportunities to bond with his hosts. Most Africans regard eating a meal provided by your host as a significant compliment and a true sign of affection. Somebody in the president's team didn't do their job properly. But then again, another American president, Harry Truman, once accepted final responsibility when he stated 'The buck stops here'.

How aware are you of special opportunities? Do you see the potential not seen by others, the possibilities ignored by others? Tigers Woods starred in an outstanding TV commercial where he bounces a golf ball off his club, again and again, through his legs, behind his back, and then flicks it into the air and belts it down the golf course. It went several shades past impressive. What the viewing public didn't suspect was everything was real, there were no computer tricks. Here's the link to leaders who have their eyes, or ears to the ground. The commercial was also totally unplanned. Tiger was waiting to film something when the director saw him having fun playing with the ball. It was so natural for Tiger they were able to film the sequence in less than 20 minutes. Who knows what happened to the original commercial. That director was a leader.

All leaders should be mentors, and have mentors. Do you have a mentor? Most of mine have been second-hand, via books. A much bigger question is 'Do you mentor others?'

Mentoring is now a buzzword in executive training courses. Typically, CEOs are encouraged to groom a subordinate for the future. This interpretation of mentoring misses so much.

When you become aware of the background of the very first mentor, you'll see the full power of mentoring. Mentor was a good friend of Odysseus in the ancient Greek epic, *The Odyssey*, written in the 8th century BC. He was chosen to protect and tutor Odysseus' young son, Telemachus, when

Odysseus sailed off for a 10-year adventure. Athena, the goddess of wisdom and counselling, took on the identity of Mentor and guided Telemachus to eventually find his lost father. This story tells us mentoring is much more than grooming an heir apparent for ongoing organisational stability. Mentoring is love in action.

If you want one year of prosperity, grow grain.
If you want 10 years of prosperity, grow trees.
If you want 100 years of prosperity, grow people.

Chinese proverb

When you think about success, do you think about Napoleon? You should! You probably associate Napoleon with his final defeat at Waterloo. But there was so much more to this leader, who ranged from an arrogant dictator to a humanitarian reformer. He had so many brilliant military successes all over Europe. Much of this success was based on a single rule that inspired every French soldier who fought for Napoleon. This was the rule. No French soldier would ever be left wounded on the battlefield. Whereas other armies abandoned their wounded, who were often then killed by the enemy, every French soldier knew he would be rescued by his comrades. Each soldier knew he was important, each soldier knew that this rule showed Napoleon cared about all of his troops. This certainly led to many brave acts plus a long-lasting devotion to Napoleon. The Duke of Wellington said this of his archrival Napoleon, 'I would at any time rather have heard that a reinforcement of 40,000 men had joined the French army than he had arrived to take command'. When your enemy gives you such glowing praise, it's likely to be very accurate.

You can study leadership anywhere, from any time. Have a good look at St Francis of Assisi. One of his contemporaries said this in 1228: 'He used to view the largest crowd of people as if it were a single person, and he would preach fervently to a single person as if to a large crowd.' He made people feel they were important to him.

Why leaders are never gods!

Too many leaders are elevated to god-like status. When Steve Waugh finished his reign as Australian cricket captain, he was front page news, everywhere in Australia. He came close to being deified. We must remember no leader is without faults. They all have feet of clay.

Beware of the adulation of leaders, whether they are in sport, politics, music, or whatever. Steve Waugh certainly showed tons of mental and physical toughness throughout his career and he also showed great humanity by sponsoring a school for lepers in India. However, he still isn't a saint. Many cricket fans felt he condoned or encouraged the practise of verbally abusing players on other teams. Worldwide television audiences saw the ugly side of Australian sport. His team and supporters justified their actions by claiming everything should be left on the field. They said it makes cricket more colourful. They call it trash talk in basketball, sledging in cricket, but the Australian team elevated and encouraged it as a tactic for the mental disintegration of their opponents. Steve Waugh led one of the most successful teams of all time, winning a host of championships, but he also led a team that often behaved like chumps. In a *Spirit of Cricket* lecture, all-time great, Sunil Gavaskar, lamented that most of the international cricketers who use verbal abuse were in the one side. Guess who he was talking about.

Winston Churchill, sometimes called the saviour of Western civilisation, was willing to 'drench Germany with poison gas'. Mandela was seen to definitely prickle when he was asked in an interview whether he ignored the AIDS problem during his time as South African President. He defended himself, saying there were so many important issues to deal with. Soon after the interview he promoted a gigantic concert to help the one in nine South Africans infected with HIV.

Rudy Giuliani was seen by the whole world as the mayor of New York who stood amongst the carnage of the September 11 attacks, supporting and encouraging rescuers, comforting the grieving. He was later voted *Person of the Year,* and then authored the best-selling book, *Leadership.* Another side was then revealed during his divorce, as he was forced to admit he had been 'cruel and inhuman' to his wife. I wouldn't put those in my *Top 1000 Leadership Characteristics*. Forces are gathering to promote Giuliani as a future American president.

When Jack Welch, the giant at General Electric retired, his company agreed to keep paying the monthly rent of $US 80,000 for his New York apartment, as well as collect and clean all his laundry, and deliver flowers every week. Is this a case of justifiable benefits, or a pig with it's snout in the trough?

Mother Teresa couldn't possibly have any flaws, could she? A film critical of her inability to make any significant changes in the public health conditions in Kolkata, was withdrawn from a film festival in India after it was opposed by the Missionaries of Charity, the order of nuns founded by Mother Teresa. The film, *Hell's Angel,* was based on the work of investigative journalist Christopher Hitchens. He claimed Mother Teresa concentrated on comforting, instead of attacking and healing the core of the constant problems.

Two of Australia's sports coaches — former Hockeyroo coach, Ric Charlesworth, and Wallabies coach, Eddie Jones — have much in common. They have both coached international teams to high levels of success, and they share the belief that being obsessive is an essential ingredient for out-standing success. I'm with sports writer Peter Fitzsimons who returned fire with 'And this, dear friends is the key problem with modern sport'.

Great ideas in, great ideas out

There's one way I enjoy finishing my seminar on coaching and leadership. I prepare everyone by saying I'm about to ask them to do something that might worry them.

They have to open their wallets and get out some money. Everyone in the audience digs out a dollar coin and then arranges into pairs. Person A of each pair hands Coin A to the other person. Person B returns the favour by passing Coin B to Person A. Simple, isn't it? What did they achieve? Was anyone richer? Was anyone poorer? That's right, we didn't change a single thing.

However, what if we replaced the coins with ideas? In less than a minute, we could have exchanged so many ideas. How easy would learning be if we could hand over ideas as quickly as that? This simple demonstration highlights the core of leadership — it's about connecting with others, connecting by sharing, both ways.

Exchanging ideas, valuable ideas, brings people together in one of the best forms of synergy. It's much more likely to happen if you keep track of the big ideas you're giving and receiving, each day, each week, and it will tell you so much about your desire to be a leader.

For it is in giving that we receive.

St Francis of Assisi (Extraordinary leader)

Leadership profile

Instructions

Decide how true each statement is about you.

1. Spreads enthusiasm to team members.

1	2	3	4	5	6	7
Never true	Very rarely	Rarely	Sometimes true	Often	Very often	Always

2. Develops team bonding.

1	2	3	4	5	6	7
Never true	Very rarely	Rarely	Sometimes true	Often	Very often	Always

3. Recognises and respects contributions of each individual.

1	2	3	4	5	6	7
Never true	Very rarely	Rarely	Sometimes true	Often	Very often	Always

4. Seeks involvement from team members.

1	2	3	4	5	6	7
Never true	Very rarely	Rarely	Sometimes true	Often	Very often	Always

5. Builds productive relationships.

1	2	3	4	5	6	7
Never true	Very rarely	Rarely	Sometimes true	Often	Very often	Always

6. Treats others fairly.

1	2	3	4	5	6	7
Never true	Very rarely	Rarely	Sometimes true	Often	Very often	Always

7. Shares ideas clearly.

1	2	3	4	5	6	7
Never true	Very rarely	Rarely	Sometimes true	Often	Very often	Always

8. Gives valuable feedback to the group.

1	2	3	4	5	6	7
Never true	Very rarely	Rarely	Sometimes true	Often	Very often	Always

9. Shows professional expertise.

1	2	3	4	5	6	7
Never true	Very rarely	Rarely	Sometimes true	Often	Very often	Always

10. Recognises problems and identifies causes.

1	2	3	4	5	6	7
Never true	Very rarely	Rarely	Sometimes true	Often	Very often	Always

11. Makes well-reasoned decisions.

1	2	3	4	5	6	7
Never true	Very rarely	Rarely	Sometimes true	Often	Very often	Always

12. Is honest and trustworthy.

1	2	3	4	5	6	7
Never true	Very rarely	Rarely	Sometimes true	Often	Very often	Always

13.Teaches skills to help others develop and improve.

1	2	3	4	5	6	7
Never true	Very rarely	Rarely	Sometimes true	Often	Very often	Always

14.Introduces new methods that improve team effectiveness.

1	2	3	4	5	6	7
Never true	Very rarely	Rarely	Sometimes true	Often	Very often	Always

15.Looks for ways to increase personal skills and knowledge.

1	2	3	4	5	6	7
Never true	Very rarely	Rarely	Sometimes true	Often	Very often	Always

16.Shares personal expertise and knowledge with others.

1	2	3	4	5	6	7
Never true	Very rarely	Rarely	Sometimes true	Often	Very often	Always

17. Is organised and uses time efficiently.

1	2	3	4	5	6	7
Never true	Very rarely	Rarely	Sometimes true	Often	Very often	Always

18.Inspires others to achieve results through example and encouragement.

1	2	3	4	5	6	7
Never true	Very rarely	Rarely	Sometimes true	Often	Very often	Always

19.Takes initiative to make things happen.

1	2	3	4	5	6	7
Never true	Very rarely	Rarely	Sometimes true	Often	Very often	Always

20.Takes well-informed calculated risks.

1	2	3	4	5	6	7
Never true	Very rarely	Rarely	Sometimes true	Often	Very often	Always

21. Follows through on commitments made.

1	2	3	4	5	6	7
Never true	Very rarely	Rarely	Sometimes true	Often	Very often	Always

22. Communicates a clear vision and goals.

1	2	3	4	5	6	7
Never true	Very rarely	Rarely	Sometimes true	Often	Very often	Always

23. Anticipates and prepares for change.

1	2	3	4	5	6	7
Never true	Very rarely	Rarely	Sometimes true	Often	Very often	Always

24. Supports those who take intelligent risks, even if they fail.

1	2	3	4	5	6	7
Never true	Very rarely	Rarely	Sometimes true	Often	Very often	Always

25. Accepts responsibility for own actions and decisions.

1	2	3	4	5	6	7
Never true	Very rarely	Rarely	Sometimes true	Often	Very often	Always

Chapter 13
Learn From the Best

Have you ever seen a Marx Brothers movie? I received sincere thanks from a fellow psychologist for introducing him to the brilliant lunacy of the Marx Brothers — Groucho, Harpo and Chico. They mixed the sense of the ridiculous with cutting satire. In their handful of movies in the 1930s, you can find the inspiration for much of the outrageous comedy that has appeared since then. They did more than elevate slapstick with lashings of sarcasm. Several long-running TV series such as *MASH, The Simpsons* and even the bizarre Monty Python skits, as well as *The Goons* on radio, all contain the Marx Brothers spirit, as do individual comedians like Robin Williams, Billy Connolly and Steve Martin. Even Jerry Seinfeld is like a very slow version of Groucho Marx. They all get laughs, but have the ability to provoke audiences to look at life afresh, often with a smirk that takes a long time to disappear. Great humour can unsettle, as well as lift you. Have you guessed why I'm attracted to great comedy? If there was more humour in the world, there'd be a lot less problems.

Like analysing the Beatles, where do you start with the Marx Brothers? You can find books filled with the witty barbs of Groucho, but you'll learn a lot more listening to the man who never spoke on screen. Find the book *Harpo Speaks!* and enjoy. It's not for movie buffs, it's for those who are captivated by observing and listening to others. Harpo was an expert. I treasure one of his anecdotes about seeking and finding wisdom.

> *Many years ago a very wise man took me aside and put his arm around my shoulder. 'Harpo, my boy,' he said, 'I'm going to give you three pieces of advice, three things you should always remember'. My heart jumped and I glowed with expectation. I was going to hear the magic password to a rich, full life from the master himself. And he told me the three things. I regret that I've forgotten what they were.*

A message from Harpo — when you discover wisdom, write it down. Better still, keep a record of useful thoughts and ideas from others, and yourself. Collect and let them incubate for great rewards in your future.

There's another eye-opener from Harpo, and it comes from his deep, loving relationship with his family. Like most psychologists, I've met many people who've been abused as children, and this probably explains why I'm constantly looking for ways to help families, even in the smallest of ways. In Harpo's auto-biography, there's a moving 'Afterword' from one of his sons. He recalls how he would call home on any pretext to hear his father answer the phone with his gentle, inquisitive 'Yeaaaaaaah? This is Haaaaah-po'. Immediately, any caller felt that Harpo was interested in what he was about to hear.

Do you make other people, especially those in your family, feel good, because they know you're interested in their thoughts and feelings? Finally, Harpo's son describes his dad as a born healer who could reduce tragedy to absurdity. Wow!

From the ridiculous to the sublime!

You could find humour as well as horror throughout the last century. So how would you sum up the 20th century? Frantic, frenzied, furious? I thought violent was a fair description until I accidentally, or should I say, luckily, came across a television program on the success of non-violence in the 20th century. Yes, you read that right. In a century littered with world wars and seemingly endless smaller conflicts, non-violence kept winning. That's hard to believe, isn't it?

The seed was planted by Gandhi back in 1908 in South Africa and it then sprouted up in many unconnected and surprising places. Non-violence triumphed in Denmark during World War II, in India under Gandhi's guidance, and in the United States under Martin Luther King's guidance. It also bore fruit and withstood the terror and brutality of General Pinochet's dictatorship in Chile. An interview with a Catholic priest from Chile left an incredible impression on me. He had warmth glowing from his eyes. His words also had warmth plus something very special. He said, only the weak use violence because they have no strength in their arguments. Now there's a message for the twenty-first century.

Gandhi, a saint in anyone's religion, said many profound things. This is one of my favourites. He said, 'Love the sinner, hate the sin'. Brief, simple, but so incredibly difficult to put into practice. Once you follow this advice, you lose any thought of revenge or being vindictive. Some think this is a call to be weak. I'm certain it isn't. Some people who have been badly hurt have shared with me bleak images they have of forgiveness. For those who won't forgive, forgiveness is like letting someone walk all over you. It's like letting yourself be a target to be hit or knocked down.

Gentleness is an awesome strength. Aesop, the ancient Greek storyteller, told a fable that highlights this apparent contradiction. The sun and wind challenge each other to see who can make a man take off his coat. The wind creates a gale but the man can't be separated from his coat. The sun then slowly warms up the air and the man soon removes his coat. Often strength is invisible and right in front of you.

Hate means never having to say you're sorry.
Alan Moir (Australian cartoonist)

I think forgiveness is gentleness in its purest form. Wayne Dyer is a best selling author, psychologist and speaker. What I find unforgettable amongst all his works, is the vivid description of the enlightenment he received after he forgave his father.

I have another unforgettable image that shows the power of forgiveness. It's a photo of Pope John Paul II shaking hands with Mehmet Ali Agca in a prison cell in Rome. Never heard of him? Two years before, Agca had tried to assassinate the Pope. What's incredible is that you can clearly see love in the eyes of both men.

Many who can't forgive, from terrorists to presidents, prefer to think that revenge is sweet. No great religious leader ever preached this, so it was comforting to find that this theme is actually a corruption of a sublime piece of wisdom from John Milton. Regarded as one of the greatest poets in English literature, he wrote that revenge at first though sweet … becomes bitter.

The thoughts of great coaches

'The prime job of a coach is not to win football games. A coach's number one job is to keep quality in the joint, to keep peace in the place … to provide opportunity.'

Jack Gibson (Rugby League)

'Too many young people hit a wall. They don't grit their teeth and give it another go. It's sad, they give up, they kill themselves. There are a lot of people hurting out there and we have to help them. I'm a football coach; I'm supposed to help young men, but if I wasn't a football coach, I'd still try to help. I'd probably be a youth leader.'

Kevin Sheedy (AFL)

'Somewhere, someplace, sometime, you simply have to plant your feet, stand firm and make a point about who you are and what you believe in.'

Pat Riley (Voted Best Basketball Coach of the 1980s)

'There is a bit of the rebel in me, quite a bit. I'm OK if you leave me alone, but just tell me I 'can't' do something, and I know it is legally and morally correct, I will try to do it to the nth degree.'

Wayne Bennett (Rugby League)

'Success is not forever, and failure isn't fatal.'

Don Shula (Most successful coach in NFL history)

'There is an art to training animals. Thoroughbred horses can become stressed very quickly. The skill is in keeping them relaxed with their reserves of strength saved for the last 300 metres of a race.'

Bart Cummings (Champion Horse Trainer)

'Obviously winning is important — but you really do have to keep it in perspective and we try to make the game fun. Sometimes it's very hard. But generally that's the quest.'

Lindsay Gaze (NBL legend)

'We all have to have a little love for each other. If you don't have it, forget it. It's not the type of love you have for your wife, your brother, your sister, your mother, your father. It's the type of love you have for your fellow man you work alongside of.'

Vince Lombardi (NFL)

Let's use a lot more four letter words

Stay calm! I'm not promoting more obscenities. My favourite four letter words are love, care and help. You've now got the core and purpose of all great religions. Remember when I explained why you're already outstanding? I said you were a coach and some great coaches were Muhammad, Mother Teresa, Jesus, Mandela, Queen Elizabeth I and John F. Kennedy. But so are cult leaders, and you can throw in Hitler and Osama bin Laden as well. So, how can you keep out of this group? It gets back to what you believe in, your principles, values, ethics, your 10 best tips to be a winner. I hope these all sound very familiar. You can have thousands of good ways to describe your principles. Sometimes you'll find great ways from great coaches. When you read my collection of thoughts from some very successful coaches, I hope you sense the presence of care and love in what they say.

In my coaching philosophy profile, there's a very special message from Vince Lombardi, a legend in American football. Nicknamed by his players as 'Saint Vinnie', he would strongly criticise without relying on abuse. He got respect. When he walked into a room and told his team to sit, one player joked that they didn't even look for chairs. They dropped to the floor. Lombardi is famous for hard nosed quotes like, 'Winning isn't everything, it's the only thing'.

I like surprising sport coaches and business managers with the very different quote at the bottom of the page. It's very special to me, and I hope it will be for you. It's a big part of why I enjoy working with teams, in sport or business. I shared my view with a gigantic footballer and he soon started to lift his teammates before and after games with his call, 'There's a lot of love in this room'. You couldn't help but smile.

There's another personal story linked to this quote. After doing several training sessions with a large sporting organisation, my notes were reproduced in a coaching booklet. The only thing missing was the Lombardi quote. Possibly it was deliberately censored as less successful coaches have told me the quote was too soft! I sometimes return serve and tell them if they had said that to Vince Lombardi, the consequences would have been messy. Lombardi had the presence of an 800-pound gorilla. He reminds me of another American strongman, General 'Stormin' Norman Schwarzkopf, the leader of the United Nations forces in the first Gulf War.

It took a long time to wipe the smile off my face when I read how Schwarzkopf wanted to be remembered, 'He loved his family, and he loved his troops, and they loved him'. You can't separate love from strength, true strength.

Where are your most important instruction booklets?

A sign in the front of a pre-school, aiming to boost enrolment, said 'No experience necessary'. I loved it! The sign was describing much more than education at school, it was describing life.

We get all our experience and learning after we're born. A lot of it just happens, but greater success and happiness happens when we deliberately search for the right experiences and knowledge. Ever bought an electrical appliance, like a VCR, a computer or a DVD player, and you went straight ahead and put it together, connected all the parts, without looking at the instruction booklet? Unless you're an expert, there's a good chance you might have missed out on something.

Are you missing out in life? We don't get an instruction booklet when we are born, and many people don't look for instructions. For them, life is all trial and error, like being blindfolded in a maze. What's the most important thing, the most valuable thing you'll ever own? It's your body and your mind, it's you, you, you! We all need instructions, guidelines, advice, wisdom.

It's easy to denigrate those who search for ways to improve their lives. If you're searching for self-help books in a bookstore, you'll probably find them next to the New Age section. I'm afraid I see that as a put-down. Another critic said you know why they call them self-help books. It's because sales of the book help to make the author wealthy. Recently I saw a Leunig cartoon showing a man reading a book with the title *How To Cure Your Addiction To Self-Help Books.*

I regularly suggest to my clients that they write their own mini-instruction booklets for topics such as 'How To Help Someone Through A Crisis' or 'How To Help Yourself Through A Crisis'. It's much simpler than you think because they're based on lists. Anyone can write a list. I love lists, not shopping lists or lists of urgent messages. I love lists of great ideas.

I also love children, so it was only natural that I put together the following list '10 ways to be a great parent'. Sir Peter Ustinov, who was always able to combine wit with wisdom, said the most painful job of being a parent is to be the bone for the young to sharpen teeth on. An amateur psychologist described parents as being the emotional punching bags for their children. I hope you disagree with both of these images.

10 ways to be a great parent

1. **Be a great role model, not just a good one.**
   Children are excellent detectives — they easily see and hear 'Don't do as I do, do as I say'. Your credibility goes out the window.

2. **Spend time with your children.**
   It has been estimated that the average amount of time a parent spends with a child, in one-on-one quality time, is 10 to 15 minutes a day. Listen to the lyrics of the song *Cat's in the Cradle.* Children hate hearing 'I'm too busy'.

3. **Listen more than you talk.**
   Talking is sharing, listening is caring. Listening is both a commitment and a compliment. It's an unseen present for your children.

4. **Smile and laugh a lot.**
   Young children often laugh several hundred times a day. An

average adult laughs no more than 20 times a day. What happened? You can enjoy being childlike without being childish.

5. **Give unexpectedly.**

   Always give more than you receive, but when your 'presents' are spontaneous they're more memorable.

6. **Turn every problem into an opportunity to learn.**

   Benjamin Franklin summed it up beautifully when he said 'Those things that hurt, instruct'.

7. **Realise you're not always right.**

   Apologising to a child is a sure sign of strength and self-confidence.

8. **Let your children teach you something.**

   Encourage them to share their ideas with you. It can be anything, from schoolwork to their dreams.

9. **Show that you can forgive.**

   Forgiveness is a very special strength that comes from caring for others, even when they've hurt you. Those who forgive, are slow to anger.

10. **Say 'I love you'.**

    These three words reinforce everything else you do. It's a sentence that lifts everyone who hears it, including you.

How many pearls have you found?

Many people, like me, are always searching for quotes that are pearls of wisdom. It's a very special feeling when you find one that hits the same target you're looking at. It's as if the person responsible for the quote reaches out, touches you, and points you in the right direction.

Keep it in mind, this whole book is about helping you find your direction in life. Quotes, aphorisms, maxims, truisms, whatever you call these guidelines, they can play an important part in putting and then keeping us on the right track. Sometimes the advice comes from those who have reached the heights of success. Sometimes they are messages from superb artisans who weave words to form memorable images — Shakespeare was one of these artisans. Throughout the book, I've sprinkled quotes that have made an impression on me.

Let me introduce one of my favourite sources of knowledge and wisdom

— Asia. It's a continent that has produced so many religions, so many philosophers and so many great leaders. Our research is going back hundreds, maybe thousands of years. With a lot of help from the Chinese scholar Gao Yuan, author of *Lure the Tiger Out of the Mountains*, I've collected proverbs and sayings from China.

To tap into their wisdom, use the imaginative right side of your brain to find everyday examples, especially in business and in relationships. One of my favourites is, 'A familiar sight provokes no attention'. In business, McDonald's the fast food giant, definitely follow this piece of wisdom. They frequently regenerate interest by introducing new products, products that are only offered for a short time before being indefinitely shelved. In relationships, staleness exists when little effort is made to add variety, to break out of set routines.

This wisdom also applies to how we look at the rest of the world. How often do we show little reaction to a major tragedy in some distant part of the world because we see vivid images like this in nearly every news bulletin? Charity organisations call this phenomenon 'compassion fatigue'. See how a single piece of wisdom can generate a flow of ideas? Use this exercise to refine your research skills. Go back many times to analyse and re-analyse each valuable piece of timeless wisdom you find, anywhere.

Wisdom from ancient China
People with different dreams can share the same bed.
When the tree falls, the monkeys scatter.
Things turn into their opposite when taken to an extreme.
Many people listen when you have the right title.
Snag your opponent by letting him off the hook.
Wild times create heroes.
Many grains of sand can become a mountain.
Pull down the ladder after the ascent.
Relax while the enemy becomes exhausted.
Make the host and the guest exchange places.
Give away a small reward to gain riches.
You can win without a fight.

Three very different kings!

Movies can help you learn a lot about life. I got a lot from watching *Three Kings*. On the surface it's just an action adventure about American soldiers searching for gold after the first war against Iraq. However, beneath the barrage of four-letter words and violence there's a moving message about humanity. If you haven't seen it, go grab a copy from a video store.

In real life, there are three kings I admire. These kings didn't inherit their titles like royalty. They earned their titles through their magnificent achievements. And I know you won't be surprised to hear their bond is sport. All three of them dominated their sports for more than a decade. Now that takes class. That takes something very, very special. But the bonds between my three kings are deeper and more important than mere success in sport.

I gained extra insights into these men from an often neglected source — newspaper articles. One of my favourite articles that I often pull out of my vault of clippings is a thoughtful review of a long-awaited clash between two kings of basketball — Michael Jordan and Earvin 'Magic' Johnson. It was written by a great sports writer, Lisa Olsen, back in 1996.

When you look at classic shots of Michael Jordan flying above his opponents you see the results of an incredible commitment behind the scenes, away from the public eye. Lisa's article gave me many insights into Jordan's phenomenal career. She writes, 'See him lifting weights in the gym, his teammates long gone. Then watch Jordan running laps in the brutal Chicago cold while everyone else sleeps. Watch him shoot thousands of jumpers a day before his teammates have shot even one.'

Jordan constantly honed his physical and technical excellence, throughout his career, right from the very start. He needed this commitment to overcome the rejection he encountered when he entered his senior high school. Cut from the basketball squad he had to wait another year before he became a member of his school team. Even then he took considerable time to show his talent and it was not until his final year that he was listed in the top 300 US college basketball prospects.

Unlike many young sports stars who never become champions, Jordan also constantly refined his mental skills. His lengthy career included two major comebacks and he was able to do this with his belief, 'There are a million ways to mentally compensate when one of your physical skills starts to diminish'. Jordan's mental strengths includes very high optimism. Here's an example when his team, the Chicago Bulls, lost the first game of the NBA Finals. The Bulls went on to win the series 4−2.

> We have an inner strength and confidence. One game does not deteriorate that. Sure, it's a pressure situation. But you don't fight that with frustration and anger. I think you have to do it with a whole different frame of mind. Smiling, when you may be frustrated inside, can help relieve the tension. I think it's that Zen Buddhism kind of stuff. One game does not dictate how the series is going to end. If you want to write us off, go ahead.

I often share Jordan's background with young people because I want them to strive for Jordan-like levels of commitment to physical and mental excellence. However, we shouldn't blindly idolise even the greatest of sports stars. I balance the view by telling how Jordan has lost huge amounts of money through gambling. He dismisses this as a valuable recreation and doesn't regard it as a problem.

Before Michael Jordan reigned supreme in the NBA, Magic Johnson was the undisputed king. In 1991, his kingdom quickly crumbled when he announced to the world that he was HIV positive. Since then he has worked passionately on his resurrection by helping others. Today he oversees a business conglomerate that owns real estate worth close to a billion dollars and employs 300 people. He has revitalised inner-city areas from Los Angeles to New York. These areas, mostly populated by African-Americans, were ignored by other business entrepreneurs. Magic has shown the way, just like he did when he was playing basketball. He leapt forward and took control when others stood back and watched.

We have to move to rugby league in Australia to look at another king of sport. Wally Lewis dominated the interstate rugby league clashes throughout the 1980s. It was not uncommon for him to single-handedly win games for his state, Queensland. He was captain of the Queensland and Australian teams and was one of the best footballers I've ever seen, in any code of football. Unfortunately, his playing success did not extend to success as a coach. Often it's easy to miss important connections in life and I thank my mother, my 85-year-old research assistant, for discovering something special.

Back in 1992, after he had retired, Wally made a surprise visit to a 9-year-old boy who lived in Tamworth, in NSW. The boy was dying of cancer and Wally had heard he was a mad Maroons supporter, the Queensland team. Wally arrived unannounced, without any TV cameras or reporters. He later took him for a holiday to the Gold Coast to play with his own young sons. When the boy died, he was buried in one of Wally Lewis' prized football jumpers.

Here's where the big message comes in. At about the same time Wally's only daughter was born completely deaf. But, three years later, in 1995, she received a cochlear implant, she was exactly the 10,000 recipient, and now has near perfect hearing. I think there's a huge connection there. I'm passionate about my work because I'm certain when you help others, something often comes back to help you, and often, like Wally Lewis, you might be completely unaware of the connection, but that never stops it happening. You're often rewarded with things that money just can't buy. Every one of us, has incredible opportunities to help others, every day of our lives.

I've shared this remarkable story with thousands of people. I've touched a lot of people but I've been touched as well. I regularly receive inspiring feedback as many people reveal to me that they have also benefited from similar experiences.

I told this story to a group of managers last year, and one of them immediately said, 'Look, I know what you're trying to say, but in my experience, it just doesn't happen'. I strongly disagreed with him. Later I was told he was famous for his selfishness. No cynic will ever stop me believing … when you help others, you help yourself. As I've been typing these words I've been humming the words of a pop song, 'You only get what you give'. It says it all.

What do your friends say about you?

Choose your friends carefully. They are a reflection of you. I discovered this slice of wisdom somewhere, back near the start of my career as a psychologist. Since then I've often asked my clients about their friends, not to be nosey, but to gain clues how to help my clients. I've collected enough evidence to disprove the belief underlying the saying that eagles don't flock together. Great people do flock together. At the other end, mediocrity attracts mediocrity. What are your friends like?

Every year since John Howard became Prime Minister in 1996, he has thrown a Christmas party at his lavish harbourside residence in Sydney. It started with 100 guests and has now expanded to 240 friends. Who are they? There are media tycoons, television celebrities, millionaire businessmen, some political colleagues, and lots of elite sporting identities.

Compare this assortment of friends with another group of guests. Sir William Deane was described as the 'most popular and well-loved Governor-General Australia has ever had the privilege to appoint'. I agree. He and his wife rejected a gigantic farewell dinner at Parliament House. Instead, on his last day in office, he invited 27 street kids, who had all suffered various forms of abuse, to a smorgasbord. Then they went on a cruise of Lake Burley Griffin in Canberra — a day they'll never forget.

> *There's no formula for happiness that's guaranteed to work. But if you open up your heart, it's a start.*
>
> G. Wayne Thomas (Pop singer from the 1970s)

If God gets so angry and he starts throwing thunderbolts at those on earth who truly annoy her, these are some of the people I would feel very safe standing near. There is a dynamic trio of Bill Deane, Nelson Mandela and his spiritual partner, Archbishop Desmond Tutu. I'd also feel very safe between a couple of aging rock stars, Sir Bob Geldof and Bono. Both have carried on the compassionate spirit of George Harrison. In 2003, the United Nations praised his staging of the 1971 Concert for Bangladesh. Kofi Annan said, 'George Harrison was the first to understand the use of rock music to motivate people to embrace causes bigger than themselves'. George had lots of friends, and he still has.

We need more outstanding women!

My wife knows I'm always chasing fascinating women. Before you start worrying about my marriage, I enjoy telling my audiences that I love my wife. The fascinating women I'm after, are those who have achieved great success, outstanding success, anywhere in life.

I want to find these women so that I can then share their stories, especially with young women, but also with men. I want to inspire these women, and encourage men to see and help remove the obstacles that exist in front of women. They've been around for a long time. There are 3,218 names in the Bible. Guess how many are female? There are only 181, that's less than six per cent!

Australian business has certainly been inspired to follow and repeat this huge imbalance. Some figures to ponder. About 44 per cent of the Australian workforce are women, but when we look up the corporate ladder, only 11 per cent of directors of Australia's top 300 companies are women. At the very top, Gail Davis of the St George Bank is the only female CEO in any of Australia's top 100 companies. As a great professor of physics used to constantly ask 'Why is it so?'

The problem won't be solved by promoting women simply because they have two X-chromosomes. Women need to be encouraged to be prime ministers, CEOs and leaders who will truly make the world a better place.

They need to be inspired by the successes of fascinating women like Diana Londish. Between 1993 to 2004, she changed her life from being a housewife in Sydney with a young son, to … wait for it, a scientist with NASA in California, working on a space telescope, investigating cosmic quasars. She became an astrophysicist because at 43 she asked herself. 'What am I going to do for the rest of my life'. Diana is an inspiration for women and men, of any age.

Are you at the end or the beginning?

Bertrand Russell, the great philosopher, described philosophy as 'something intermediate between theology and science'. That's how I see psychology. It's more than the study of human behaviour, it's a love of humanity. Discovering psychology, at the ripe old age of 39, was possibly my resurrection. As a school teacher I was down and out. The study of psychology relit a flame within me, and it got even better when I practised as a psychologist. I feel so privileged when complete strangers come to me for help and share the very personal sides of their lives. Being given so much trust, produces a special feeling that I enjoy over and over. Some sessions with individual clients, and even with groups, have produced a spiritual feeling. It's uplifting.

What's this got to do with you? You're not a psychologist. Yes you are! Go back to the very first page of this book where I asked you some big questions. You've kept reading because you agreed you wanted to help others. That makes you an honorary psychologist. Remember the wise words of Kirk Gibson, a retired baseball star. He had a powerful effect on a large audience in the Crystal Cathedral in California when he told everyone, 'We're here to care for each other'. Combine this with a gift from my favourite basketball coach, John Wooden. He said, 'You can't have a perfect day without doing something for someone who will never be able to repay you'.

The growth of learning is linked to so many things — happiness, maturity, fulfilment, success, loving relationships — the list is endless. Once you see this, life can be wondrous because there are so many opportunities to learn all around us. Everywhere!

I opened a Sunday newspaper and found a message for life staring at me from an advertisement for the *Australian Geographic* magazine. It said, 'Besides love, your most precious gift is knowledge'. I thought, that's beautiful! Then later on the same day I watched a British TV series called *Badger*, about a policeman who spent much of his time helping animals. Staring at a wild wolf, he said so much when he simply stated, 'You're beautiful'. His caring for animals was contagious. Other human strengths can be contagious when you become more aware of the beauty in front of us and you become more aware of the love within us.

Australian television has recently highlighted a disappointing change in our society. We've been swamped with programs on home renovation. It's wonderful to truly enjoy your home, but it's very misguided when you retreat into your home, and focus on little outside. Location, property, investment and auction are the popular words of a generation who rarely contribute to the community.

A second wave of renovation TV programs centre on the human body. Some give fashion and appearance tips to transform the plain into the beautiful. Then there are the much more extreme makeovers with volunteers who undertake major surgery to change their bodies. We should all be renovators, always learning, looking for ways to improve our lives, and others. A close friend described those professional sportspeople who make the headlines for all the wrong reasons as incomplete human beings. I think we're all incomplete, to varying degrees. Those who chase selfish goals need to renovate their lives by changing and reinforcing their foundations. Some of them will never do this.

5 best books I've read

_____

_____

_____

_____

_____

5 best movies I've seen

_____

_____

_____

_____

_____

5 best sporting events I've seen

_____

_____

_____

_____

_____

5 best moments in my life

_____

_____

_____

_____

_____

5 best decisions I've made

_____

_____

_____

_____

_____

Education is not filling a bucket but lighting a fire.

William Butler Yeats

A few pages back, I mentioned how charity organisations are now faced with the phenomenon of compassion fatigue. Many people feel overwhelmed by the world's major problems of starvation and disease, especially when they are graphically shown on television. Compassion fatigue lets some people escape from caring by switching off. Fortunately, some wonderful people have limitless supplies of compassion. Have you ever heard of two wonderful Australians, Heather and Neville O'Malley? They had, at last count, fostered 167 children. For 22 years they opened their hearts and their home to many distressed children. If the O'Malleys were as famous as sports stars, I'm certain compassion fatigue would quickly wither.

Take a special deep breath, a breath that invigorates your body and mind. I reward myself with these special breaths when I finish jogging. When I discover an exciting jogging track, sometimes hidden in the bush, I go back time and time again. Please revisit many of the places we've been to. Your company has been special and I want to finish by sharing a special story with you. A very talented therapist ended a long training session with his group by telling the following tale. It had a profound effect on everyone who heard it.

There was a very wise Arab who had three sons, and on his death bed he asked them to keep a sacred promise. He owned 17 camels and he asked them to divide them in a very peculiar way. The oldest son would receive one half of the group, the second son would receive one third, and the youngest son would claim one ninth. They quickly agreed for they all deeply loved their father. After his death, they were greatly perplexed. How was it possible to keep their promise without slaughtering some of the camels to achieve the strange fractions? They went to a friend of their father's. This old Arab loved the boys like they were his own and he was determined to solve their problem. He knew his beloved friend had left a deep and profound message for his sons. After much thinking, he smiled for he understood. He told the boys, 'I will give you one of my camels so you can add it to your father's herd'. It was now very easy to divide the camels. The oldest son received nine camels, the next son got six, and the youngest was given two camels. Their father's wish had been satisfied. But, there was one camel left over. The wise friend said he would take it back and return it to his own herd of camels. He told the young men, when you give something away, something that is truly important, like understanding, caring and love, it never leaves you. It will always return. It's the best form of sharing.

I hate the thought that I could die without having truly explored my capabilities. Swimming has been a wonderful vehicle of self-exploration for me.

Shelley Taylor-Smith (Seven-time world
marathon swimming champion)

Recommended Reading

Albom, Mitch, *Tuesdays with Morrie: An old man, a young man and life's greatest lesson,* Hodder, 1998.

Bennett, Wayne, *League's A Lot Like Life,* HarperSports, 1996.

Bennis, Warren, *Managing People Is Like Herding Cats,* Kogan Page, 1998.

Blanchard, Ken & Terry Waghorn, *Mission Possible: Becoming a World-Class Organisation While There's Still Time,* McGraw-Hill, 1997.

Boldt, Laurence, *Zen Soup,* Arkana/Penguin, 1997.

Charlesworth, Ric, *The Coach: Managing For Success,* Pan Macmillan, 2001.

Chopra, Deepak, *How To Know God,* Rider, 2000.

Chu, Chin-Ning, *Thick Face, Black Heart,* Allen & Unwin, 1992.

Chungliang Al Huang & Jerry Lynch, *Thinking Body, Dancing Mind,* Bantam, 1994.

Coelho, Paulo, *The Alchemist,* HarperPerennial, New York, 1998.

Covey, Stephen, *The 7 Habits of Highly Effective People,* The Business Library, 1990.

Covey, Stephen, *Principle-Centered Leadership,* Simon & Schuster, London, 1992.

Csikszentmihalyi, Mihaly, *Flow: The Psychology of Happiness,* Rider, 1992.

Dalai Lama & Howard Cutler, *The Art of Happiness,* Hodder Headline, 1998.

Dando-Collins, Stephen, *The Penguin Book of Business Wisdom,* Penguin Books, 1998.

De Pree, Max, *Leadership Is An Art,* Australian Business Library, 1989.

De Vos, Rich, *Compassionate Capitalism,* Dutton/Penguin, 1993.

Dyer, Wayne, *Wisdom of the Ages,* HarperCollins, 1999.

Edwards, Betty, *The New Drawing on the Right Side of the Brain,* Tarcher-Putnam, 1999.

Ferguson, Howard, *The Edge, Getting the Edge Company,* 1996.

Frankl, Viktor, *Man's Search For Meaning,* Pocket Books, 1985.

Gawler, Ian, *Meditation: Pure and Simple,* Hill of Content, 1996.

Gibran, Kahlil, *The Prophet,* Knopf, New York, 1965.

Gibson, Jack, *The Last Word,* ABC Books, 2003.

Gibson, Jack, *When all is said and done,* Ironbark/Pan Macmillan, 1994.

Goleman, Daniel, *Emotional Intelligence,* Bloomsbury, 1996.

Graham-Pole, John, *Illness And The Art Of Creative Self-Expression,* New Harbinger, 2000.

John-Roger & Peter Williams, *Life 101: Everything We Wish We Had Learned About Life in School — But Didn't,* Thorsons/HarperCollins, 1992.

Kouzes, James & Barry Posner, *Credibility: How Leaders Gain and Lose It,* Jossey-Bass, 1993.

Kriegel, Robert & Louis Patler, *If it ain't broke … break it!,* Warner Books, 1991.

Kushner, Harold, *Living A Life That Matters,* Pan Macmillan, 2001.

Lee, Blaine, *Influence With Honor,* Simon & Schuster, 1997.

Macqueen, Rod & Kevin Hitchcock, *One Step Ahead: On The Field And In The Boardroom,* Random House, 2001.

Marinoff, Lou, *Plato Not Prozac!* HarperCollins, 1999.

Marx, Harpo, *Harpo Speaks!* Virgin Books, 1992.

McCormack, Mark, *What They Don't Teach You at Harvard Business School,* Collins, 1984.

McCormack, Mark, *What You'll Never Learn On The Internet,* HarperCollins, 2000.

McGinnis, Alan, *The Power of Optimism,* HarperCollins, 1990.

Melohn, Tom, *The New Partnership: Profit By Bringing Out the Best in Your People, Customers, and Yourself,* John Wiley & Sons, 1994.

Moran, Aidan, *The Psychology of Concentration in Sport Performers: A Cognitive Analysis,* Psychology Press, 1996.

Morita, Akio, Edwin Reingold & Mitsuko Shimomura, *Made In Japan: Akio Morita and Sony,* Signet, 1986.

O'Boyle, Thomas, *At Any Cost: Jack Welch, General Electric, and the Pursuit of Profit,* Vintage Books/Random House, 1998.

Peters, Tom, *Thriving On Chaos,* Pan Macmillan, 1989.

Peters, Tom, *The Circle of Innovation,* Hodder & Stoughton, 1997.

Player, Gary, 'Swinging Hard on Life's Course', *Psychology Today,* April 1999.

Robbins, Anthony, *Awaken the Giant Within,* Fireside/Simon & Schuster, 1992.

Roberts, Monty, *Horse Sense For People,* HarperCollins, 2001.

Roddick, Anita, *Take It Personally,* Thorsons, 2001.

Rose, Colin & Malcolm Nicholl, *Accelerated Learning for the 21st Century,* Dell, 1997.

Saul, John Ralston, *On Equilibrium,* Penguin, 2001.

Seligman, Martin, *Learned Optimism,* Random House, 1992.

Seligman, Martin, *The Optimistic Child,* Random House, 1995.

Semler, Ricardo, *Maverick!,* Century, 1993.

Semler, Ricardo, *The Seven-Day Weekend,* Century, 2003.

Senge, Peter, *The Fifth Discipline: The Art & Practice of the Learning Organisation,* Random House, 1992.

Shula, Don & Ken Blanchard, *Everyone's A Coach,* HarperBusiness, 1995.

Snyder, Alan, *What Makes A Champion!* Penguin, 2002.

Stanley, Thomas, *The Millionaire Mind,* HarperBusiness, 2000.

Waitley, Denis, *Seeds of Greatness,* Brolga, Melbourne, 1983.

Walton, Gary, *Beyond Winning: The Timeless Wisdom of Great Philosopher Coaches,* Human Kinetics, 1992.

Yuan, Gao, *Lure the Tiger Out of the Mountains,* Judy Piatkus, 1991.

Ziglar, Zig, *Over the Top,* Thomas Nelson, 1994.

Answers To Exercises

Conflicting advice

Contradicting pairs are: 1–28, 2–7, 3–10, 4–23, 5–27, 6–21, 8–17, 9–18, 11–24, 12–20, 13–19, 14–15, 16–26, 22–25

Some simple arithmetic

1000 + 40 + 1000 + 30 + 1000 + 20 + 1000 + 10 = 4100

(Most people answer 5000)

Optimism at work

Ratings of explanations for 'Customer makes an angry complaint about your service':

3, 4, 1, 2, 5

Ratings of explanations for 'A survey shows that staff morale is low':

5, 3, 4, 2, 1

About the Author

Paul Smith is a registered psychologist and a member of the Australian Psychological Society. In the world of sport his individual clients have become world, national and state champions. He has also trained elite groups such as NSW Cricket (senior and junior squads), NSW Netball team (Under 21s Australian champions), NSW Rugby League team, NSW swimming squads, nine National Rugby League clubs, Sydney Kings and West Sydney Razorbacks basketball teams, as well as the Sydney Swans.

His outstanding reputation as a sports psychologist has led to training with corporate clients such as Amcor, Fuji Xerox, IAG, Toyota, NSW Department of Corrective Services, NSW Local Government & Shires Associations, plus many Councils.

Paul is passionate about helping young people. He presents seminars to students and teachers in schools throughout NSW, and helps the Youth Insearch Foundation and Father Chris Riley's Youth Off The Streets. He still maintains his private counselling practices in Sydney and on the NSW South Coast.

Paul is also the author of the *Mental Toughness Training Manual.* He is regularly interviewed in major newspapers about the mental side of sport and is a guest lecturer at Wollongong University.

In all of Paul's seminars, speeches and individual sessions, he sets out to activate his clients to help them reach even higher levels of success, whether it is academic, business, personal or sport. His driving belief is 'Be outstanding!'

Paul and his wife live near the Shoalhaven River, one of the most beautiful regions of Australia.

Notes

....
....
....
....
....
....
....
....
....
....
....
....
....
....
....
....
....
....
....
....
....

Notes

Notes

....
....
....
....
....
....
....
....
....
....
....
....
....
....
....
....
....
....
....
....
....
....

Notes

....
....
....
....
....
....
....
....
....
....
....
....
....
....
....
....
....
....
....
....
....

Notes

....
....
....
....
....
....
....
....
....
....
....
....
....
....
....
....
....
....
....
....
....

Notes

Notes

....
....
....
....
....
....
....
....
....
....
....
....
....
....
....
....
....
....
....
....

Notes

Notes